Politics of Belief

POLITICS OF BELIEF

in Nineteenth-Century France

★

LACORDAIRE: MICHON: VEUILLOT

by Philip Spencer

FABER AND FABER LIMITED

24 Russell Square

London

First published in mcmliv
by Faber and Faber Limited
24 Russell Square, London W.C.1
Printed in Great Britain by
Western Printing Services Limited, Bristol

For

JOAN

Contents

9

CONTENTS

VEUILLOT'S TRIUMPH

10

Illustrations

Preface

A nyone who has written many pages about the Church must feel impelled to preface them with an apology. To have explored the plan of so vast an organization, tracing some of its devious ins and outs and peering into its dusty nooks and crannies, is to realize how much more is still unseen, unspoken of and unguessed at. Whole wings remain unentered for lack of the knowledge of how to enter; whole stories remain unsurveyed for lack of the ability to climb them. The edifice is too huge for any one visitor to master its pattern; he can hardly hope to know a single section thoroughly. But within his own limits he is free to wander at will. Poking into forgotten closets and trying the keys of unsuspected cabinets, he can idly indulge his curiosity; and sometimes he may find portraits and encounter people at least as interesting and significant as the inhabitants of more frequented chambers.

If, then, this book is confined to nineteenth-century France, it is partly from necessity; but it is also from choice. For France has always been crucial to the understanding of Christianity in the West. The proud title of elder daughter of the Church was not won for nothing, and no country has given more saints to the calendar or sent more men and women to the mission fields. The Church, too, has dominated French domestic history from Charlemagne to Clemenceau. The casual intruder into contemporary France who hopes to understand the country from his knowledge of present conditions finds that long-distant feuds still echo in the minds of Frenchmen, reverberating down the corridors of the Chamber and adding curious overtones to current controversies.

13

PREFACE

It is, of course, an arbitrary choice to pick out Lacordaire, Michon and Veuillot; they represent three points on a personal itinerary which might vary widely with another traveller. Nor will the informed reader fail to observe that the accompanying description of events is necessarily selective; he will look in vain for a paragraph on the Curé d'Ars, a chapter on Renan, or incidental references to Schleiermacher, Newman and many other great figures in the religious consciousness of the nineteenth century. But if the path followed is personal, the geography is, I believe, accurate. Perhaps it should be added that throughout this book, ignoring controversial subtleties, I have spoken indifferently of the 'Church of Rome', the 'Roman Church', the 'Roman Catholic Church' and the 'Catholic Church'. For any offence given unwittingly I should like to apologize in advance.

Certain particular debts I acknowledge with pleasure and gratitude. Mr. Patrick Bury has lent me an inaccessible volume; the Cassel Trustees have generously financed an essential trip to France in search of unpublished material; Dr. Alfred Cobban has given me bibliographical advice; M. Pio Corrêa, Junior, of the Brazilian Embassy in London, has helped me to uncover a plausible forgery in French anticlerical literature; Miss B. Schlumberger has supplied me with elusive information; the Librarian of the University Library, Cambridge, has allowed me to plunder his books for illustrations; and—perhaps my greatest debt of all—Mlle Monique Laroche has begrudged neither time nor trouble in investigating the private papers of the Abbé Michon, gathering personal memories of his character and copying out many documents bearing on his career.

Cambridge, 1953

14

PART ONE

Lacordaire's Hour

CHAPTER I

Saint-Germain-l'Auxerrois

February 14th, 1831, a damp, bleak day, dawned on the quiet streets of Paris with no hint of disturbance. While Louis Philippe dozed peacefully in the Tuileries, the ex-king Charles X, now condemned to obscurity as the Comte d'Artois, slept harmlessly at Holyrood, seven hundred miles away. If bourgeois Orleanists looked across France a little nervously, if they wondered how long it would take to strengthen the new regime against revolutions from the left and *coups d'état* from the right, their contentment was none the less justified; they were sleek, they were prosperous, they had power.

M. Alexandre Dumas was at the Vaudeville, rehearsing his actors with his usual intolerable zest. His confidence in the country's stability was hardly less than his confidence in his own genius. Shortly after noon, when the actors were already beginning to flag beneath his demands, a door burst open and the *chef de claque* ran on to the stage, panting with excitement. Outside the Louvre, he explained, stood rows of glittering coaches emblazoned with coats of arms. The street was thick with Bourbon supporters. Trouble was in the air.

Checking a phrase of complacent disagreement, Dumas interrupted the rehearsal and stepped into the street, where he joined a small crowd making in the same direction. He found a glossy line of coaches drawn up in the rue des Prêtres, outside the church of Saint-Germain-l'Auxerrois and only a stone's throw from the mean, pathetic graves that recalled the street-fighting of the previous July. A memorial service was apparently in progress—a Mass for the Duc de Berry, Charles X's younger son, who had died by the assassin's knife exactly eleven years before. Countermanded at Saint-Roch, the service had been transferred to this equally ancient but less conspicuous church. Carlists—adherents of the exiled king—filled the pews, splendidly attired, displaying a defiant loyalty to the Bourbon cause. As Dumas pushed through the crowded doorway, the frail old priest, who forty years earlier had attended Marie Antoinette on the scaffold, was just bringing the service to an end. The congregation stirred and rose. Suddenly there was a flutter of white round the catafalque and four Bourbon flags unfurled at the corners.[1] At the same time an officer pinned to it a lithograph of the Comte d'Artois, and a woman, standing behind him, flung up a crown of everlasting flowers—*immortelles*. The priest, quickly stretching to unpin the lithograph at each of its four corners, appeared to bless it and was greeted with shouts of anger from the intruders. Confusion turned to uproar. Fighting their way in from the street, bourgeois and workers wrestled with legitimists who were trying to escape. A young man broke out of the church, leapt high on to the bar of the iron railings, and flinging his arm towards the graves outside the Louvre, shouted to the gathering crowd: 'Citizens! Fifty yards from the last resting-place of the victims of July a service is held to honour the family we have driven from the country! Will you allow this service to continue?' His cry was hailed with angry applause. While the coaches clattered away across the cobbled Place du Louvre, the priests, taking advantage of this brief diversion, managed to shut the church doors and to push home the bolts of the presbytery. Scarcely had they withdrawn than the crowd, swelling rapidly, seeking some outlet for its passion, balked by the speedy departure of the legitimists, turned menacingly on the two buildings. It was in an ugly mood; weapons sprang from nowhere; there was a threat of blood. Someone hurled himself against the main door and at once, as though they had only been awaiting this signal, a determined group of ruffians pushed forward and began to batter down the woodwork, while another group moved round to the presbytery and attacked it with beams and paving-stones. Trapped inside, the priests could only wait.

[1] Louis Philippe had accepted the tricolour as the national flag of France instead of the white flag of the Bourbons. The latter had therefore become a standard of revolt, rather more provocative than the red flag is today.

Just as the defences were yielding, a detachment of the National Guard arrived at the double, and forcing a path through the rioters, escorted the clergy to safety. But the church had no protectors. A man slumped outside on a pile of rubble, head gloomily sunk in hands, was furiously accused of being a 'Jesuit!', seized and overpowered; and while he was roughly bundled and tossed towards the river—only to be saved from a cruel death at the last minute by the Prefect of Police—the mob broke across the threshold of the church and poured down the aisles. There was no holding them. The Prefect of Police and the Prefect of the Seine each made brief appearances, uttered a few ineffectual words, then vanished. The *maire* of the *arrondissement* even gave his approval as the great cross that crowned the church, adorned with three golden fleurs-de-lis, was caught in a rope, tugged down, torn to pieces and trampled on. Within the building a horde of rioters eddied round, drunk with aimless destruction, breaking crucifixes, snapping statues, rending pictures. From the sacristy a man emerged in full sacerdotal dress, and climbing on to a pile of debris, beat a measure while his comrades broke into a grotesque dance.

The mob was further inflamed by an unfortunate incident. An officer of the 12th Legion, marching with his troops to the scene of the disturbance, rhetorically swung his sword wide and high to emphasize some impassioned remark, and a working man standing harmlessly by the roadside fell mortally wounded. The riot thus acquired the excuse of retaliation. Crowded out of the church, a section of the mob repaired to the Archbishop's palace under the shadow of Notre-Dame.[1] Though damaged the previous July, it was still standing: now it was doomed. The iron gates that barred admittance were wrenched apart by the weight of a dozen men and the mob swirled past. What furniture remained in the rooms was tossed through the windows, piled high on the lawns and chopped up for firewood. When the early darkness of winter fell on the scene, it was illumined by the glow and flicker of three great bonfires; but the demolition was still only half-completed, and the rioters broke off in disappointment, arranging an early rendezvous for the morrow.

[1] The Archbishop, Mgr de Quélen, was in hiding.

On the 15th they were speedily at work. The presbytery of Saint-Germain-l'Auxerrois was stripped till not a scrap of paper decorated the walls and not a stick of furniture adorned the rooms. A withering fire seemed to have burnt its way through the building, consuming all but the stone and plaster. In the church itself only the tabernacle and the choir went unscathed. Stumbling across piles of rubbish, the crowd lurched round in grotesque dances, while a few figures in priestly vestments administered a mock blessing. 'There weren't only workmen in smocks', says one witness: 'I saw coats and fine hats.'

The other churches in Paris were shut, but from almost every one the cross was broken down and replaced by a tricolour. Only by the ingenuity of the Prefect of Police did Notre-Dame itself escape mutilation. Outside Saint-Paul a huge fire was lit and fed throughout the day with objects bearing the fleur-de-lis. Nor were the troubles confined to Paris. At Conflans the Archbishop's country house and the adjoining seminary were pillaged. As far afield as Lille and Nîmes, Dijon and Angoulême, seminaries and episcopal palaces were sacked.

But the greatest destruction was visited on the Archbishop's palace against Notre-Dame. This building, which had been erected by Maurice de Sully in the thirteenth century and had endured six hundred years of war, siege, insurrection and revolution, was levelled in exactly five hours. The finest ecclesiastical library in the country perished. Books were flung through the windows to children in the garden, who tore them up and dropped them in the river. A few bibliophiles who rashly intervened, all but paid for their indiscretion with their lives. When all the valuables had been looted, when all the furnishings and hangings had been wrenched away, when nothing that could be removed still remained in the building and the Archbishop's palace was reduced to a naked skeleton, a swarm of men clambered on to the roof—they numbered about a hundred, one bystander tells us—and grappled with slates and tiles. Brick by brick the chimneys fell away. Every now and then an unusually heavy splash marked the dislodgement of a beam. All day long a jubilant crowd packed the Pont-Neuf and derisively watched the flotsam—ornaments, chasubles, robes, books, bookcases, beams, cassocks—as it drifted downstream. And when at last nothing remained of the palace but broken walls and heaps of rubble, an obscene parody of the Mass was executed amid the ruins.[1]

In this disturbance the Government remained neutral: it seemed almost indifferent. A junior minister named Thiers came to observe the destruction, for it was doubtless a salutary spectacle for a politician. But he prevented the National Guard from interfering, and a few days later he was speaking of the 'legitimate indignation' of the people. As early as February 16th *Le Journal des Débats*, the official organ of the regime, told Catholics and legitimists: 'You are not only to blame for your own madness: you are to blame for the madness of others.' It was a hard saying: but the riots of February 14th and 15th found their excuse and explanation in the history of the previous forty years.

It is a crucial and disastrous feature of French religion in the nineteenth century that Church and Revolution came to represent incompatible ideals: cross and tricolour were made into contrasting symbols. It is true that when the States General met in 1789, the lower clergy favoured constitutional changes, urging reform on their reluctant bishops. But the reform movement quickly outran their purposes. The Church, burdened as it was with the great wealth it had acquired during its centuries-old association with the crown, quickly became a target for the reforms that many of its priests advocated for the rest of society; its riches were altogether too tempting not to arouse cupidity. Less than a year after the first meeting of the States General the Assembly therefore voted the complete expropriation of the French Church. Perhaps this measure would not in itself have set the ecclesiastical hierarchy at permanent odds with the

---

[1] The details of the sacking are confused and disputed, and precisely what happened in the church is particularly obscure. The official account, published some months later, denies that flags were produced and states that the lithograph represented the Duc de Bordeaux. But this is doubtful in view of the admissions made by Catholic legitimists immediately after the outbreak. See particularly Alexandre Dumas, *Mémoires*, 2ᵉ série, IV; *L'Avenir*, 1831; *l'Ami de la Religion*, 1831; P. Thureau-Dangin, *Histoire de la monarchie de juillet*, I, pp. 189 ff.; Louis Blanc, *Histoire de dix ans*, II, pp. 283 ff.; G. de Berthier de Sauvigny, 'Mgr de Quélen et les incidents de Saint-Germain-l'Auxerrois', *Revue d'histoire de l'Eglise de France*, XXXII, pp. 110–20. (For all bibliographical details, see the bibliography.)

Revolution, but it was soon followed by a much graver step touching the articles of belief—the Civil Constitution of the Clergy, by which the structure of the Church was democratized and its role reduced to that of a mere department of State. Erastianism could hardly go further. In retrospect the Civil Constitution of the Clergy seems to have been one of the Revolution's most decisive acts of legislation. It precipitated a schism;[1] it provoked a revolt; it was largely responsible for the King's disastrous flight to Vincennes; and it incurred papal condemnation. At once the Revolution became unacceptable, in one of its most vital aspects, to all orthodox Catholics; with this one stroke all sympathies with reform were quelled in seminaries and presbyteries throughout the land.

An impossible situation was thus created in which the Church was divided and its larger section was unrecognized by the State; and one of Napoleon's earliest acts after the *coup d'état* of 18th Brumaire was to give to the French Church a proper legal status. But the Concordat of 1801, though its terms were to be all-important in the subsequent course of the century, was drained of effect by the Organic Articles which were simultaneously brought into operation. Although the Church reached an agreement with Napoleon which it could never have reached with the Revolutionary Governments, relations between Rome and Paris were only temporarily eased. Napoleon, it is true, used the Pope as a convenient tool; and the Pope, lured on by the hope of concessions, seemed to acquiesce, even travelling to Paris to place the imperial crown into Napoleon's hands. But once back in Rome, he could see that his journey had gained him no advantage and cost him much of his prestige. As Napoleon's demands grew more pressing, his attitude stiffened. He ignored blandishments and resisted threats. The conflict between the two men, sharpening when the Pope refused to annul Jerome Bonaparte's American marriage, culminated in his kidnapping and removal to Savona, and only declined when in 1814 Napoleon, bowing to events, allowed him to return to Rome.

When, therefore, Louis XVIII was recalled to France in 1814 and became king in fact as well as in name, it seemed that with the upset of the revolutionary tradition and the overthrow

[1] Only four diocesan bishops out of a hundred and thirty took the oath.

of Napoleon, the Church had lost its worst enemies. Bishops who had been in exile since the early days of the Revolution returned to take possession of their dioceses; and with them returned the *émigré* nobles. But to the mass of Frenchmen the Bourbon regime was an imposition, an image of authority with a shadow of power; and by allying itself with the Bourbons the Church took on an aura of remoteness, a taint of unpatriotic privilege. 'Vive l'empereur! A bas la calotte!' was the cry that greeted Napoleon when he rode again into Paris after his escape from Elba. And when the Hundred Days were over, the sentiment could still find an echo both inside and outside the capital.

On the whole, however, the Church was well regarded by the mass of the people. In their eyes it was the supernatural ingredient in society, and though it sometimes went too far, it was necessary for the proper conduct of birth, marriage and death. While only a fraction of the population consisted of practising Christians, the majority were nominal Catholics, and the enemies of Christian dogma and tradition could muster little general support for their attacks on an organization that had suffered from a quarter of a century of intermittent persecution. The priesthood, therefore, enjoyed a position of security and influence; and immediately abused it. The sympathy which they originally felt for the States General had foundered in the blood of the Terror, and they were instinctively, unreflectingly, royalist: it was a matter of faith, not of politics: the Revolution was anti-Christ. They were buttressed by the *émigré* nobles, who had shed the anticlericalism so fashionable in 1780 and now perceived in the alliance of throne and altar the only guarantee against social disintegration. It is not true that either priests or nobles had forgotten nothing and learnt nothing: they had forgotten their mutual hostility and learnt their common interest. They now co-operated to re-create a normal society, by which they meant the society of the *ancien régime*: if there was some delay in the pacification of the realm, the Revolution and Napoleon would, in the end, be not so much superseded as ignored.

As he presided precariously in the Tuileries, Louis XVIII, that cold, cynical but astute king, shared none of these illusions; he was embarrassed by the vehemence of his own supporters, uneasy at their extravagant clericalism, skilful in modifying their plans. When, for instance, the Chamber carried a measure restoring to the Church many forest lands in possession of the Government, he hastily declared the session closed, acknowledging with relief the less reactionary character of the succeeding Chamber. But this was not before the ultras had achieved one great triumph in the abolition of divorce; and if they were temporarily frustrated in Parliament, they prospered elsewhere. *Missionnaires* appeared throughout the country, in town, commune and village, preaching routine religious observance and automatic salvation; but their successes, though spectacular, were not lasting. They contrived merely to embarrass their wisest friends and to incense their bitterest enemies. Bands marched through the streets chanting:

> *Vive la France!*
> *Vive le roi!*
> *Toujours en France*
> *Les Bourbons et la foi.*

When the *missionnaires* had departed, the secular clergy, infected by their mood, showed a similar fervour and presumption. In Rouen diocese, for instance, many, following their Archbishop's advice, fastened to the church door a list of non-communicants and kept a register of concubinaries. Almost everywhere a religious burial was refused to revolutionaries and actors, Jansenists and remarried divorcees.

Now however well-intentioned these manifestations of Catholic enthusiasm, the resultant combination of intolerance, royalism and reaction was politically inept. Failing to recognize and cope with the growing power of the bourgeoisie, the Church committed itself to preserving the old order, and the bourgeois, already liberal in inclination, became automatically anticlerical. They had no alternative. To many thinking men who had no stakes in the *ancien régime* and refused to follow blindfold in the steps of the clergy, it seemed folly to reject all the benefits evidently wrought by the Revolution. In any case, freedom, once tasted, lingers on the palate; and it was clear that the Church aimed at doing away with many forms of freedom. Moreover, the priest, as he dispensed offices to the faithful, incurred the dislike of those who were less faithful but more competent.

'The *curés* almost became political authorities by the weight

24

attaching to their recommendations', Alexis de Tocqueville wrote to an English correspondent.[1] 'Positions were often filled out of consideration for the candidates' beliefs, rather than for their abilities. . . . This period marked a revival of the *esprit voltairien*, that is to say, a spirit of mockery and hostility towards not only ministers of religion, but towards religion itself and Christianity in every guise.'

If Christianity did not incur still deeper hatred, some credit at least belongs to the Protestants, for they were free from reactionary associations. Exchanging persecution under the *ancien régime* for tolerance under Napoleon, they gave the Revolution their praise and the Empire their support. Even had they been tempted to welcome the return of a Bourbon regime (and such a supposition is highly unlikely), they were immediately antagonized by the White Terror, which, condoned as it was by the Restoration Government, claimed many victims in their ranks. The Protestants indeed were represented by several Independents in the Chamber.[2] In the country they comprised a small minority, at no time numbering more than 700,000 in a population that swelled from 29,000,000 in 1815 to 39,600,000 in 1914;[3] but this minority was an influential one, steadily extending its power and heightening its reputation as the century grew older.

The ultras, on the other hand, did everything possible to unite moderate, liberal-minded men in opposition to Christianity: they recognized no Christians but Catholics, and no Catholics but their own party. As he declined into senility, Louis XVIII succumbed to the charms of Mme du Cayla, a companion provided by an eminent minister and supervised

---

[1] A. de Tocqueville, *Œuvres et correspondances inédites*, II, p. 45.

[2] Guizot, however, belonged to the Constitutionalist centre party and therefore generally supported the Government; he was in many ways an exception among Protestants.

[3] The religious census of 1806 showed 680,000 Protestants as against 639,000 in 1896; but the apparent drop is more than accounted for by the loss of Alsace and its Lutherans in 1871. As for Catholics, the Abbé Pététot estimated in 1847 that some two million Frenchmen were Catholic to the extent of practising confession (T. W. Allies, *Journal in France*, p. 113); in 1815 there cannot have been more than a million. But of course the Frenchman without Protestant or atheist associations generally becomes a Catholic on his deathbed.

by an eminent cleric, and under the influence of this seductive *dévote* he abjured personal temperance and political moderation. The law of Sunday observance was strictly enforced; an army which crossed the Pyrenees to restore that cruel despot, Ferdinand VII, was delightedly hymned; a measure giving the King unrestricted personal right to authorize religious communities of women only collapsed when it came before the Upper Chamber; and large sums of money were voted to protect religion from the attacks of the Press.

After the death of Louis XVIII in 1824, this policy was pursued still more vigorously; for Charles X, though a better man than his brother, was a more foolish one—more fanatical, rigid and credulous. Crowned at Rheims in all the splendour of the *ancien régime*, anointed even with oil from the sacred phial of the Kings of France, which though once thought to have been destroyed at the Revolution, was now most fortunately rediscovered and replenished, he regarded himself as the modern representative of Saint Louis. With his approval, sacrilege became a legal offence, punishable by imprisonment and death. At the same time the number of religious congregations grew apace, and rumour spoke, in particular, of the increasing power of the Jesuits, who had been unpopular in France since the days of Pascal's *Provinciales*. Their presence was not officially authorized, and the country probably contained no more than three hundred, personally unostentatious and politically discreet.[1] But the sight of a single Jesuit was enough to set a cabaret in uproar. For the Jesuits were known to be the secret organizers of the Congregation of the Blessed Virgin, a society of laymen which had been founded in 1801 to prosper Catholic social work and to affirm loyalty to the Pope. The Congregation, which expanded fast after 1815, drawing to itself *émigré* nobles and bishops, writers and journalists, lawyers and civil servants, was regarded by its enemies as a vast conspiracy reminiscent of the Jacobins. Was it not significant that so many public men—generals, Prime Ministers, Foreign Ministers—were suspected of being members? Alarming anecdotes were recounted. One day late in 1825, a young man named Louis de Carné, calling at the Foreign Office, was received by a high official, who conversed with him

[1] The order had been restored (though not in France) by a papal bull of 1814.

for some time about politics. Then, quite unexpectedly, says Carné, he stretched out his hand and 'placed his fingers in mine in an embarrassing fashion—though I saw no particular meaning in his gesture'. Carné mentioned the interview to a more experienced friend. 'Ah! you silly fellow,' replied his friend. 'It was the *chain*. You ought to have slipped your thumb in the ring. You have missed the chance of a lifetime.'[1] It seems, however, that the Congregation itself was entirely innocent, but that alongside it there existed a shadow organization, the Society of Banners, whose secret purpose was to promote by all possible means the cause of Bourbon legitimacy.

The picture is altogether confused by the intervention of the Jesuits; for there were many Catholic royalists, who in spite of their loyalty to Charles X regarded all Jesuit influence as sinister and detestable. This explains the sudden outburst of an elderly Catholic peer, who in 1826 produced a book covering with generous obloquy the Jesuits and the Congregation, and assaulting the aggressive spirit of the clergy and their dependence on Rome.[2] Deprived by the Government of his pension, he was acclaimed by the liberals as 'the torch of France', gaining the support not only of the Cour Royale but of several bishops. His exaggerations, grotesque as they were, were echoed by Paul-Louis Courier, in some of the most skilful pamphlets that have ever been written, and by Béranger, in songs that were heard all over France. As the jesuitical turkey-cock remarks to the peasant-woman in one of Béranger's well-known pieces:

> *Vous êtes surtout bienfaisante,*
> *Le pauvre au pauvre le redit,*
> *Mais la bonté reste impuissante*
> *Lorsqu'on est chez nous sans crédit.*
> *Voici les parts qu'il faut qu'on fasse:*
> *A nous l'or, aux pauvres les sous.*
>   *Glous! glous! glous! glous!*
> *Reconnaissez la voix d'Ignace:*
> *Pleurez et convertissez-vous.*

[1] L. de Carné, *Souvenirs de ma jeunesse*, pp. 30–1.
[2] Le Comte de Montlosier, *Mémoire à consulter sur un système religieux tendant à renverser la religion, la société et le trône*, 1826.

This opposition, though far too heterogeneous to do more than combine in hatred of the Jesuits and of the Congregation, represented a passion that was mounting all over France. 'About 1827', says Sainte-Beuve, 'the unpopularity of the clergy was at its height: the century which, at its dawn, had greeted the restoration of the Catholic cult with approval and even a tremor of joy, had slipped back into its old hatred of the priesthood: insults bespattered the cloth.'[1]

To many it might indeed have seemed that the Restoration had already restored too much, but not to Charles X and his advisers. They persevered. In 1829 the King, dissolving a ministry which by a year of moderation had contrived to cool the temper of the people, appointed Prince Jules de Polignac as his Prime Minister. Polignac, who represented the right wing of the right wing, failed to secure the support of the Chamber; but rather than dismiss him, Charles dissolved the House, thus offering the country an opportunity to elect more ultras. The country, however, failed to comply, and the opposition emerged from the elections of July 1830 with its strength substantially increased. While the pulpits resounded with the praise of absolutism, Charles hesitated. Should he take the hint? At length, encouraged by the Archbishop of Paris, he published four ordinances, dissolving the Chamber and suppressing the liberty of the Press, limiting the franchise to landed proprietors and appointing a date for new elections. If technically he was acting within his royal rights as prescribed by the Charter of 1814, no one failed to realize that his ordinances amounted to a *coup d'état*. It was therefore unfortunate that Charles did not support them with a show of force, and for the rest of his life he was to regret the omission. Four days after the publication of the ordinances he scratched the royal coat of arms off his coaches and drove hurriedly out of St. Cloud, while in Paris Louis Philippe, Duke of Orleans, received a group of deputies and cautiously consented to become Lieutenant-General of the Kingdom.

The July Revolution was, indeed, directed as much at the altar as at the throne. The crisis, though precipitated by Charles's bid for power over the Chamber, would not have turned to revolution without accumulated resentment against

[1] Sainte-Beuve, *Nouveaux lundis*, V, p. 422.

the Church. While Pius VIII wept in Rome, a number of bishops took ship for England and America. Sporadic outbreaks of violence in Paris forced priests to walk through the streets in civilian dress. In the theatre enthusiastic audiences applauded plays with such resounding titles as *The Jesuits, The Congregations, Cloistered Victims* and *Nuns and Soldiers*. Pamphlets accused the Archbishop of Paris of whoredom and even murder. A group of Saint-Simonians, meeting at Versailles, were set upon and dispersed because hostile posters had described them as a 'Jesuitical sect'.

The July Revolution was indeed a bourgeois revolution, and with it political power over the country was seized by those who already wielded economic power. There is some evidence that Charles's fall was directly engineered by industrialists, who on July 26th, seeing the drift of events, closed their factories and put their workmen on the streets; for unemployed make willing insurgents. Certainly there is nothing surprising in the coats and fine hats that were glimpsed at the sacking of Saint-Germain-l'Auxerrois six months later. The bourgeois were celebrating their triumph, rejoicing over the defeat of their foremost political enemy. Who could be altogether shocked if the members of the National Guard, always a middle-class organization, themselves joined in the looting they were supposed to prevent? Or entirely astonished if the Abbé Liautard, generally known as the spiritual supervisor of Mme du Cayla, was with difficulty saved from an ugly death at the hands of the mob?[1]

The casual observer might be forgiven if he concluded that Christianity in France had had its day. The Roman Catholic Church was discredited politically, while the Protestants, after generations of persecution, lacked the organization and experience to go over to the attack. Now that the Church had no prop, it tottered visibly, and the masses seemed only too ready to complete its downfall. Certainly no one could foresee the transformation that would be worked in less than a decade.

[1] There had been occasional outbreaks of violence since July 1830. On September 5th, the Abbé Guibert wrote from Le Lans: 'Les catholiques sont abattus. On a voulu crucifier le curé de Thiers; c'eût été une belle mort. Vous voyez que la tempête s'approche de nous.' J. Paguelle de Follenay, *Vie du Cardinal Guibert*, I, p. 248.

For some time country priests remained faithful to the Bourbon regime. In the diocese of Angers, for instance, *Domine salvum fac regem*, which continued to be sung according to the local rite, became almost a manifestation, for *regem* evidently referred to Charles X. The Bishop hastily intervened. But his instruction to insert the two names of Louis Philippe was not generally observed, and a few priests, exploiting the fact that the new king's second name was used as an insult by Carlists, maliciously intoned *Domine, salvum fac regem Philippum*. This vulnerable accusative, pronounced as it was *Philippom*, released a spate of jokes about *Philippe-pomme*, *Philippe-poire* and *Philippe-poireau*. In other churches Carlists departed noisily as soon as the anthem began, leaving Philippistes ostentatiously at worship.

Louis Philippe himself deprecated excess. If he sometimes argued testily that as a descendant and representative of St. Louis he was a defender of the faith and therefore qualified for its protection, his attitude was not hostile, only cautious. On the one hand, a coronation without ceremony; on the other, regular attendance at Mass with his family. Entertaining Catholics at the Tuileries, he agreeably passed the time with questions about the difference between *Dominus vobiscum* and *Pax tecum*, or inquired the exact number of candles necessary to validate the sacrament of marriage. Nor did his caution go unrewarded. At the first sign of hostility from the bishops, the Papal Nuncio was secretly informed of Louis Philippe's filial love for the see of Saint Peter; and the Pope immediately restrained his higher clergy, reinforcing his private representations with a brief. In return Louis Philippe observed a delicate neutrality, assailed from either side. At his casual use of the word 'Providence' in a speech to the Chambers, the *Constitutionnel* at once accused the Government of 'tending towards mysticism'. But in Rome the new Pope, Gregory XVI, told a French visitor, 'I am very well satisfied with Louis Philippe; I wish that all the sovereigns of Europe resembled him'.

But it would have been politically disastrous and psychologically eccentric for the Government to have wooed the Church. The most that Catholics could reasonably hope for was toleration. Not till they quelled the suspicion that they favoured a counter-revolution, not till they outlived their reputation for reaction and obscurantism, could they expect the smallest degree of popularity. In preventing the National Guard from interfering with the riots in the Archbishop's palace, Thiers exercised the calculated policy of the Government: for if the Church had triumphed six months earlier and the rebels had succumbed, Charles X would still be ruling from the Tuileries. *L'Ami de la Religion* might bewail the preferential treatment accorded to Protestants, who were not as a body politically minded but generally welcomed the Orleanist regime, but there was no gainsaying the reason for this preference. The hardships inflicted by Louis Philippe's administration—the reduction in the Church's budget, the expulsion of Carthusians, Trappists and Capuchins from the country, the abolition of regimental chaplains—were meant to annoy and enfeeble an organization whose influence had declined and was neither expected nor intended to revive.

But the Church itself was changing fast. Though allowed to receive gifts and legacies, it enjoyed little prospect of regaining the wealth it had disposed of under the *ancien régime*, and the fact that, since disendowment, its clergy were paid by the State, meant that its finances were constantly subject to revision at the whim of whatever party was in power. This, though a disadvantage, was not an unqualified misfortune. Formerly, when the wealth of abbeys, bishoprics and archbishoprics had been at the disposal of the Government, it was regularly dispensed to the younger sons of the nobility who aspired to a comfortable existence. Ecclesiastical promotion was a reward for gentle birth. Of the 134 bishops and archbishops who belonged to the Church of France in 1789, only five were of humble origin. A hundred years later, when a bishop's maximum income had shrunk to reasonable proportions, there were only four nobles out of ninety bishops and archbishops.[1] To this change there was an immediate corollary. A bishopric, ceasing to be a sinecure, also ceased to attract men whose only qualification for high office was their taste for high living. One no longer encountered prelates like the famous Loménie de Brienne, who were proud of their atheism. The bishops returned to their task as fishers of men.

Not that the Church of France before 1789 had been corrupt

[1] See H. Taine, *Les Origines de la France contemporaine. Le Régime moderne*, II, pp. 65–6.

or self-seeking: on the contrary, it contained many priests of exemplary piety and devotion. But they belonged to a particular class and owned to a particular loyalty. During the Revolution and the Empire many of them died, were killed, or went into exile, so that in 1816 a third of the country's livings were vacant. For the next four or five years it seemed improbable that more than 6,000 men could be ordained, whereas calculations on the death-rate showed that at the end of that time 20,000 parishes would be unprovided for.

By 1830, however, most vacancies were filled; and if the change in the quality of the clergy was not immediately apparent, it was none the less radical. While the bishops of the Restoration were still *grands seigneurs*—the Duc de Rohan, for instance, was made Honorary Vicar-General of Paris the day following his ordination and six years later became Archbishop of Auch—the parish priests sprang from the common people, pursuing vocations that were untainted by any worldly aims. They had little hopes of advancement. Who could foresee how soon the three principal members of the espicopate would be a cobbler's son, a tailor's son, and the illegitimate son of a peasant girl? As to their training, it is described for us by Renan, who attended the little seminary at Tréguier about this time. 'The education I received', he writes, 'was the same as was given two hundred years ago in the strictest religious societies. It was none the worse for that. It was the same sound and sensible education, at once pious and unjesuitical, that shaped the youth of old France; one emerged from it with an earnest and a Christian mind.'[1] But it had its shortcomings. To bring up men on a narrow selection of Latin classics, with no knowledge of modern history, literature or apologetics, was to create a priesthood which, however exemplary in morals, was unable to cope intellectually with the problems of the time —a priesthood excellently suited to the peasantry, but bewildered and indignant if it was forced to grapple with serious doubters and instructed opponents. Only at Saint-Sulpice, in Paris, was there any genuine scholarship or sound theology. Most seminarists wrestled clumsily with bookish learning— mastodons studying the humanities, as they were described— but stopped short of criticism. Instilled with a deep but narrow

[1] E. Renan, *Souvenirs d'enfance et de jeunesse*, p. 132.

piety, they were too shocked at any exercise of intellectual independence to sympathize with men who had not yet found a religion; their ministrations were for the faithful alone. Similarly, so indoctrinated were they with royalist ideas, so convinced of the Christian necessity of the Bourbon regime, that the July Revolution struck them with the force of a hurricane, and it was left to the more worldly-wise bishops to restrain their indignation, reminding them that obedience was due to every government, whatever its political complexion.

Once the storm was over, however, it was clear that the ship had not capsized. In 1830 it was the Church that was unpopular, not religion, and priests who remained aloof from politics were despised rather than hated. They ministered to a generation that for ten years of Revolutionary Government had been virtually bereft of organized religious instruction and whose most active members—the new bourgeois—were superior to them in influence, social background and education. But the bourgeois comprised only a small section of society. The illiterate masses, whose only means of political self-expression was to erect barricades, loved Louis Philippe as little as Charles X. At the most, they were indifferent to this new bourgeois edition of old Bourbon. *Their* hero was Napoleon, Emperor and man of the people, whose legend, fed deliberately by poets and inadvertently by politicians, overspread the memory of his oppressions and became a mystical cult. This fact was discovered by a seventeen-year-old boy called Louis Veuillot in July 1830. Caught in the Paris street-fighting, he was trying to escape when an old workman seized him by the arm. 'If you want to go, lad,' he said, 'you can; but first take a look at the man I am fighting for.' And pulling open his shirt, he revealed Napoleon's face tattooed on his chest.

The Napoleonic legend, still attached to no particular person, was vague and undefined—a hankering for ancient military glory, a longing for the open society that every efficient army must become in time of war, a distrust for the pacific respectabilities of bourgeoisie and Church. But although in the name of Napoleon working men would overturn carts and carriages, heave up paving-stones and brandish muskets, they had drunk in the supernaturalism inherent in every glorious tradition. And this supernaturalism overflowed into other channels.

C

Priests, whatever their failings, represented powers that really existed—powers that must be placated and propitiated. Involved in politics and identified with a particular cause, the clergy checked this feeling; but once they were relieved of power, hampered and harassed by the Government, their real function came into focus. They survived the Bourbon *débâcle* because, however slow they were to appreciate the fact, their loyalty was not addressed to a dynasty or to a form of government. The labouring classes, who had often been anti-Christian but had never been atheist, observed that the Church not only persisted, but gradually cast off its ancient allegiance. Slowly they began to shed their suspicions; slowly they began to respect it as an agency of the divine. The priest and the people, at length, almost imperceptibly, drew closer together. There was a possibility that the sacking of Saint-Germain-l'Auxerrois would be the last outbreak of mob violence against the Church, a possibility that Christianity would overcome the stigma of privilege, a possibility that religion would revive in the hearts of Frenchmen. But only if the Church could speak with the right voice.

CHAPTER II

The Priest and the Prophet

Like those other great orators, Bossuet and Saint Bernard, Lacordaire was a Burgundian; he was born at Recey, not far from Châtillon, in 1802, of middle-class stock. For a Frenchman who had no particular vocation law was the obvious career, and at twenty Lacordaire was in Paris, drudging in an advocate's office, an uneasy, restless student whose gifts were not quickened by any genuine ambition. Not that he was unsuccessful. After witnessing his first few appearances in court, the famous orator Berryer told him, 'You have enough forensic talent to put you in the front rank, but you also have great dangers to avoid; in particular, you must not abuse your fluency of speech'. But this impulsive, versatile and eager young man, who had amused himself translating Anacreon, reading Alfieri in Italian, writing a republican tragedy, nurtured other ideas —ideas so various and conflicting that he lost himself in their complexity. One minute he longed for glory; the next for a quiet life. He would pursue a career at the hub of events; he would settle as a farmer in a Swiss valley; he would travel—how the mere words *la Grande Grèce* brought tears to his eyes!—to the four corners of the world; he would—he, a sceptic—become a country priest. But he was vexed with his own vagaries; worried; lonely; depressed.

'Errant dans le secret des solitudes ou dans les splendides carrefours des villes célèbres', he was later to write, 'le jeune homme se sent oppressé d'aspirations sans but; it s'éloigne des réalités de la vie comme d'une prison où son cœur étouffe, et il demande à tout ce qui est vague et incertain, aux nuages du soir, aux vents de l'automne, aux feuilles tombées des bois, une

35

impression qui le remplisse en le navrant. Mais c'est en vain; les nuages passent, les vents se taisent, les feuilles se décolorent et se dessèchent sans lui dire pourquoi il souffre, sans mieux suffire à son âme que les larmes d'une mère et les tendresses d'une sœur.'

That was Lacordaire's suffering—an unassuaged hunger, but for what he did not know: a hunger not relieved by success at the bar, by fame or by friendship. It was the burden of Romantic sensibility superposed on eighteenth-century scepticism— the soul of a tortured hero like René and the philosophy of a desiccated theorist like Royer-Collard. With Lacordaire it was this Romantic sensibility that eventually triumphed and led him to religion; for the occasions of emotional experience were desperately inadequate when he came to explain it, to reconcile it with his philosophy. He needed a faith to make his own feelings real to himself; he wanted to tear aside the curtain of reality, wanted to attain the greater reality that lay behind. Something forced him to penetrate beyond appearances in order to achieve some degree of personal contentment. But his need was not exclusively personal or individual; he was also continuously and earnestly concerned with the conditions that gave stability to society, with the ideals that might one day transform it into another paradise. But where, he asked himself, were those conditions and ideals to be found? Certainly not in the easygoing liberalism that he had hitherto accepted.

Lacordaire's crisis was painful and prolonged, but it was some time before he admitted—even to himself—that there was a crisis at all. 'I am sated with the world without having known it', he wrote, and apparently foresaw no end to the condition. It is a complaint that one often hears from French youth of the Romantic generation—from Lamartine, Flaubert, Baudelaire. But Lacordaire's misery was so deep and destructive that it must be overcome. One of his friends found him in his rooms, holding his head desperately in his hands. Another glimpsed him in Saint-Germain-des-Prés, kneeling before a pillar. Finally, suddenly, he took his decision: he announced his conversion. But that was only part of the change. 'My mind is made up', he said abruptly, bursting in on an acquaintance: 'I am going to a seminary.'

But Lacordaire was the favourite son of an ageing widow.

LACORDAIRE

THE PRIEST AND THE PROPHET

One moment, moved by her piety, she was delighted at his conversion; the next, moved by the ambitions she had cherished for his future, she was shocked at his avowed intention of entering the priesthood. Lacordaire, foreseeing this difficulty, had delayed some months before breaking the news. When at last it reached her, she replied with no less than ten letters of remonstration. Would he abandon his legal career, so promisingly begun, forfeit the money already spent on his training, condemn himself to poverty and obscurity? Would he disappoint her hopes and despise her sacrifices? She could hardly think so. But in this storm of reproach and entreaty Lacordaire was obdurate: he displayed towards his mother the same tenacity of purpose with which he defied his friends. For they were equally shocked and surprised. Most were scandalized at such a desecration of talent: while a few, shrugging their shoulders as men of the world, suggested that his conversion was not altogether disinterested. Surely the Church still offered its prizes and rewards?

He entered Issy seminary on 12th May 1824, and at once threw himself heartily into the discipline of Saint-Sulpice.[1] But although, after a year, he was transferred to the great seminary in Paris, there was a disquieting delay in his ordination. Quick-tempered, impulsive and passionate, free from all doubts on the genuineness of his vocation, he failed to control his tongue or to check his speculations. Continual misgivings assailed the minds of his superiors. There had been an unfortunate occasion when, irritated by the ugly square caps worn by his fellow seminarists, he seized a number and set them on fire. There was his sermon, too. For at Issy it was customary for one of the hundred and thirty students to preach to the others while they were dining in the refectory—a searching test for any rhetorician. Lacordaire's experience at the bar stood him in good stead. His sermon was highly effective—in fact, far too effective, for although his friends were generous with their compliments, his superiors looked at him askance, and while the Professor of Oratory warned his pupils not to imitate Lacordaire's style,

---

[1] How Lacordaire regarded this discipline is apparent from the short passage about Issy in Sainte-Beuve's *Volupté*; for Lacordaire, on being approached by Sainte-Beuve, not only took him round the seminary but sent him a detailed account of conditions.

the Council of the seminary laconically dismissed his effort as 'one-half verbiage, one-half nonsense, the whole an absurdity'. Nor was Lacordaire entirely happy in mind; in donning his religious habit, he had not thought it necessary to discard his political opinions; he remained what he had long been—a liberal. To the other seminarists liberalism was as shameful a sin as adultery: that it should not only be committed but proclaimed —and Lacordaire did not fail to proclaim it—only served to increase their distrust of a man who, to their patient minds, though aggressively talented, was devoid of the more conventional virtues of piety and deference.

Occasional priests looked on him with a more discerning eye. One day the Abbé Boyer, a spiritual director noted for his firm friendships and vigorous decisions, announced his intention of making Lacordaire a cardinal: the Minister of Education, he explained, was seeking a candidate of outstanding personality and exceptional learning for the vacant post of Auditor of the Rota at the Vatican—a situation which invariably brought ecclesiastical preferment. Lacordaire protested with an incredulity not far removed from tears. He brushed away the preposterous vision of a cardinal's hat. Such promotion he did not desire. After two and a half years in the seminary he had at last hastened his ordination by threatening to leave Saint-Sulpice and join the Jesuits; but when, on 22nd September 1827, he became a priest, he had reached the summit of his ambition—*sacerdos in aeternum secundum ordinem Melchisedech.*

It is a curious commentary on the administration of the Paris diocese that he was made to wait some months before receiving an appointment, at a time when the French Church was still suffering from a severe shortage of men. Eventually he found himself chaplain to the convent of Visitandines, a post which involved little more than supervising religious instruction at a girls' school. The nuns were baffled rather than inspired by his ardent, ambitious dialectic, and the relief was mutual when, towards the end of 1828, he was transferred to the Collège Henri IV. Even there, however, he chafed. His mother, who had come to Paris to live with him, took fright at his loneliness, his brooding sense of dissatisfaction. Conversion, though soothing his private distress, had sharpened his awareness of what was amiss in contemporary society. It was some relief to be

entrusted with the task of drawing up a report on the physical
and moral conditions of the royal colleges in Paris; for no one
knew better than Lacordaire the manner of life that Musset
was to describe in the early pages of *La Confession d'un Enfant
du Siècle*, and there was always hope of stirring the Minister to
action. But he needed work of wider scope, and in spring 1830,
acting on a sudden impulse, he visited Lamennais at La
Chesnaie.

Lamennais was twenty years older—a tormented, headstrong
Breton priest who had won a reputation for violent polemic and
tenuous orthodoxy. 'An unhealthy, unkempt little bourgeois,'
said a contemporary, 'with a parchment face like a lawyer who
is as dusty as his files and has never written on anything but
papier timbré.'[1] 'You'd take him for the local vestry keeper',
Lacordaire had remarked on their first meeting in 1823. But
this scruffy little figure was the visionary genius of his age. He
foresaw with uncanny precision the collapse of temporal power,
the declaration of papal infallibility, the separation of Church
and State, the triumph of democracy and its ultimate reconciliation with the Church; and what he foresaw, he declared with a
ruthless and intimidating clarity. 'That Frenchman', said Pope
Leo XII, 'is one of those lovers of perfection who, if they were
allowed, would turn the world upside down.' There is some
possibility that Lamennais was the Cardinal reserved *in petto*
of whom the Pope spoke in a consistory of 1827 or 1828; but
if so, his supporters were soon frightened first into neutrality,
then into opposition.

It is said that while Lamennais was celebrating his first Mass,
he heard a voice, 'I call you to bear my cross, my cross alone:
do not forget that'. His burden was never light and by 1830,
when Lacordaire visited him as a disciple, had become almost
intolerable. His rigidity of purpose had already alienated all
but a handful of loyal supporters. At first, at the time of his
essay on religious indifference (1817–24), he had been a royalist,
one of the most ardent supporters of the Bourbon cause, regarding the legitimate monarchy as an indispensable means of gaining the ultimate triumph of Catholicism. But by overturning
the traditional method of apologetic and appealing to the

[1] L. de Carné, *Souvenirs de ma jeunesse*, p. 250.

authority of the *sensus communis*—the universal testimony of the human race—he implanted suspicions; and these suspicions took root and flourished when it became clear that by exalting authority he was asserting the preponderance of the Pope over the national Church. Almost all the ecclesiastical hierarchy combined legitimist politics with Gallican[1] theology; they used the king as a symbol of divine approval for their own policies. If the Pope became supreme, their independence would vanish overnight. Denounced and delated, Lamennais submitted a defence to Rome; and after a considerable pause the Pope awarded oblique commendation. Rejoicing in this encouragement, Lamennais pressed ahead and in 1826 produced the second volume of his *De la religion considérée dans ses rapports avec l'ordre politique et civil*. In this he denounced Gallicanism, proclaiming that the Pope was infallible and had a directive and ordinative power over kings and peoples. There was no surer way of confirming the Gallicans in their hostility, alienating royalists and infuriating liberals. For Lamennais knew no mean: waving away any Erastian compromise between Church and State, sweeping aside the Restoration because of its parliamentary system and its toleration of heretics and atheists, warding off with horror any educational system that was not based on religion and religion alone, he announced his own plans for the new City of God. He was immediately fined thirty francs.

In fact, his alliance with the royalists was wearing thin. With every year that passed, he could see more clearly that the Bourbon monarchy, even when it protected the Church, did not protect the Catholic religion; his doctrine of *sensus communis* already inclined him to exalt the vast numbers of ordinary Catholics; and the moderate ministry of 1828, swinging against the ultras, decided his change of mind. Lamennais had no respect for tolerance, moderation or caution: given a goal, he marched straight towards it, ignoring the dangers that beset himself or others. He dealt in glorious certainties, absolute necessities, irreformable dogmas. No shadow of fallibility blurred the outlines of his policy. As soon as he realized that even royalists were practical politicians, obliged to court heretics and atheists if they wished to retain power, he discarded them;

[1] See below Chapter VII and the Appendix.

and holding fast to his conception of the Pope as the supreme authority of Christendom, he proposed a new ally—the People.

'If you are afraid of liberalism, then catholicize it': such was the theme of his new book.[1] It was a theme that would appeal to a generation that had not forgotten Napoleon or the achievements of the Revolution. Diplomats might demand Lamennais's condemnation by Rome; bishops run to the capital; the Archbishop of Paris fulminate; Jesuits fret; in spite of them all Lamennais had an enthusiastic following, small perhaps, but devoted. At his humble property at La Chesnaie, near Dinan, he had formed a kind of Third Order, based on the teaching congregation at Malestroit of which he was nominally head. Gousset, Donnet, Gerbet, Salinis, Guéranger—most of the men who were to stand out in the French Church for the next thirty or forty years gathered around him; and this untidy wisp of a man moved among them as a master, giving instruction, hearing confessions, directing consciences, planning a synthesis of all human knowledge to be published by his disciples.

To La Chesnaie Lacordaire now went.

He quickly succumbed to the spell. Lamennais's alliance of Pope and People answered so completely his own longings— his conviction of Catholic truth and his respect for political liberty: here at last was a man with a vision equal to the times. But Lamennais, instead of attempting to keep Lacordaire in his entourage, encouraged a different scheme; for Lacordaire had long been attracted to foreign missions. Did it not seem that in the United States, where religious liberty went hand in hand with political liberty, there was a great chance to investigate and prove his own ideas about the relations between Church and State? 'To free the Church from the condition of incorporation (*engrènement*) from which she suffers in France', he wrote to a friend, 'and to give her that absolute independence she enjoys in America—that is our primary task.'[2] Now his opportunity occurred. The Bishop of New York, who was visiting La Chesnaie, unexpectedly offered him a post as Vicar-General; and Lacordaire, excited and exultant, returned to

[1] *Du progrès de la Révolution et de la guerre contre l'Eglise*, 1828–9.
[2] Quoted by M. Foisset, *Vie du R. P. Lacordaire*, I, p. 143.

LACORDAIRE'S HOUR

Paris to obtain the Archbishop's consent and his mother's approval, planning to start for America immediately.

At this point the news of the July Revolution broke upon him; but after a moment's reflection Lacordaire clung to his decision. Indeed did not Charles's fall confirm his diagnosis of the deplorable subjection of the Church to a particular brand of State? While, however, he was visiting Burgundy to take leave of his family and friends, news came that transformed his future.

CHAPTER III

L'Avenir

⸎━━━━━━━━━━━━━━━━━━━━━━━━━━━━━━━━⸎

The accession of Louis Philippe proved to Lamennais how accurate was his appraisal of the situation; there could be no possible hesitation about the proper course for the Church to adopt, and the only difficulty was to urge it on priests and people. If the clergy looked back wistfully to the reign of Charles X, linking themselves with legitimists whose day was over, they would lose their chance. As one of Lamennais's disciples put it: 'Did the Son of God die on a gibbet 1,800 years ago in order to set the Bourbon family back on the throne?'[1] The obvious policy was to embrace the cause of liberty, the cause of the people; and if the bishops were too much caught up in their ancient habits of allegiance to see their present duty and to impress it on their inferiors, some other way must be found of explaining the situation, dinning it into the reluctant heads of priests all over France. Someone suggested the starting of a paper; Lamennais snatched at the idea; one of Lamennais's lieutenants wrote to Lacordaire, asking for his participation; and on 16th October 1830 the first number of *L'Avenir* was on sale, bearing the emphatic motto *Dieu et la liberté*.

This is not the place to recount the complex and passionate history of *L'Avenir*. While Lamennais, as editor in chief, wrote many of the leading articles, the bulk of the work fell on Lacordaire and a young nobleman who joined him a few weeks later—Charles de Montalembert. Montalembert was barely twenty—passionate in his hatreds, generous in his enthusiasms; a man whose aloof and disdainful manner was curiously

---

[1] Quoted by A. Dansette, *Histoire religieuse de la France contemporaine*, I, p. 296.

matched with a burning eloquence and a zeal for reform. He flung himself forward with the unshakeable conviction that his cause was right. The French nobility, he saw, was out of date and ineffective; but his ideal remained an aristocratic one, a return to the Christian—and feudal—Middle Ages. In his eyes the July Monarchy was a half-way house between legitimist folly and republican abjection; and this house he prepared to defend and fortify against all assailants. It offered a condition and protection for the Catholic religion.

Lacordaire remained a liberal, in sympathy with Montalembert but readier to grant the principles of democracy, while Lamennais, having abjured all forms of royalism, had become a fervent republican. Between them, these three men drew up a formidable programme of reform.[1] In education, the State (represented by the University[2]) must lose control; in journalism, censorship must be abolished. The right of association must be granted, primarily to religious congregations but also to workers. In short, education, Press, and labour must all be free; and it was clear not only that universal suffrage was essential to this freedom, but that, were universal suffrage granted, the State, becoming still more non-Catholic, would no longer be an ally of the Church. The two would evidently have to be separated. The programme of L'Avenir was, in fact, one of radical liberalism, a consistent and thoroughgoing demand for freedom. The primary freedom must be that of the Church; but together with the Church other oppressed minorities—workers, teachers, journalists, even nations like Belgium, Ireland and Poland—should be set free.

No wonder the Government was suspicious; in the first five weeks two numbers of L'Avenir were seized by the police, and opposition waxed rather than waned. Prosecuted and acquitted for attacking the Government; defeated in bringing an action for libel; prosecuted and fined for opening a school in defiance of the law—the editors of L'Avenir lived precariously from week to week. Lamennais, who in private life could seem so gentle and compassionate, assumed a new character with a pen in his hand, becoming a virtuoso of abuse. It was not to his advantage.

[1] A fourth member of the *Avenir* Committee was the Comte de Coux.

[2] The University (*L'Université*) was the State organization responsible for all departments of education, primary, secondary and advanced.

LAMENNAIS

By accusing the royalists of deliberately inciting the mob to sack Saint-Germain-l'Auxerrois, he incurred their hatred, and a group of the more malevolent bishops, led by the exiled Cardinal de Rohan, plotted his destruction. Many bishops forbade their clergy to read *L'Avenir*; in some dioceses ordination was postponed because seminarists were suspected of a Mennaisian taint; and the number of subscribers, which had never exceeded two thousand, sank rapidly.

It would be easy to exaggerate the influence of *L'Avenir*. It was read principally by the younger members of the clergy, and in spite of their enthusiasm, they were few. But although the immediate impact was narrow, it was deep. 'This *Avenir* business must not be neglected', a confidential correspondent named Dupanloup informed the Cardinal de Rohan in 1832; 'all the younger clergy in France are lost. M. de Lamennais is not merely the idol of young priests, betraying them into political independence and religious rebellion, but the scandal of all the old clergy and all pious believers.' These are the partisan words of one of Lamennais's enemies, briefing a rigid reactionary, but they express the fear and hatred which *L'Avenir* often aroused. Nor was Dupanloup's anxiety ill founded; Lamennais had the future on his side, and although *L'Avenir* was discontinued in November 1831, after a life of barely a year, it had worn away deep inlets in the ancient stronghold of Gallican royalism—inlets through which the flood-tide would come sweeping less than half a century later.

A more immediate effect of *L'Avenir*, and a no less deliberate one, was to demonstrate to Catholics the potentialities of the Press and the spoken word. The fervour of Lacordaire and Montalembert, both in the courts and in the columns of *L'Avenir*, and the caustic invective of Lamennais, were a proof that a bourgeois anticlerical paper like *Le Constitutionnel* could be challenged and surpassed in its own field. It was the editors' misfortune that their very success should be cast against them, that the urgency with which they pressed an unpopular case should be twisted into an excuse for destroying them.

But they had no intention of being destroyed. Within France Lamennais's enemies might circulate a forged letter in which he apparently preached the demolition of the episcopate; outside France the Chanceries of Europe might request the Pope to administer a severe reprimand: the three men, still confident in their essential mission, stuck to their arguments and, on Lacordaire's suggestion, decided to consult the oracle and go to Rome. At any time it would have been a dangerous idea; for the Holy See is perennially reluctant to judge any doctrine unless it must, and still more reluctant to give official approval to a minority that is out of favour both with its Government and its episcopate. But even the immediate conditions were unfavourable: in 1832, when the pilgrims arrived, Gregory XVI had been Pope for just a year, and in that time he had called on Austria—Metternich's Austria—to help in suppressing a revolt in the Papal States. He was an elderly man of jovial disposition, fond of gossip and *bonbons*, addicted (it is said) to the novels of Paul de Kock. But his training as a monk had done nothing to widen his mind, and politically he adhered to the forces of blind reaction, hating liberalism in all its forms, frowning on the Polish revolt, refusing to send a chargé d'affaires to the upstart Catholic state of Belgium till 1842, and then only on Metternich's intervention.

To expect in Rome, capital of the most backward state of Europe, propped uneasily (as its enemies averred) on the coffers of the Rothschilds, undermined with political intrigue and sustained by the tortuous contrivances of a Metternich—to expect in Rome more support for *L'Avenir* than could be found in Paris, was to stray so far from reality as to prove beyond all doubt the unworldly sincerity of Lamennais and his friends. His own honest, simple, rigid mind was never more clearly exemplified. Lacordaire and Montalembert were still young enough to have illusions, but Lamennais, who had visited Rome before and was now almost fifty, hoped as pathetically as they for a triumphant vindication of his doctrines. Perhaps he presumed on his support for the papacy against the French episcopate; perhaps he imagined that by championing papal infallibility he had protected himself against its exercise. At any rate he was unprepared for the forbidding silence that greeted his arrival, and refused to heed the semi-official hints that his cause would prosper better if he left. Accordingly Lamennais, Lacordaire and Montalembert were granted an interview with his Holiness. It was a chilly half-hour, made chillier by the disapproving presence of Cardinal de Rohan and the urbane insouciance with which Gregory offered them all a pinch of snuff, talking the while of Michelangelo.

Gregory had apparently made up his mind. 'That dangerous man', he said of Lamennais shortly afterwards, 'deserved to be brought before the Holy Office.'[1] The blow fell in August, when the encyclical *Mirari vos* declared to all patriarchs, archbishops and bishops that it was wicked to propose the separation of Church and State, wicked to seek alliance with liberal revolutionaries, wicked to defend liberty of conscience or to claim freedom of the Press and of opinion. There was a pause for anxious heart-searching. Then on September 10th, the three editors of *L'Avenir* made their formal submission.

But two of them, at least, had all kinds of mental reservations. While Montalembert called *Mirari vos* 'the most disastrous act in the annals of the Church of France', Lamennais, gradually recovering his dogmatic self-confidence, drew an appalling picture of Roman corruption for the benefit of his intimates, casually dismissing Gregory as a 'cowardly and imbecile old man'. Lacordaire, meanwhile, was sorely distressed. For a long time he had been suspicious and nervous of Lamennais's indocility; even during the journey to Rome Lamennais had sometimes seemed to look ahead, beyond his condemnation, to a decisive struggle with authority. By a strange coincidence Lacordaire, like Montalembert, had been in Munich independently of Lamennais, when *Mirari vos* was published, and welcomed with relief Lamennais's immediate decision to yield. But his relief turned to misgiving one day as they were climbing a hill near Saverne; for Lamennais turned to him suddenly, saying, 'Lacordaire, suppose we add to our declaration of submission the words "Just for the present"?' By the time they had reached Paris, their disagreement was manifest. Visiting the shabby apartments the two men had taken in the rue de Vaugirard, Sainte-Beuve found Lamennais downstairs, enlarging on everything that had displeased and shocked him in Rome, while in the room above Lacordaire was cautiously outlining his disappointments. 'I concluded', says Sainte-Beuve, 'that entire harmony did not exist between the ground floor and the first.'[2]

---

[1] Quoted by E. L. Woodward, *Three Studies in European Conservatism*, p. 265. The Holy Office was, of course, the Inquisition.

[2] Sainte-Beuve, *Nouveaux lundis*, V, p. 451.

From Paris they went to La Chesnaie, where Lamennais was once again surrounded by his disciples. With mounting distress Lacordaire watched the growth of a schismatic spirit. Lamennais had put his heart into *L'Avenir*, and though he might tolerate the failure of the paper, might even acknowledge correction from the Pope, he could never admit the falsehood of his basic suppositions. Had he not been assured in Rome by such authorities as Father Ventura and Father Olivieri that his opinions were irreproachable, proof against any condemnation? Did he not feel intellectually and morally the master of that crass old dotard on the throne of Peter? It was true that no one had done more than he himself to exalt the Pope's authority, but his conviction of that authority derived from no more certain source than his conviction of his own rightness. Once he had believed in the Bourbons; but when they betrayed him he had turned his venom against their cause. Now he still believed in the Pope, maintaining that should the Pope err, he could not be disobeyed; but if even the Pope failed him, if even the Pope denied the very philosophy from which Lamennais's defence of papal authority had sprung . . . what then?

It was too early to answer that question, but Lacordaire could sense what the answer would be. Lamennais categorically prescribing his remedies for the mortal diseases of the Church; Lamennais declaring his respect for the papacy and in the next breath mocking at ignorant, monkish, reactionary old Gregory; Lamennais gathering disciples, preaching error, ignoring *Mirari vos*, identifying the future of Catholicism with himself alone, spitting defiance at prelate and Pope—that was not the master for Lacordaire, with his deep, unshakable fidelity to the Church and its head. For three months he stayed on at La Chesnaie, financed by the man he had once loved and now feared. A stinging retort of Lamennais's pricked him into a decision. Packing his bag, he left a note for his host, and, in the evening, walked out of the house. As he was making his way through the grounds, he suddenly caught sight of Lamennais's head over the top of a thicket, silhouetted against the darkening sky, engaged in earnest discourse. It was a pregnant, almost a symbolic, moment. Lacordaire stopped, hesitated, and walked on.

While his decision was probably inevitable and certainly

right, Lacordaire could never feel proud of the circumstances of his departure. But he was in deadly fear—fear of being fascinated back into heterodoxy and revolt. The two letters that he wrote to Lamennais were unhappy and ungenerous disavowals of the immediate past. The second, coming from a favourite disciple, was particularly wounding. 'It is,' said Lamennais, 'cold as a winter's night after the *bise* has blown.' Indeed if anyone suffered during the cruel months of 1833, it was not Lacordaire but Lamennais, writhing in humiliation, condemned to ignominious silence, watching his disciples break away one by one, and yet forbidden by his own pride and purposefulness from giving up the course on which he was set. Orthodox historians hint that he lost his soul. With his companions dismissed and the school at La Chesnaie shut down, he was committed to his final struggle with the Pope. He prepared for battle. But it was Gregory who opened hostilities. Alarmed at a letter in which Lamennais had announced his intention of thinking and acting as he saw fit 'in the purely temporal order', incapable of the act of generous magnanimity that might still have kept in the Church the only one of its servants with undisputed genius, Gregory demanded an explicit assurance that Lamennais would follow absolutely the doctrines set forth in *Mirari vos*. There was a long pause, which ended in Lamennais's submission without reserve. But his submission was neither sincere nor lasting. Pressed and harried by his friends, Lamennais had given way—'J'ai signé, j'ai signé, j'aurais signé que la lune était tombée en Chine'—but it was his final concession. He would abandon the Pope as he had abandoned the Bourbons, and with the Pope he would abandon the Church. In March 1834 he gave to Sainte-Beuve the manuscript of *Les Paroles d'un croyant*, which had long been in his possession. Its publication advertised his loss of Catholic faith.

CHAPTER IV

The Opportunity

Thus ended—or seemed to end—a movement which for a moment had glowed with the promise of a new future for the French Church. Lamennais's band of disciples fell apart; the bright flame of Lamennais's own genius spluttered into rebellion and was quenched. The inertia of tradition, the political habits of a displaced generation, the power of the past —all seemed to bear so heavily upon the living Church that its life was in danger of being extinguished. Perceptive Christians might be forgiven if they felt disheartened and oppressed; scarcely a glint of hope could be seen as they scanned the horizon.

It is true, as we have observed, that the poorer classes were slowly drawing nearer to the Church; but this movement was hardly yet apparent. Elsewhere the Church met with hostility or indifference. Among intellectuals, in particular, it enjoyed no more than a supercilious toleration. It received the polite and insincere tributes accorded to a distinguished old man who lies impotent on his deathbed; soon the curtains will be drawn and the will published. 'The time is coming', an eminent politician told a priest in 1831, 'when your only supporters will be a handful of dotards.' 'Gentlemen,' said the Inspector-General of Rennes University in the same year, 'we are marching forward to a great period in our history; we may see the obsequies of a great religion.' 'Philosophy is patient', observed Victor Cousin, the eclectic philosopher, with the serene confidence of a universal heir. 'Rejoicing to see the masses of the people (that is, almost the whole of the human race) reclining in the arms of Christianity, we are content to stretch out a helping

50

hand and to raise them higher still.' Some even declared that
the final scenes were already over. 'Since the nasty jolting it
received in 1789, the Catholic religion has been very sick',
wrote a famous journalist: 'the July Revolution has finished
it off.' And Heine added a clinical note: 'The average Frenchman doesn't want to hear a word about the corpse; he puts his
handkerchief to his nose when the Church is mentioned.'

Now that the Church's political power was broken, intellectuals did not worry about its impact on the moral and emotional
life of the country. No one is afraid of a corpse. Instead, they
discussed and disputed the succession, arguing about the precise
degree of symbolism and mythology necessary to the new
religion. For of the need of religion itself few had any doubt.
Already there existed the so-called Eglise française, which
preached a Christianity devoid of dogma; and Ballanche's attempts to reconcile the old faith with new ideas met with increasingly sympathetic understanding. Among the philosophers
Royer-Collard had begun to lecture earnestly and aridly on the
spiritual meaning of life, and from the complacent peaks of
eclecticism Victor Cousin looked down benevolently on any
religious system that had contributed to his own superior
synthesis. Of the sociologists Pierre Leroux, who popularized
the word 'socialism', vied with less radical theorists to establish
his system on a relatively Christian basis: while the revolutionary
Barbès, languishing under a death sentence that was happily
only temporary, eloquently invoked the name of Christ. The
Saint-Simonians, after the death of the Duke their founder,
wallowed ever deeper in emotional abstractions, which were
regularly expounded by the genial, handsome Enfantin in a
series of mystical sermons in the Salle Taitbout. Wherever one
might look, it seemed that scepticism and its prophets were in
disgrace. While Le Globe itself, one of the principal Romantic
organs, assailed Voltaire's thought as fiercely as it attacked his
writings, Creuzer's religious interpretation of the myths of
antiquity found eager readers. In short, it was clear to all but
the blind that the eighteenth-century tradition of analytical
materialism had failed to convince the new generation.

Now this chorus of aspiration was not exclusively or even
primarily intellectual in origin: as soon as a need is seen, it
begins to be felt. 'If Le Globe made no conversions,' says one of

51

its readers, 'its polemic manifestly added to the burden of incredulity.'[1] Many leading Romantics—Hugo and Lamartine, for instance—were definitely, if precariously, Christian, and those, like Michelet or Vigny, who had rejected Christian dogma, preserved a kind of mystical deism which protected them against the despair of unbelief. The air was full of nebulous religion; the verb of believing was daily conjugated without an object. One of the earliest to notice the change was the popular philosopher Jouffroy, whose famous—too famous—article on *Comment les dogmes finissent* had appeared in *Le Globe* in 1825. Lecturing in the Ecole normale in 1832, he remarked: 'Five years ago, the only objections I received were based on materialism; spiritualist doctrines met with a most vigorous resistance. Now, the general attitude has quite altered: the opposition is entirely Catholic.'[2] Probably this is an exaggeration, for Catholicism proper hardly made such rapid headway; but at any rate the trend of opinion showed that the so-called spiritualist doctrines were no longer spiritualist enough for the times. In the course of the next few years there is a startling unanimity among all who refer to the younger generation's attitude to religion. To speak of a metaphysical *Angst* would be going too far, for the critical exegesis of the Bible had not yet created a taut discrepancy between intellect and emotion, and there are few at any time who undertake a dispassionate analysis of the basis and pattern of their belief. Rather, disparagement of the Church and of the Christian religion, which had long been a conventional coinage of intellectual society, came under stress and suffered a rapid devaluation. It was a difficult transition from the superior smile of delicate mockery to the bowed head of humble respect, but the difficulty was emotional—the task of adapting oneself to live in another atmosphere. Just as Voltairian scepticism, reinforced by political liberalism, had once created conditions in which an intellectual required high originality in order to appreciate, much more to accept, the Christian religion and especially its Catholic form, so the discovery that social morality and vague deism left a deep void where it was least comfortable produced the exact opposite—a spiritual environment in which atheism became

[1] Louis de Carné, *Souvenirs de ma jeunesse*, p. 143.
[2] Frédéric Ozanam, *Lettres*, I, p. 49.

not merely stupid, but what was worse, insensitive and out of date. At first this change affected only a small section of society. Hardly touching the older generation of radical anticlericals, its main appeal was to young men who had yet to adopt a considered attitude to life. But this small section was a most important one.

Jouffroy himself spoke cogently on the subject: 'The void is everywhere: it is in every heart—darkly felt by the masses, more clearly perceived by distinguished minds. This void must be filled; as long as it remains unoccupied, I do not believe that society will achieve tranquillity. . . . Such is the deep, the fundamental cause of our social malaise.'[1] Musset was asking:

> Et que nous reste-t-il à nous, les déicides?
> Pour qui travailliez-vous, démolisseurs stupides,
> Lorsque vous disséquiez le Christ sur son autel?
> Que vouliez-vous semer sur sa céleste tombe,
> Quand vous jetiez au vent la sanglante colombe
> Qui tombe en tournoyant dans l'abîme éternel?[2]

By 1835 a prominent critic was writing: 'Our true feeling is one of emptiness; an uneasy need for faith; a sort of astonishment and horror at the isolation in which both man and society have been left by eighteenth-century philosophy—man struggling against the hazards of life with no help to sustain him, no torch to guide him, and society struggling against revolutions with no public faith to moderate them and reduce them to one or two basic principles.'[3]

Meanwhile, the Government, while showing no enthusiasm for religion, allowed itself a few gestures of tolerance. Touring the country, Louis Philippe was polite and even genial to bishops and parish priests. In 1833, for the first time since the July Revolution, the Chambers interrupted their sittings on Ascension Day; and the next year, as a cautious expression of neutrality, an allegorical representation of Justice, with sword and scales, was introduced into the Paris assizes to replace the crucifix that had been removed on the downfall of Charles.

[1] Quoted by Thureau-Dangin, *Histoire de la monarchie de juillet*, II, p. 345.
[2] *Rolla*, 1833.
[3] S. de Sacy, *Variétés*, II, p. 6. He regarded the religious reaction as the last spasm of a dying faith.

It seemed, in short, that all the necessary preconditions existed for a religious revival: the Church, no longer the target of political passion, enjoyed extensive liberty, without being compromised by the regime; and with deism, materialism and even spiritualist philosophy failing to supply the void left by the decay of dogma, the younger generation groped helplessly for some support, some stanchion, some assurance that the gods were not mere figments. But nothing happened; and the man in whom the revival was to centre was still living in obscurity in Paris, out of favour, suspected of heresy.

Unnerved by the violence of his own self-questioning, Lacordaire had yielded entirely to the Pope and to the Archbishop, who had restored him to his post as chaplain at the Visitandines. He was anxious to repudiate his errors—indeed too anxious; for he was prevailed on to write a book against Lamennais, *Considérations sur le système philosophique de M. de La Mennais*, which appeared in May 1834. No doubt his purpose was good: he wished to show that in flirting with Mennaisian philosophy his intentions had been honourable, and to contrast its impropriety with conventional virtue. But his book won him no friends and convinced few who were not convinced already. Lacordaire was no philosopher, and only successful as a polemist within the narrow limits of a given brief. To go into battle against Lamennais with the slender weapons of a seminarist was to expose his own weakness; for Lamennais, though usually dogmatic and often illogical and preposterous, was a writer of evident force and striking originality. Lacordaire, though he had just turned down the offer of a chair at the Catholic University of Louvain, was not thereby endowed with honorary rank as a thinker—certainly not as a thinker of the calibre to challenge his recent master.

His principal adviser was Mme Swetchine, and she it was who betrayed him into the blunder of writing his *Considérations*. This acquaintance revived him at a crisis, when plunged in his darkest moods of doubt and lassitude. 'You,' he told her a year later, 'you took me up at a moment when my disasters had warned me of the difficulty of life and the pride implicit in my past. I can *never* forget that.' At this time Mme Swetchine was in her early fifties, the hostess of the principal Catholic salon in

Paris. Born in Moscow and brought up in the sceptical atmosphere of the court—her father was confidential secretary to the Empress Catherine II—she had formed a close friendship with the Ultramontane philosopher Joseph de Maistre and under his influence had undergone conversion. The bewildering fluctuations of Russian politics, by which both her father and husband, falling from favour, were obliged to retire to their estates, disturbed the even progress of her social life, and in 1825, when the accession of Nicholas I inaugurated an era of brutal autocracy, she left Russia and settled in Paris, opening a salon in the rue Saint-Dominique which was immediately distinguished from its rivals by the personal piety of its devotees.

Perhaps the competition in piety was not severe; but it was characteristic of Mme Swetchine that she maintained a private chapel as part of her establishment. While young women used its amenities to pray against the temptations of the world, the flesh and the devil, earnest discourse was heard in the adjoining salon, where this middle-aged widow with the ugly face and slightly foreign accent gathered to herself a galaxy of talent, from the precise small-talk of Cuvier to the passionate generalizations of Montalembert, from the confident eloquence of Ravignan to the hesitant subleties of Tocqueville. She revelled in obscurity: 'I plunge into metaphysics like a bath', she said of herself. And from these periodic immersions she emerged with a desire to dive yet deeper. She was never so happy as when she could indulge in long and stupefying speculations, unimpeded by the discipline of history or the evidence of established fact.

Almost at first sight she picked on Lacordaire as her favourite, and the feeling was reciprocal. 'I never met anyone', he said, 'with so bold a spirit of freedom combined with so solid a faith.' In some ways she was another mother for Lacordaire—she even invited him to live in her *hôtel*; in others, a spiritual director. Having discovered in this downcast young priest a heart like her own, ineradicably Catholic but given to the cause of freedom, she determined to create his future—to hoist him up from his pit of loneliness and to set him high above his contemporaries. To this end she urged him to practise and develop his gift for eloquence, that natural facility of which Berryer had spoken over ten years earlier. Lacordaire was reluctant, but let himself be persuaded, and at 7 p.m. on Sunday, 5th May 1833, he delivered his first sermon in Saint-Roch before a group of friends and priests.

The emissaries whose return Mme Swetchine anxiously awaited came back with long faces. 'He will never be a good preacher', said one. Lacordaire felt the same. 'I can see', he wrote, 'that I lack the necessary strength of body and suppleness of mind. I have not sufficient understanding of the world; I have lived—I shall always live in it—as a stranger. I possess none of the qualities one needs to be a real preacher.' And he cancelled all the twenty sermons he had promised to deliver in the neighbouring parishes.

There were, however, other possibilities. He had already given two lectures in the Collège Stanislas which had been well received, and when he was invited to deliver a course on religious subjects in the same chapel, he accepted, arranging the first lecture for 19th January 1834. Only a few of the pupils and staff thought it worth disturbing their afternoon to hear him, but those who did were startled. At the second lecture there was a crowd; at the third, most of the pupils had to be excluded to make room for visitors who flocked from outside. It was, in fact, apparent that Lacordaire had struck his true vein, that the alleged heretic had grown into a powerful apologist, and the halting preacher of Saint-Roch become an orator of power and persuasion. In a few weeks the chapel was packed two hours before the lecture was due to begin; Chateaubriand, Lamartine, Hugo were prominent among the audience; and Berryer himself, arriving late one day, climbed up a ladder and through a window rather than go away disappointed.

It is difficult for us to imagine the effect of Lacordaire's lectures. They were like resurrection in a mortuary, or a sudden glory of blossom in a waste land. They aroused, says one witness, 'an admiration verging on stupor'.[1] 'There is nothing to match that eloquence and inspiration', wrote a young poet who had chanced to attend. 'In philosophic and religious circles people talk of nothing else.'[2] By the time April came round, the college authorities had erected a new gallery in the chapel, to cope somehow with the avid and still multiplying public.

[1] *Annales de la philosophie chrétienne*, 1844, p. 215. Quoted by J. Favre, *Lacordaire orateur*, p. 217.

[2] M. de Guérin, *Journal, lettres et poèmes*, p. 291.

In private life Lacordaire was cold and a little forbidding; shy of his own emotions and apt to check them. As he realized, his manner of habitual reserve frightened, when it did not repel, those who sought to know him intimately. 'People do not distinguish enough between the real man and the unreal man within me', he said: 'between what I am and what I wish to appear. I cannot, like Sterne, weep before others; I am ashamed of tears.' And again, penetrating deeper into his own psychology: 'There are two contrary principles ceaselessly at war in my breast, often making me most unhappy: cold reason blights my glowing imagination; I am disenchanted in exact proportion to my former illusions.' His stilted hesitations and intellectual misgivings followed him into the pulpit; if, as at Saint-Roch, he had a written sermon before him, they sapped his confidence, cramped his vocabulary, weakened his voice and reduced him to a condition of feeble incompetence. But once let him throw aside his manuscript, relying, as he did at the Collège Stanislas, on the impulsions of the moment, and his inhibitions dropped away. He no longer wavered about his purpose or muttered uncomfortable clichés: the stimulus of an audience drew out of him an eloquence of which he had been unaware, and the excitement of responding to a mass of listeners, themselves increasingly excited and moved, drove him on past his immediate goal into a bolder world of high paradox and deep emotion, into which he was carried headlong and carried with him the pliant assembly, till together, exhausted and over-wrought, they reached the climax and the end, and stumbled out into the street, wondering in what experience they had been engulfed.

There are no proper records of the lectures at the Collège Stanislas; it is not even clear what Lacordaire said, for the audience took away a memory of his oratory rather than of his theme. But the publicity and success of the lectures woke up his enemies, who had been reposing contentedly on *Mirari vos*. Was it just or right than a man of Lacordaire's avowed opinions and acknowledged past should step out before all the orators of France as *the* spokesman of the Catholic Church? Was it even safe? Grounds for complaint were not lacking. One of the few sentences that has survived from the lectures comes from the first. There seems no doubt that Lacordaire, leaning towards

57

his audience, tartly admonished them: 'Never forget that the first tree of liberty was planted in the earthly Paradise.' Trees of liberty indeed! What place had they in the accepted apologetic? And within a few weeks Lacordaire had been denounced for dangerous and heretical opinions to the Government, the Holy See and the Archbishop of Paris. While the Government announced that they viewed the lectures 'without distrust', the police were less generous, apparently writing secretly to the Archbishop, stressing their outraged theology;[1] and the Pope referred the matter to the same quarter. Mgr de Quélen was therefore left with the unwelcome task of making a decision. It was a task for which he was hardly qualified; but after a pause for reflection his prudence overcame his lethargy and he suspended the course. Stung at this second failure when he thought to have found his bent, Lacordaire remonstrated; and as a concession, Quélen replied that the lectures could be resumed on condition that they were first written out in full and submitted to him for approval. 'I counted on two men', Lacordaire wrote with some bitterness. 'The first I left because he betrayed the hopes of us all. The second forsakes me. Henceforth I count on God alone.'

Mgr de Quélen was a Breton—a Catholic royalist of the old school who had readily encouraged Charles X's attempt to dispense with deputies. He was a tall gracious figure, with an imposing presence, a sound classical education, and a negligible acquaintance with theology and religious history. As Archbishop, his avowed aim was to 'clean up' the episcopate, by which phrase he meant that it should be restricted to men of noble blood. Not for him the democratic egalitarianism of Lamennais. 'Not only', he once declared in the pulpit of Notre-Dame, 'was Jesus Christ the Son of God, but he was also of very good family on his mother's side, and there are excellent reasons for seeing in him the heir to the throne of Judea.' How fortunate that the genealogy of Joseph the carpenter was not in question! Moreover the general benevolence of Quélen's character was of no help in foreseeing the trend of events; he was unable to compromise with the present, much more with the future. Clear-headed enough to be vaguely uneasy about the relations between Church and people, he halted in nervous

---

[1] Foisset, I, p. 299; Favre, p. 216.

bewilderment when it came to taking action. He was sufficiently enlightened to distrust his own judgement, now that no Bourbon king stood at his side. The decisions he took were negative. Beholding his dignity entangled in a net of apparent error, he therefore hastened to extricate himself. The unorthodoxy of Lacordaire's methods, he reflected, might well indicate a corresponding unorthodoxy of doctrine.

It was not the first time that Quélen had drifted into a decision in regard to Lacordaire. About ten days before the inauguration of the lectures at the Collège Stanislas he received a deputation from a number of young men led by Frédéric Ozanam, who had been associated a few months earlier in the foundation of the Société de Saint-Vincent-de-Paul. Distressed at the spread of free-thought, they asked that some outstanding Christian thinker or orator should be given an opportunity to defend the faith from the pulpit of Notre-Dame; they suggested the Abbé Bautain or Lacordaire. The Archbishop, who listened with his customary courtesy, nodded his head at their proposals, agreeing on every point except the most important—the choice of speaker. Instead of Lacordaire (who was contaminated with Mennaisianism) and instead of Bautain (who was tarnished with fideism) he would choose a group of highly talented preachers suitably qualified to deal with the problems of the modern world. So on 16th February 1834, while the Collège Stanislas was crowded to suffocation, Mgr de Quélen himself inaugurated the new series in Notre-Dame; and every week he was followed by a preacher of fame and ability.[1] It was an excellent scheme and was carried out with skill and ingenuity. It had only one disadvantage. The sermons were delivered to an empty cathedral.

Ozanam and his friends were not alone in regretting the virtual interdict imposed on Lacordaire; indeed a pamphlet of expostulation by the Abbé Liautard, Mme du Cayla's friend, who had founded the Collège Stanislas, circulated widely among the Paris clergy. Liautard still wielded considerable influence both in the Church and outside it, and his intervention was probably decisive. At any rate, one cold morning in January 1835, while Lacordaire, dispirited and rather bitter, was walking through the Gardens of the Luxembourg, he met a priest of

[1] Dupanloup, of whom we shall later hear much, was one.

his acquaintance. 'What are you doing?' this man asked. 'You
ought to see the Archbishop and come to some agreement with
him.' Lacordaire had not walked many steps further before he
met another priest, who remarked, 'You are wrong not to see
the Archbishop. I have some grounds for thinking he would be
glad to have a word with you.' Mildly bemused by this curious
coincidence and always ready to see the hand of Providence in
the most trivial event, Lacordaire turned towards the Convent
of Saint-Michel, where Quélen was now unostentatiously living,
and rang the bell. The door was opened, not by the portress,
but by a choir nun who knew and liked Lacordaire. The
Archbishop, she said, was not at home to visitors, but could
perhaps be seen. Lacordaire was ushered into the study. For
some minutes Quélen pursued a desultory conversation. Then,
fixing a sharp eye on Lacordaire, he exploded his charge: 'I
propose to entrust to you the pulpit of Notre-Dame. Will you
accept it?'

CHAPTER V

Notre-Dame

Lacordaire was to deliver eight lectures—or *conférences*, as they were called—differing from sermons proper by not being part of a service: the first to begin at 2 p.m. on 1st March 1835, during Lent. Because of the high reputation he had won at the Collège Stanislas and because of the strong feeling—approval or disapproval—aroused by any mention of his name, the Cathedral filled early. There were people in the nave at 8 a.m., and the pious ladies who arrived an hour later for the Canons' Mass were startled to find their pews occupied by strangers. These strangers were men, and what was even rarer, young men: evidently unused to waiting in pews, for they spent the morning reading papers—*La Dominicale, La Nouvelle Minerve, Les Débats, Le National*, and even *Le Constitutionnel*. One horseman, after dismounting on the Parvis, was seen to walk in still wearing riding-boots and brandishing a stick. When the procession bearing the archiepiscopal cross entered at one o'clock, the Archbishop started with noticeable alarm as he saw the tide of humanity that had swept into his Cathedral, flowing down the aisles, swirling round the pillars, lapping against the walls. It was a sea of people numbering at least five thousand.

At two o'clock, after the Archbishop had celebrated Mass, Lacordaire mounted the pulpit, a slim figure with bony head, high brow, and dark, flashing, close-set eyes. His first words were drowned by the footsteps of late-comers, who meandered down the aisles looking for seats; but when the clatter had subsided, he was heard in absolute silence. The Archbishop, says Lacordaire, 'listened with his head slightly bowed, completely impassive, like a man who was not only a spectator and a judge, but ran personal risks in this solemn venture. When I had fairly come to terms both with my subject and my audience, and my breast was swollen with the need to grip such a huge gathering of men, I uttered one of those cries which, if sincere and deeply felt, never fail to be moving. The Archbishop started visibly. A pallor which even I could see covered his face, he raised his head and cast on me a look of astonishment. I realized that the battle was won in his mind. It was also won in the audience.'[1]

There seems no doubt that the passage which shook the Archbishop and the audience, tearing them almost bodily from their seats so that they were no longer spectators but participants, was the following:

'Pourquoi ai-je pris la parole dans cette enceinte? Si je jette les yeux autour de moi, je découvre des fronts de tous les âges, des cheveux qui ont blanchi dans les veilles de la science, des visages qui portent la trace de la fatigue des combats, d'autres qu'animent les douces émotions des études littéraires, de jeunes hommes enfin qui viennent de cueillir à peine la troisième fleur de la vie. Assemblée, assemblée, dites-moi: Que me demandez-vous? Que voulez-vous de moi? La vérité? Vous ne l'avez donc pas en vous, vous la cherchez donc, vous voulez la recevoir, vous êtes venus ici pour être enseignés.'

With his authority established and the weakness of his audience revealed, Lacordaire could proceed to affirm his advantage, to assert the doctrine of a teaching Church, whose need was proved by the very presence of his hearers. His voice, which was at first subdued, grew in breadth and flexibility till he displayed all its range and power, pausing suddenly on the brink of emotion or dropping to a barely audible whisper, slowing to a plodding rhythm or whipping up his speed till the words of a sentence almost coalesced. His dryness of timbre was forgotten; especially as he began to move about the pulpit, swinging from side to side, raising his arms and shouting with the passion he had induced in himself. He was carried away on a torrent of spontaneity; and when the last echo of his voice had died away in the galleries of Notre-Dame and he had withdrawn to the sacristy to recover some gleam of energy,

[1] *Le Testament du Père Lacordaire*, p. 83.

the crowd gushed on to the Parvis, overpowered and entranced by the performance it had witnessed.

So the following seven *conférences* brought, not a decline in numbers, but an increase. Men who had first come out of curiosity came again out of interest. Barriers had to be erected to hold back the crowds, and stewards appointed to control them. By the time Lacordaire delivered his third address, there was a strong possibility that many intending spectators would be excluded for lack of space—and that in one of the greatest cathedrals of Europe. Overcoming his initial hesitations and uncertainties, Lacordaire had cast off whatever awkwardness of gesture had first been apparent; and with full confidence that he could possess his audience, he responded freely to its stimulus, becoming naturally and completely himself. His personality, which so often struck his intimates as cold and reserved, seemed to burgeon in the pulpit, as though he needed the glow of public excitement in order to unfold the true extent of his gift. As he stood before them, he appeared to his listeners larger than life.[1] But it was more than that. His personality was a compression of their personalities; his feelings condensed their feelings; his experience sounded like their own. Only his beliefs were different.

Lacordaire, then, was a popular hero. At the end of the course, Quélen, in a public speech of thanks, referred to him as 'that excellent and faithful friend who is at once the solace and joy of my heart'; and shortly afterwards offered him an honorary canonry at Notre-Dame. A large crowd, waiting patiently outside the Cathedral at the end of this last *conférence*, refused to be dispersed, and when Lacordaire at length emerged, greeted his appearance with a flurry of pleasure, making a narrow path through which he could walk. A shade of green that had become the rage at Longchamp was even christened *vert Lacordaire*.

If, however, there is no doubt about Lacordaire's success or about the quality of the eloquence that brought the most distinguished connoisseurs of language—from Chateaubriand and Berryer to Lamartine and Vigny—flocking together in the pews of Notre-Dame, it is much harder to assign reasons, to say why he succeeded when so many others failed. He was, of course, an orator of unrivalled power; but Dupanloup, who had preached

---

[1] Delpech quoted by Foisset, II, p. 528.

the year before to a handful of *dévotes*, was an orator, certainly not in Lacordaire's class, but of no mean gifts. Lacordaire had, it is true, a well-deserved reputation for liberalism; but so had Lamennais, whose adherents were slipping away with increasing rapidity. And if his loyalty to the Church was the attraction, there were surely other men whose past was less erratic and whose improvisation was more predictable.

No: if we are to explain Lacordaire's success, it cannot be in terms of one particular endowment but in the combination of them all. In other words his appeal lay in his character, or in as much of his character as he cared to show from the pulpit. He stood there as a man of the modern world, acknowledging the same problems and answering to the same enthusiasms as his audience; and his approach, necessary as it might seem for any apologist, was as rare and refreshing as spring-water in high summer. For the gifts of his predecessors had been parched by tradition; their prospects of success had wilted and withered through the long desiccation of precedent. Since the death in 1742 of Massillon, the last of Louis XIV's pulpit orators, there had been no preacher to receive and revive the tradition of Bourdaloue and Bossuet. Inevitably the method that had once been brisk and original ossified into a model. First came the text; then the exordium, in which the preacher developed his text, sketching the main points of his sermon and ending with an invocation to the Virgin—'la chute à l'Ave Maria', as it had been called. After the exordium, the points themselves, two or three in number, but often divided so that the sermon contained seven or eight sections; and finally the peroration, in which the exordium was re-echoed and recalled. In addition, there was a prescribed pattern of apology: it was the custom of centuries that the preacher should start with the existence of a supernatural order and gradually narrow it down to revelation, to Christianity and to Catholic doctrines; while as for the style of the sermon, congregations for a hundred years were treated to careful imitations of Massillon, even to his sentence rhythms and verbal mannerisms.

Now Lacordaire shattered this model. Confident in his own authority, he dropped the old appellation of 'brethren' and called his audience 'Messieurs'; for like him they belonged to the nineteenth century. 'Brethren' had a flavour of pious archaicism—precisely the flavour of 1835 Christianity; and Lacordaire's first aim was to create an atmosphere of contemporary urgency. For the same reason he discarded both text and *Ave Maria*, simplified and shortened the exordium, and dispensed with all artificial divisions within the sermon itself, so that he could move freely within its framework, quick to follow any metaphor or picture that occurred to him under the stress of improvisation. Sometimes he did without exordium at all, or so abbreviated it that he could quell his audience within the first few minutes with a cry like 'Assemblée, assemblée'.

Turning to apologetic method, he paid more respect to his audience than to his masters of rhetoric. The men who filled Notre-Dame belonged to a generation that had grown up since the Revolution and the First Empire; soldiers, lawyers, students, doctors, drawn partly by curiosity, partly by the awareness of a blank within themselves, they had few of them any first-hand acquaintance with religion, and even if they were kindly disposed to his doctrine, it was less from conviction than from sentimental aspiration. To have followed the dusty track of tradition, beginning with a so-called demonstration of the existence of God, would have been folly: he would have outstripped his audience in the first ten minutes. Instead, therefore, of inaugurating his sermons by an attempted proof or a bold hypothesis, he started with a fact—a fact admitted even by those in his audience who had taken part in the sacking of Saint-Germain-l'Auxerrois and the Archbishop's palace: the fact of the Church. From that point his way was clear: he could go on to discuss, in successive sermons, the necessity of the Church; its constitution and authority; its establishment and the teaching of mankind before its foundation; its relations with the temporal order and its disciplinary power; thus drawing a long perspective of history in which the Church came to fill its appointed place—in which all was naturally, authoritatively organized for the soul's salvation. History not merely revealed God: it was almost dictated by Him.

Lacordaire's general aim was limited: it was, he said, 'to prepare the way for faith'.[1] But what won him acceptance as a leader was not merely the power of his oratory—for even Romantic France was suspicious of oratory by itself—but the

---

[1] Lacordaire, *Œuvres*, II, p. 5.

self-revelation that was part of his eloquence. In its new form the sermon was a vehicle of social, philosophical and political ideas and feelings which had hitherto escaped it; and Lacordaire's sentiments were those of his generation. Hearing him, the audience reflected, as one contemporary put it, 'Lui aussi, il a donc connu cela?'[1] By basing his course on the fact of the Church, he had adopted an experimental method in his search for truth: the Church, on his argument, was its own justification. But his experimental method applied to the emotions just as much as to the more logical faculties of the mind: for if *he*, sharing the sympathies and aspirations of his century and suffering from their widespread sense of futility and hopelessness, had been able to satisfy his needs and heal his wounds within the Church, was that not in itself an encouragement for others to follow his example? 'The crowd . . .', wrote a critic, 'does not believe that one *can* believe. . . . It comes not because it believes, but because it would like to.'[2] Realizing that though the barrier to faith had been erected on the arguments of the enemies of Christianity, it was now emotional and not logical, Lacordaire assaulted it with pertinacity, striving to clear an open path for the explorations of the lonely mind; and his audience asked for the barrier within themselves to be removed, for the inhibitions of scepticism to be broken down.

Such was always the essence of Lacordaire's appeal: he moved his hearers, often in spite of themselves. This preacher with his love of liberty, his respect for the Revolution and his sympathy for the perplexities and hesitations of the contemporary world, could find bold pictures that struck the mind like a blow. Sometimes it was a stark juxtaposition:

'Si l'on était venu dire à Auguste se promenant dans ses jardins avec Horace ou Mécène: Il y a là-bas un homme avec une besace et un bâton qui se dit envoyé de Dieu pour entendre l'aveu de vos fautes, n'aurait-il pas regardé cet homme comme un fou? Eh bien! Messieurs, cette folie a prévalu.'[3]

More rarely it was a simile so apt to the mood of the audience that it was received with a shudder:

'L'infini est établi mathématiquement; il existe. Et vous

[1] Delpech quoted by Foisset, II, p. 523.
[2] Philarète Chasles in *La Revue de Paris*, 1835, XVII, pp. 17, 19.
[3] Lacordaire, *Œuvres*, II, p. 119.

croyez que vous m'emprisonnerez dans le fini, comme dans une Sainte-Hélène entourée de l'océan?'[1]

But always there was a verve and vigour that masked whatever deficiencies his argument might reveal (precisely what, for instance, was this 'infinite' that had been proved mathematically?), and brought home to his audience the immediate, instant quality of the experience lying behind his words.

Superficially Lacordaire was a Romantic preacher, appealing to the Romantic generation and listened to by the acknowledged masters of Romantic literature; and it is true that he had learnt nothing from Bossuet, who was curiously neglected at the time, and everything from Rousseau and Chateaubriand, the former giving him his oratorical movement, the latter his sense of colour. But of literature since Chateaubriand he knew next to nothing. Even in the past his taste was strangely old-fashioned: probably he never read a word of Shakespeare, Schiller or Calderon (which is curious in a man who publicly proclaimed the value of literature in education[2]), and when he used a poetical quotation, it usually came from one of Voltaire's tragedies, and even then not from the best. What is his one passage from Lamartine beside this pseudo-classical hotch-potch? Even Montalembert, in a book that exalts Lacordaire to the skies, is forced to admit that 'mythology and Greek and Roman history were his great quarry. Never, at least in our time, has anyone made greater use or misuse of Brutus and Socrates, Epaminondas and Scipio. It was no use telling him that if you want to find Voltaire, you do not look for him in his tragedies.'[3]

If one opens a book of Lacordaire's sermons today, in the stern black binding that the house of Mme Veuve Poussielgue has thought fit for works of this kind, one's reaction is of surprise and disappointment: surprise that for more than a decade these slipshod arguments and loosely constructed sentences captured and held the admiration of believers and sceptics alike; disappointment that so little of the original fire and passion has survived the transition to print. For these sermons are flat and dull, not redeemed by the occasional flash of

[1] Lacordaire, *Œuvres*, II, p. 149.
[2] Lacordaire, *Lettres à des jeunes gens*, p. 359 (in 1858).
[3] Montalembert, *Le Père Lacordaire*, p. 147; see also Foisset, II, p. 517; le Comte d'Haussonville, *Lacordaire*, pp. 143–4.

originality that hints at their original power. To men who saw and heard Lacordaire in Notre-Dame, these little black volumes must have possessed a quite different significance; reading through the sober pages they could still catch the intonation of his voice and glimpse his familiar gestures. But the echoes have faded away; and for us the lines are dead. All that great eloquence has evaporated, leaving only the pattern of its progress.

Lacordaire, of course, had his critics, even among men receptive to novelty. There is, for instance, a letter to Lamennais from one of his disciples, a pathetically hostile letter in which Lacordaire is humbled by comparison with his former master.

'Last Sunday [it runs] Notre-Dame was crowded. The Abbé Lacordaire was to preach. . . . I was astonished at such eagerness to hear a man who cannot satisfy the needs of his audience because he lacks both the necessary depth and logical power; and I reflected that he owed his reputation to his one-time association with you. His appearance before the young people was one more concession to "new ideas", and you ought to have seen how all the old canons, surrounding the Archbishop as he superintended the ceremony, pulled wry faces and displayed their hostility to the man they were obliged to hear. . . . I found his sermon desperately weak, and I am not the only one.'[1]

But his shortcomings, though apparent to the hostile critic, did not strike the mass of his listeners; and one can understand the reason by turning over the pages of these sermons. For if there is one shining quality that illuminates every line Lacordaire ever wrote, it is his sincerity: a conviction of the absolute truth of what he was saying and an appealing frankness in its expression. He might be a dupe; at least he was not a fake. Together with this frankness there went a consuming desire to make his message acceptable, to induce an appetite so strong that it could no longer be resisted. And so he had no hesitation in proclaiming his belief in progress, affirming his faith in the people (were they not the poor of the New Testament?), and welcoming the advance of science.

But the very attraction of his eloquence was its weakness. Admittedly he did not try to dilute Catholic doctrines in order

[1] A. Roussel, *Lamennais intime d'après une correspondance inédite*, pp. 259–60.

to administer them more easily to the people, and in his first course of eight sermons he argued strongly in favour of the infallibility of the Church and the primacy of the Roman Pontiff. But for a preacher who was always taking his stand on experience, Lacordaire displayed a surprising vagueness about historical fact, a vagueness none the less real because it was camouflaged by dogmatic assertions. No doubt this distorted account of the past made his preaching more palatable, especially to a generation which had not yet learnt to value even the historical accuracy of Michelet, but in the long run his reputation suffered. Had it not been for his outstanding honesty, he would have appeared disingenuous in neglecting inconvenient facts: for what other orator would have contrived to speak at length of the persecutions to which the Church had been subject, without even mentioning the persecutions of which the Church had been guilty? As it was, his neglect sprang from mere ignorance. Montalembert suggests that his historical knowledge was confined to Plutarch and Cornelius Nepos.[1] And there is no doubt that even when Lacordaire was sufficiently familiar with his subject to have misgivings, he somehow avoided them. He was endowed with a comfortable faculty of being certain: objections, exceptions, logical flaws—his mind passed serenely over them into the oratorical absolute.

Other criticisms struck his audience when they read his sermons in cold blood. There was a certain ingenuity of reasoning, a courting of danger, an almost complacent fondness for the precipices of thought, which he might cultivate voluntarily but which was certainly not discouraged by Mme Swetchine. His love of paradox, too, overflowed from his ideas into their expression, with the result that his metaphors, though often powerful, jostled together and gave an impression of incoherence. Moreover, the detail, especially in his first sermons, revealed frequent lapses from taste. Chance appeared as 'Dieu gardant l'incognito'; honour as 'la ligne équinoxiale de l'humanité'. It was clear that Lacordaire's rhetoric often overweighted his thought, draping a frail little idea in robes of great splendour: the voice became so loud, rich and conscious of its own sonority, that its message was no longer audible.

When, however, an orator's supreme gift lies, as did Lacor-

---

[1] Montalembert, *Le Père Lacordaire*, p. 146.

daire's, in the quality and passion of his improvisation, the
faults of detail that mar every page are the conditions of his
eloquence. To stand up in the pulpit after an hour or two's
reflection on the general aspects of a subject, provided with only
a scrap of paper bearing the merest outline of what one has to
say, is to command and welcome the promptings of the moment;
and these, however well suited to the mood of the audience, are
bound to be largely compounded of commonplace ideas, trivial
metaphors and stock expressions, which would be blotted out
had the sermon first been written. But for Lacordaire the cost
of writing was too heavy; he lost his spontaneity and conviction.
When the sermon had been delivered and when—to his disgust
—shorthand reporters had already circulated copies, he usually
recorded a version of his own, which was eventually published
as the definitive edition; but if, in fact, one wishes for an
accurate account of the sermon as delivered, the reporters are
more reliable, and the best text lies not in the black volumes of
Veuve Poussielgue, but in the files of *L'Ami de la Religion* and
L'Univers.

CHAPTER VI

Revival

Had he not struck the right moment all Lacordaire's qualities would have been spent in vain. It happened that he delivered his sermons when they were most needed, to an audience that delighted in his virtues and largely ignored his defects. Germany had already witnessed a Catholic revival in the 'twenties, with Görres, Baeder, the Brothers Schlegel and Döllinger; and this movement now spread to France. It was no accident that the German group, which stressed the need to free the Church from state control and to reconcile the traditional teaching of Christianity with modern research, was on a particularly friendly footing with the authors of *L'Avenir*; for both schools owed their main attraction to the forthright, unprejudiced spirit with which they approached the modern world, denying any inevitable rift between the nineteenth century and the old religion. Lamennais's impulsiveness and Gregory's distrust broke up the party of La Chesnaie and, it seemed, obliterated any hope of a revival in France. But as soon as Lacordaire stood forth in a church and declared in sonorous accents his attachment to the present and his faith in the past, the people flocked to hear him.

The revival lit a flame within the Church as well as outside it; for many of those who habitually practised their religion did so with some insincerity, as though it were a picturesque social ceremony too ancient and amusing to be discontinued. At Périgueux, for instance, which was a fairly typical provincial town, a routine parade took place every Sunday morning. At about half-past twelve a crowd of men assembled before the Cathedral—young bourgeois, young noblemen and a sprinkling of their elders—drawn up in two lines outside the main door. The service over, a slow procession of ladies emerged, girls and young matrons in full array, older women in more decorous attire, sailing gorgeously past their admirers, acknowledging their friends with demure smiles and delicate inclinations of the head. When the last worshipper had received her due, the street was empty save for a wake of heavy perfume.[1]

Now all this changed. 'Gentlemen,' said a speaker in the Chamber of Deputies in 1837, 'whether you like it or not, the feeling for religion has, in the last six years, regained a power which no one could have foreseen.'[2] And there was evidence for this revival on all sides. By 1837 the Abbé Desgenettes, who three years earlier was appointed to Notre-Dame-des-Victoires in Paris, a parish with an unenviable reputation for viciousness, had seen the number of communicants rise from 720 to 9,950.[3] Nor was there any great falling-off as the novelty of devotion subsided. When he was touring the country in 1847, Mr. Thomas Allies, an Anglican clergyman with an interest in Catholicism, discussed the subject with two French priests. 'They give', he wrote, 'the most astonishing account of the change which has taken place in France in the last fifteen years in religious matters. Formerly a young man dared not confess that he was a Christian, or show himself in a church; now the bitter sarcasm and ridicule with which all religious subjects were treated has passed away; earnestness has laid hold of the mind of the nation, and even those who are not Christians appear to be searching for the truth, and treat Christianity as a reality and religion with respect.'[4]

But, of course, the conditions favouring revival were not peculiar to Catholicism, and there was a parallel movement in the Protestant Church. The support and encouragement that the Protestants had received from Voltaire, particularly in the cases of Calas and Sirven,[5] inclined them to perceive much

---

[1] E. Veuillot, *Louis Veuillot*, I, p. 76.

[2] Quoted by Thureau-Dangin, *L'Eglise et l'Etat sous la monarchie de juillet*, pp. 14–15.   [3] *Dublin Review*, 1844, XVI, p. 11.

[4] T. W. Allies, *Journal in France*, pp. 112–13.

[5] Calas, a Protestant merchant of Toulouse, who, wrongly charged with killing a son who wished to become Catholic, had been found guilty and executed, was rehabilitated by Voltaire's efforts. Voltaire also proved the innocence of the Sirven family. The parents were Protestants from

virtue in Voltairian philosophy, and during the early years of the century it was as much deist as Christian morality that was taught from their pulpits. They were, on the whole, united, for the recurrent threat of persecution, and the ugly fact of the White Terror, closed their ranks against the danger of dissension. Their only divisions were on matters of theology and doctrine; for unlike the Catholics they were not disturbed by the question of temporal power, and their relations with the State were always correct and sometimes friendly. The Church, however, was split into two sections: the 'liberals', who clung to the intellectual freedom inherent in Protestantism, forswearing the confessional yoke that was imposed on the Roman Church; and the 'orthodox', who wished to re-establish the discipline of the heroic age of Protestantism and return to the definitive expression of faith as set forth in the 1571 Confession of La Rochelle. For many years a desultory and inconclusive polemic between the two sections had brightened their periodicals, sharpening their pens and elucidating their differences. But now a new impulse emerged from Geneva to strengthen and encourage the orthodox—a movement ultimately called *Le Réveil*. Its purpose was to organize the Church more strictly, teaching justification by faith and the complete inspiration of the Bible, inculcating the need of salvation and the fear of hell. Surging across Protestant France, *Le Réveil* brought new crowds into the churches and old doctrines into the sermons. Welcomed though it was by the leading spokesmen of the liberal school, it gave a special stimulus to the orthodox. If they always remained a minority in the consistories, unable to carry out the Calvinist reforms which they had at heart, their number and influence grew fast, especially under the leadership of Adolphe Monod.

The son of a minister who had belonged to the old school of pulpit exhortation, Monod became the outstanding figure of *Le Réveil*, while his brother Frédéric was its publicist. Dismissed in 1831 from the church at Lyons for disturbing its members by his exacting doctrinal requirements, he spent some years as a Professor at Montauban and ended as a minister in Paris. Monod was the Lacordaire of Protestantism, but Lacordaire

---

Castres, whose second daughter was forcibly removed to a convent and there went mad. When she broke out and committed suicide, they were accused of her murder, but fled in time to escape execution.

with a difference. His attitude was tenser and more doctrinal, the attitude of a man who foresaw the main danger to his faith in relaxed theology and subverted traditions; and his preaching was therefore much less suave and seductive, aimed rather at drawing together the threads of the ancient creed than at injecting Protestantism with modernity. For Protestantism was modern enough; perhaps indeed too modern, too ready to accept the ephemeral clichés of the century. It was hampered even by its lack of prejudice, its cool appraisal of contemporary trends. One had only to compare the Protestant *Le Semeur* with the Catholic *L'Ami de la Religion* to realize how much wider, more liberal and humanistic was the Protestant attitude to all the problems of the day, whether political, social or moral. Armed with greater cogency and less charm than Lacordaire, Monod, whose sermons were widely read after 1850, carried on a limited war against liberal humanism, achieving gains which, if not extensive, were safely consolidated before his death.

It seems, then, that the religious revival of the thirties and forties was a definite movement away from extremes to a compromise position, though to many in the churches it appeared precisely the opposite. Within the Catholic communion the revival was led by men who had been linked with Lamennais and who, in spite of abjuring his ideas, preserved much of their liberalism, while among the Protestants the revival centred on the conservative group of *Le Réveil*. It would be misleading to suggest that Monod and Lacordaire felt any mutual sympathy; but accidentally and unconsciously they had come far closer than ever Mgr de Quélen and the first Protestant beneficiaries of the Organic Articles.

But how deep did the revival go? It is one thing to fill Notre-Dame week after week with sympathetic crowds who savour eloquence like wine on the palate; it is another to induce them to practise the religion that underlies the orator's conviction. The figures from the Abbé Desgenettes's parish are proof enough—and there are many similar figures—that there was a real increase in the number of practising Catholics. But how far these people were swayed by Lacordaire's sermons, how far they followed the drift of opinion, it is impossible to say. We can guess from the history of the Church under the Second Empire that many of those who later swung away from Catholicism when it ceased to be a church proclaiming and demanding freedom, cared primarily for the values that were taken for granted in lay society. As soon as the Church turned against freedom of discussion and freedom of education and revealed its lack of enthusiasm for the apostolic virtue of poverty, these men left the Church: their submission had never been absolute.

Catholics themselves tended to exaggerate their gains. In 1838, for instance, shortly after his own conversion, the young journalist Louis Veuillot spoke gaily of 'five hundred conversions' among the young people of the *hautes écoles* and even imagined that *Le Journal des Débats* was run by fervent Christians. But Balzac's novels are surely a strong indication that a very different spirit was abroad in society, a spirit of egoistic ambition and greed; and though we may suspect Balzac, in his dark and terrible world, of disfiguring and defacing the real world before him, his picture is borne out by Frédéric Monod in the following analysis of the state of France in 1835:

'Taking a general view of our country, I find, apart from individual exceptions, appearances, not realities; phrases, not deep feelings pregnant with good deeds; passions, not love; the word philanthropy, not charity; egoism and ambition everywhere; everywhere envy and often hatred; everywhere ignorance of the Gospel or the completest indifference; gold and silver set up as gods; the bonds of morality, the family and society in general loosened; the yoke of subordination, which God established on earth for the good of all, rejected as a burden which no one will bear; each man seeking to escape his obligations and to rise above his neighbour; the theoretical materialism that invaded the educated class at the end of the last century transformed into a practical materialism and brought down to the masses without leaving their masters; God forgotten everywhere; everywhere the creature usurping the place of the Creator!'[1]

This is the background for Rastignac and Vautrin, Gobseck and Goriot. Pseudo-Romantic phrase-making, which Flaubert was later to assail as *blague*, infected religion and morality as deeply as it infected literature and art: it was so much easier to traffic in sonorous abstractions than to translate the pose into action. Not that the pose was insincere; but however well

[1] *Le Semeur*, 26th August 1835, p. 265.

meant, it did not commit the whole personality. These 'appearances, phrases and passions' which Monod perceived among his fellow Frenchmen were no substitute for reality; and the façade of piety and reform, impressive though it might be to foreigners who had known Paris in the later years of the Restoration, covered a ramshackle, crumbling fabric.[1]

Moreover, the revival did not pervade the whole of society. It impinged most sharply on the upper and middle classes—those who saw the need for faith and desired some foothold in the shifting tides of opinion. In spite of Lamennais's emphasis on the masses and in spite of Lacordaire's anxiety to popularize religion, working men were hardly touched. True, their hostility towards the Church gradually ebbed, but only because the Church was an independent power in the State, and no longer a weapon brandished by authority. It was a far cry to the acceptance of Christian doctrine; at the most they venerated the priest as a kind of witch-doctor whose black robes betokened the power of commanding and controlling supernatural forces. Peasants, of course, particularly in the south and west, still obeyed their local *curé* with scarcely a murmur; if he was a shepherd, they were sheep. But already the Church had lost its control over the peasants in eastern and central France, who, while knowing nothing of politics, often forsook their Christian allegiance for more ancient and primitive reasons. Though to conservative eyes this was disquieting enough, it was nothing beside the universal and continual drift from country to town, which meant that the docile labourer, evading his ancient duties, went to swell the mounting numbers of working men employed without proper supervision or welfare facilities in the great factories of the wealthy bourgeoisie. The great age of French industrial expansion was yet to come; but there already existed a substantial literature dissuading countrymen and girls from leaving their fields in order to grasp at the bubble of wealth and happiness. Novels like the Comtesse de Gasparin's *Allons faire fortune à Paris!* (1844) drew a forbidding picture of the penury and temptation, the vice and misery that overtook the peasant expatriate. For the multiplying proletariat spelt danger to the State. Indeed there is no doubt that some at least of the Catholic converts between 1835 and 1845 were swayed by fear

[1] Compare Thackeray, *The Paris Sketch Book*, pp. 299 ff.

—fear of godless, debauched, poverty-stricken working men who hated their masters; fear of rumbling discontent among those whom the sociologist Frégier, in a resounding and much-quoted phrase, had called *les classes dangereuses de la société*.

But fear is an uninspiring leader; and with Lamennais Catholicism had already cast off the only man who possessed enough constructive genius to rouse thinkers outside the Church. While Lacordaire preached liberal sermons, his audience listened with *Mirari vos* at the back of their minds, remembering that Lacordaire had barely escaped destruction in Lamennais's downfall. In fact, by 1835 the brightest chance of winning over the post-1800 generation had already evaporated: many, once moved and excited by the bold doctrines of *L'Avenir*, had concluded that Gregory and his bishops were too heavily bogged in the social and theological assumptions of the Middle Ages ever to stride out freely into the nineteenth century; and turning aside from a Church that seemed caught in the more obscurantist traditions of its past, they sought salvation elsewhere, in the Protestantism of many republicans or in the brand-new religions of Saint-Simon and Comte.

Meanwhile, in February 1836 Lacordaire had inaugurated a second series of *conférences* in Notre-Dame, dealing with the doctrines of the Church in general. At the first *conférence* he preached to the Archbishop of Aix and the Bishops of Nancy, Meaux and Icosium; and the regular attendance of the lords spiritual encouraged his supporters to believe that he was cleared of all hostile insinuations. Did not Archbishop Quélen ask the papal chargé d'affaires to write to Rome, describing the wonderful effects of his preaching? For in spite of dispiriting forecasts, the crowds were as plentiful as ever; they admired—they even clapped—his power of speech. His talent seemed to have blossomed in the previous twelve months, as though his self-realization had enabled him to discard empty rhetoric and incongruous metaphors.

All the sharper, therefore, was Lacordaire's impact on literature. The merest glow-worm in the Romantic coruscation could not escape his influence. A minor novelist like Ulric Guttinguer allowed one of his heroes to be converted by the *conférences* of Notre-Dame, for in this way he portrayed a characteristic spiritual pilgrimage. Victor Hugo, by contrast, was incensed. Had not Lacordaire, in the ninth *conférence*, issued a challenge to statesmen, kings and poets, arguing that none of them, in spite of their pretensions, could rival the supernatural power of the Church? 'Je les prie de s'entendre pour faire un prêtre. Ils verront!'[1] It touched Hugo on a tender spot. Gathering his sacerdotal robes about him, he issued his reply in *Les Mages*:

> *Pourquoi donc faites-vous des prêtres*
> *Quand vous en avez parmi vous?*[2]

Priests?—the true priests of the modern world were the poets, the magi, the Hugos in fact. But the most typical of his generation was Alfred de Musset. His unhappy disavowal of all belief in *Rolla* (1833) had not destroyed every trace of faith within him. If it was not, as he explained, a faith that could be expressed in dogma or observance, it existed none the less. And he unfolded it in the nebulous terms of *L'Espoir en Dieu* (1838). Whether or not Musset thought of Lacordaire as he wrote, the central passage on the inscrutability of God almost certainly echoes the thirteenth *conférence*, which Musset had attended. In fact the poem is a reasonably accurate guide to the permanent effect of Lacordaire's oratory. For Lacordaire encouraged a tenuous hope, nothing more. While stimulating a rapid increase in Catholic devotion, he failed to make many converts tenacious enough in spirit to cling to the French Church when it forsook liberalism; and slender though it may seem, his real contribution lay in the impact of his personality, dissolving prejudices against the priesthood, sowing doubts about doubt and hesitations about hesitation, speaking a contemporary language from an ancient pulpit, and implanting a Catholic leaven in the educated and professional classes.

Now although Lacordaire had renounced Lamennais, he could not renounce all his works; the imprint of *L'Avenir* on his personality and ideas was too deep ever to be expunged. It is true that even when living at La Chesnaie he had attenuated Lamennais's doctrines, shrinking from their categorical logic, nor had he ever stood so close to Lamennais as to choose

[1] Lacordaire, *Œuvres*, II, p. 165.
[2] See M. Souriau, *Histoire du romantisme en France*, II, pp. 152–3.

him for confessor. But from his association with Lamennais Lacordaire had made two permanent acquisitions. He had enlarged his recognition of the inherent greatness and power of the modern spirit, and he had acquired a new sympathy for the common people. When, therefore, he stood by himself, he still uttered ideas that had been familiar in *L'Avenir*, ideas that he had so completely assimilated as to take them for his own. One finds him maintaining that liberty, like gregariousness, is part of man's nature; treating society as a compound of families; arguing that property is essential to liberty. And all these notions sprang from the fertile brain of the man he had abjured.[1]

It is easy for us today to see the intellectual contrast between Lamennais and his former disciple: all the tumultuous originality is on one side, all the submissive humility on the other. But Lacordaire was explosive enough in his own right, especially to minds that denied the concept of progress and considered the Church an immutable structure permanently organized by Saint Peter for the instruction of the human race. Novelty of expression, it seemed to such men, implied novelty of doctrine, and novelty of doctrine deserved condemnation and suppression. The upstart orator must be fought and broken.

When Lacordaire occupied the pulpit of Notre-Dame for the second time, he already knew that twenty-seven propositions extracted from his sermons had been delated to Rome by a provincial priest and, in addition, that the Bishop *in partibus* of Carystos was preparing a two-volume work of censure. With the people he was as popular as ever, nor had his friends any idea of the hostility accumulating against him. Admittedly after his second sermon both *L'Univers* and *L'Ami de la Religion* saw fit to defend him against certain unspecified attacks, but in general the opposition eschewed publicity. It was tortuous in its methods and secretive about its aims, striving to wound Lacordaire not from below, with a falling-away of his audience, but from above, with the disapprobation of ecclesiastical authority. Gradually the pattern of attack took shape. While *L'Ami de la Religion* received from Toulouse twenty propositions taken from Lacordaire's sermons as worthy of theological censure, a hum of gossip and anecdote ran round the palazzi

---

[1] See also Souriau, II, pp. 141–3; J. Poisson, *Le Romantisme social de Lamennais*, pp. 84–5, 432–4.

of Rome. We can see the tactics of Lacordaire's enemies from a pamphlet published the next year. 'Properly understood', it says, 'the sermons of the Abbé Lacordaire amount to newspaper articles which even today would be well suited to another *Avenir*. To our mind they represent a vile degradation of the spoken word and a complete relaxation of the rules of thought —we cannot call this thought theological but merely philosophical.'[1] Lacordaire, in fact, was always the victim of malice; far more seriously its victim than his former associates Gerbet and Salinis, whose implication in Mennaisian ideas had been deeper and more prolonged. He was marked for life. Refusing to abjure his liberalism, refusing to deny his belief in political freedom, he preserved an uneasy reputation as an incendiary. While Gerbet and Salinis pursued their tranquil road towards the episcopate, he remained a perennial suspect, branded by his association with genius, branded by his belief in the people.

Small wonder, then, that the older clergy detested his name and his works. Perhaps unhappy, vacillating Mgr de Quélen would have stood by him, allowed him to remain in the pulpit, refrained from imposing restraints. But who could tell? And knowing that the Archbishop had been approached about ending the series of *conférences*, Lacordaire sprang his own surprise. It was with a shock of dismay that the audience at his last sermon heard his concluding words:

'Je laisse entre les mains de mon évêque cette chaire de Notre-Dame, désormais fondée, fondée par lui et par vous, et par le pasteur et par le peuple. Un moment ce double suffrage a brillé sur ma tête: souffrez que je l'écarte de moi-même, et que je me retrouve seul quelque temps devant ma faiblesse et devant Dieu.'[2]

Lacordaire had decided to return to Rome in search of refreshment and support.

He did not see clearly into the tangle of his motives. No doubt his main purpose, or at least his most immediate purpose, was to rebut the accusations levelled against him and to prove how utterly he was devoted to the Holy See. He may, too, have felt

---

[1] *Lettre aux membres du clergé et aux auditeurs de Notre-Dame.* Quoted by Chocarne, *Le R. P. Lacordaire*, I, p. 194. This pamphlet now seems to be unobtainable in any library.

[2] Lacordaire, *Œuvres*, II, p. 238.

a dimly stirring desire to lead the life of a religious. But it is also probable that he was dissatisfied with his own achievement, dissatisfied with the limited scope of his sermons, anxious to reach, not merely inquiring laymen, but parish priests. At any rate he was confident of his own powers; indeed over-confident. 'Our clergy is divided', he wrote from Rome in January 1837. 'One section desires the ancient Church of France with all its maxims and methods; the other believes that France is in an entirely new situation. I am the leader—potential but unrecognized—of the second section. This the people feel, and the deep hatreds that already split the parties are sharpened by personal hatreds surviving from the past.'[1] We can now see that Lacordaire deceived and flattered himself, wrongly diagnosing the political and theological trend of the Roman Church. But it is time to ask what was this second section of the clergy whose leader designate he imagined himself to be.

[1] Lacordaire, *Correspondance avec Mme Swetchine*, p. 103.

CHAPTER VII

The Gallican Decline

It is one of the paradoxes of modern history that the Pope owes his power and influence in the world to the man who scourged and humbled the papacy and came near to destroying it altogether. For though Napoleon was not the father of Ultramontanism, he was its obstetrician. Had he not overthrown the ancient defenders of the faith, the Pope would still have enjoyed the support, and suffered the rivalry, of his traditional allies. By 1801, however, Pius VII was virtually bereft of assistance; and the beginning of the new order can be dated from the Bull of November 29th of that year, *Qui Christi Domini*, which imposed the terms of the Concordat on the Church of France. Pius had already demanded the formal resignation of all his bishops; and as some, particularly those in exile, did not comply, he deposed them by what Lord Acton called 'the most arbitrary act ever done by a Pope'. It was, in fact, a reasonable and perhaps inevitable exercise of ecclesiastical authority in a perplexing situation; there was no doubt that the authority was his. But by deposing thirty-eight bishops who were his colleagues and co-bishops, being members of the same order and successors of the apostles by the same right, he asserted his power in a way that would have been resisted far more vigorously had he not seemed himself virtually powerless. Who, looking at Europe in 1801, only a few months after Marengo and Hohenlinden, could see any threat of absolutism in the almost indecent compliance which the decrepit papacy showed towards the new master of the Continent?

But this was not the Pope's only debt to Napoleon. After the Restoration it became gradually clear that Rome was much strengthened by the destruction of the great Catholic states of the Rhine, which had been stubborn supporters of anti-papal theory. It also followed from the abrupt break with the past that as soon as stable political conditions were restored, Concordats had to be negotiated both in the Old World and the New, to settle terms between the civil and the religious order. The great number of Concordats signed after the Restoration —Bavaria (1817), the two Sicilies (1818), Prussia (1821), Württemberg, Baden, Nassau and the two Hesses (1821), Hanover (1824) and so on through the century[1]—meant that these Churches were new: they depended on Rome and had been created by Rome, owing both their internal structure and their external form to the politicians of the Vatican.

In such conditions Gallicanism stood little chance of survival. The essence of Gallicanism as expressed in the Articles of 1682,[2] lay in the independent existence of a national Church, supported when necessary by a Christian king against the Pope. The Gallicans did not deny the Catholic teaching that the Church was one, visible and infallible, nor did they dispute the Pope's position as Vicar of Christ and head of the Church on earth. Their distinguishing mark lay in affirming the independence of the civil power and in limiting the Pope's infallibility to the occasions when he had obtained the universal assent of the Church. So long as a king was on the throne of France who was evidently a successor of Clovis and a descendant of Saint Louis, the Gallicans could plausibly invoke the ancient customs and liberties of the Church of France. Although no one denied that in 1690 the Pope had declared the Gallican Articles to be null and void, his expressed opinion that they were without theological censure had guaranteed their survival, and they were, in consequence, taught in Catholic schools, all over Europe and particularly in France, right up to the Revolution.

But once break the tradition, once create a new church far more dependent on Rome than the old, and Gallicanism is undermined. Even had it not already been discredited by the use to which it was put by Napoleon, Gallicanism would have seemed an anomaly under the Restoration. The modern world no longer hung on differences between popes in Rome and

---

[1] See particularly Taine, *Les Origines de la France contemporaine. Le Régime moderne*, II, pp. 56–7. [2] See Appendix.

Catholic kings in Paris. The conflict lay between the Revolution
on the one hand, and the Church and the monarchy on the other.
The opponents of revolution, unless they wished to encourage
disaster, were obliged to compose their differences and to close
their ranks.

After Waterloo, however, the new situation was apparent to
only a few. The Bull *Qui Christi Domini* had provoked a minor
schism with the formation of La Petite Eglise, which refused to
acknowledge the Concordat, claiming (as it still claims) to
represent the Catholic Church in its uncorrupted state. But
further defections were guarded against. It is significant that
after the Restoration the English Vicars Apostolic imposed a test
on all French clergy living in England: they were asked to
declare that Pius VII was 'not a heretic nor a schismatic nor
the author or abetter of heresy or schism'.[1] But though only a
handful anathematized the Pope, the French clergy of 1815,
encouraged by the returning exiles, persisted in the Gallicanism
of their youth. It was part of their cultural heritage. In 1820,
for instance, a cardinal delivered a powerful attack against
papal infallibility, and his attitude was shared by teachers in
seminaries[2] and pungently expressed in the popular religious
encyclopaedia, Bergier's *Dictionnaire de théologie*. When that
elderly peer Montlosier criticized the Jesuits six years later, he
did so in the name of Gallicanism. But the effects of his book
could not be confined to any one party in the Church, falling
on the mass of the clergy indiscriminately. Nor was this without
justice, for by 1826 the Gallicanism of the lower clergy could
no longer be counted on. Realizing the situation, the Government, which looked to the national Church for support in all
disputes with Rome, tried to extract from the bishops a declaration adhering to the Articles of 1682. But the bishops were
wary; they were ready enough to censure Lamennais and to
maintain the vague 'maxims received in the Church of France',
but as for a positive declaration, they were content to proclaim
'the full and absolute independence of sovereigns from the
authority, whether direct or indirect, of any ecclesiastical
power'.

By this time, in fact, all the old props of Gallicanism had

[1] Wilfrid Ward, *William George Ward and the Catholic Revival*, p. 88.
[2] See for example C. Guillemant, *Pierre-Louis Parisis*, I, pp. 24–5.

cracked, and the July Revolution was to sweep them away. No longer could a young man entering the Church look greedily at its endowments and its privileges: bishops had to pay taxes; monseigneur was only a courtesy title. The lawyers of the Parlement, who, by inciting the bishops to claim their common rights, had always been the main strength of Gallicanism under the *ancien régime*, dropped all interest in the theology of the matter now that the State was secularized; while as for the theologians, they wielded only a shadow of the authority that had been theirs when Rome trembled at the learning of the Sorbonne.

But in addition to these negative reasons for the decline in Gallicanism, there were positive ones: in short, the Ultramontane crusaders. The policy of the popes has, of course, always been to centralize power in Rome and to whittle down particularism in doctrine and administration; but they have had to contend with two main threats—the self-sufficiency of the General Council, which nearly triumphed in the fifteenth century, and the autonomy of the national churches, which grew swiftly in strength as the ideal of medieval unity decayed, and were stiffened by their association with the civil power. Both struggles ended during the nineteenth century with a complete victory for the Vatican; but it was the Church of France, still loyal to the traditions of Gerson and Bossuet, which offered the toughest and boldest resistance.

It is curious, however, that the Ultramontane champions were also French. After Joseph de Maistre and Bonald, came Lamennais, and though it can be argued that the first two maintained a residual and unwitting Gallicanism, there can be no doubt about the downright and categorical Ultramontanism of their successor. To Lamennais's mind the position was crystal clear: the Church, being a world-wide society divinely ordained, must have a supreme head to administer and control it; to do without a head or to leave the direction to the national churches would mean social and spiritual anarchy; the Pope was therefore entitled to the absolute submission of Catholics everywhere, and even should he err, must be obeyed. It was as simple as that; and Lamennais saw it simply because his mind was not blurred by dynastic loyalties or personal privileges. He had little time even for the regime of Charles X: why bow to a king when one could kneel to a pope?

These ideas steadily took hold of Catholic youth. The old Gallican episcopacy represented by Mgr de Quélen fumbled pathetically when it tried to deal with the needs of the new generation, and Lamennais's emphasis on liberty and his anxiety to appeal to the Pope against his traducers encouraged the belief that the Pope was ready to defend individual priests against the oppressions of authority. Among young laymen there was little talk of theology and no talk of papal infallibility. But, says one of them, 'they were brought to think and speak of themselves as Ultramontane because they hoped to find in the Holy See the support for their ideas that was refused by the Gallican episcopate of France'.[1] Even the bishops yielded to the Ultramontane contagion. In 1822, when the Grand Almoner of France was obliged to propose names for twelve newly created bishoprics, he consulted his secretary: and his secretary, who was in fact the Abbé Jean de La Mennais, a brother of the man we know as Lamennais,[2] submitted a list of priests eminent for their zeal, learning—and hostility to Gallican ideals.

Meanwhile the lower clergy, coming as they did from humble families, found no reason to treat Gallicanism as an ancient, unbreakable tradition. Many of them first heard the doctrine in the seminary, and from the lips of men with a different background and a divergent outlook. Some seminarists were undoubtedly convinced of the validity of the 1682 Articles; but the majority, whose youth had been marked by a steady growth in the prestige of Pope and papacy, questioned a doctrine that seemed to exalt a king who was not personally popular—whether his name was Louis or Charles—over a pope who was. Thinking in this way, they were particularly amenable to Lamennais's ideas; and when, with the advent of Louis Philippe, the Government ceased to favour the Church, the only two authorities still worthy of their respect were the bishop and the Pope.

But in the 1830's bishop and Pope were very different ideas. One was near, the other remote; one stern, the other paternal; one linked with the old aristocracy, the other bound by no ties

[1] L. de Carné, *Souvenirs de ma jeunesse*, p. 167.
[2] *Dublin Review*, 1844, XVI, p. 20. Lamennais was born as La Mennais, but ran the two words together after his break with the Church; one word was more plebeian than two.

of class. Whereas in the eyes of the average priest the virtues of
the Pope, far away in his Holy See, seemed to grow in proportion to his distance, the bishop was a very present evil. For
another of Napoleon's legacies to the nineteenth century was
the vastly inflated power of the episcopate. It suited him well to
tighten the hold of the bishops on their priests provided he
himself controlled the bishops, and he therefore allowed them
to evade the limitations imposed by the Organic Articles and to
seize the power once held by the Chapters. Only after his fall
was it apparent that the parish priest enjoyed far less freedom
than under the *ancien régime*. Indeed of all the provincial powers
of pre-revolutionary France—landowners, justiciaries, local
parliaments—the only one to emerge into the Restoration period
stronger and more formidable was the bishop. Whereas before
the Revolution he might have disposed of perhaps a tenth of
the benefices in his diocese and was legally unable to remove his
subordinates, he now controlled nearly all benefices and dismissed his subordinates at will.[1] And it was not an empty
threat. One bishop, for example, interchanged one hundred and
fifty priests in the space of a month: another dispatched thirty-
five dismissals by a single post. In the year 1837 3,500 priests
left their *cures*: indeed the bishops were so fascinated by the
problems and possibilities of permutation that between 1836
and 1842 all the lower clergy of some dioceses were interchanged
like ciphers in a party game. 'It was both sad and amusing',
writes a detached observer, 'to meet, on different roads, a pile
of shabby bags followed by an old woman in tears and a priest
reciting his breviary.'[2] Nor were these men all appointed to new
cures: far too many, destituted without proof, without even
knowing the names of their accusers, sank into extreme poverty
or drifted into employment as coach-drivers and road-sweepers.

An extreme type of Gallican bishop was the Duc de Rohan,
whose swift rise had culminated in his appointment as Cardinal
Archbishop of Besançon. Shunning vulgar worshippers as

---

[1] The bishop could dismiss all but the *curés*. Of the 40,000 parishes in
France less than a tenth (generally the larger ones) were *cures*; in addition to
the incumbents of these *cures*, both *archiprêtres* and *doyens* were technically
curés. All the rest of the lower clergy were *desservants* and could be removed
by the bishop at will. See also Taine, II, pp. 66–70.

[2] E. Ollivier, *L'Eglise et l'Etat au Concile du Vatican*, I, 285.

though they were cattle, he would only consent to say the offices in a private oratory decked with satin hangings and attended by a chosen band of personal servants. On his rare episcopal visitations he insisted on the presence of the local *maires*, sword at side, behind his chair as he dined. We must not of course imagine that all or even most bishops resembled Rohan; but he had enough imitators to drive parish priests into the opposite camp and to taint Gallicanism with an odour of antique tyranny. For the most part rebellion was confined to grumbles, insinuations and sarcasms, but sometimes it took a more explicit form. In 1839, for example, two brothers named Allignol published a pamphlet describing the wretched conditions to which the lower clergy had been reduced by the Concordat regime,[1] and advocating a return to the safeguards provided by canon law, particularly irremovability. The bishops intoned a chorus of anger, muttering darkly of presbyterianism: and eventually the two brothers were destituted. But not before the elder had visited Rome and laid his case before Gregory XVI, who remarked, 'I had no idea that the French bishops were such popelets', and put a private chapel at the disposal of the two men.

This, then, explains the welcome which the lower clergy accorded to Lamennais's Ultramontane doctrines, though they were not linked and interpreted according to his intention: and these were the men who represented the 'second section' which Lacordaire now hoped to lead.

[1] C. and A. Allignol frères, *De l'Etat actuel du clergé en France*, 1839.

CHAPTER VIII

Friar Preacher

While Lacordaire was in Rome, Lamennais's *Affaires de Rome* were noisily published. Amid the cloud and dust of controversy they inspired Mme Swetchine with one of her phrases—'Only an angel or a priest could sink so low'—and Lacordaire with a book in the Pope's defence, entitled *Lettre sur le Saint-Siège*. At Mme Swetchine's suggestion the text was submitted to Mgr de Quélen, who, after a single glance at its outrageous Ultramontanism, strongly advised Lacordaire not to print it. But blank discouragement is not the wisest way to deal with an inconvenient author, and a series of proud and testy letters ran to and fro between the Archbishop in Paris and the priest in Rome. Had it not been for the Archbishop of Cologne, the *Lettre* might even yet have gone unpublished; but when, in spite of the Pope's entreaties, this prelate was locked in a German fortress, Lacordaire sent his manuscript to the printer in the hope that where the Pope's protests had not availed, his own prose might be more successful. Though it was not a book of high merit, its publication was a shrewd tactical measure. It failed to liberate the Archbishop, but it could and did release Lacordaire from all allegiance to Quélen. His future was now tied to the Pope at the cost of estrangement from the Archbishop of Paris. He felt sufficiently strong to discard the Gallicanism to which he had hitherto been uneasily allied. Had Lacordaire been more cunning or even more clever, one would attribute this move to calculation: as it was, it happened almost by accident, confirming him in the new direction of his life.

Certainly Gregory looked with a kindly eye on the young

priest who had come to Rome, discontented with his nation-
wide reputation and groping towards a more settled career.
Why indeed should Gregory frown on one of the most warm-
hearted advocates of papal power, especially seeing that he
was endowed with the ancillary virtue of submissiveness? At
one of Lacordaire's audiences with the Pope there was a
pamphlet from his enemies lying on the desk, and picking it
up, the old man ripped it in half, saying, 'There you are: that
is how I deal with the works that are written against you'.
Usually, however, he observed the precaution of first reading
the attacks. It seems that when one of the early pamphlets
arrived, he examined it thoughtfully, then, turning to the
emissary, remarked: '*Caro mio*, we must discover, firstly, whether
the propositions attacked do in fact deserve censure, and
secondly, whether the censure already passed is not more
censurable than the propositions themselves.'[1] For Gregory had
no illusions: if Lacordaire's enemies sought his opinion, it was
not from belief in his spiritual insight, but from knowledge of
his disciplinary power.

One of Lacordaire's first actions on reaching Rome had
been to choose a Jesuit confessor—a prudent step in view of
Jesuit influence at the Vatican, but a significant one too in
relation to his future. For his mind was increasingly exercised
by the idea of entering a religious order. Jesuit, Benedictine . . .
or what? He did not know; but his imagination was caught.
When the Abbé Guéranger, who had recently restored the
Benedictines to France, pointed out that the Dominicans had
still to return, a spark was kindled in Lacordaire's mind. Were
the Dominicans not a preaching order? Had they not led and
inspired the people? He consulted his friends in Paris, who were
discouraging. He spoke to Quélen, who was frigid. He reflected.
But in spite of almost universal attempts to dissuade him,
Lacordaire's decision crystallized, and in July 1838 he set out
again for Rome, determined to embark on a fresh and hazar-
dous career.

No doubt there were personal advantages in his becoming a
religious. Not only would a man so easily overwrought benefit
from periods of solitude and contemplation, but he might no

[1] From Régnier and Lacroix, quoted by A. Ricard, *L'Ecole menaisienne,
Lacordaire*, pp. 198-9.

longer find it necessary—as he had found it in 1835—to spend months sea-bathing. But there were disadvantages. Community life was onerous. 'One of the trials of being a monk', he later told an inquirer in a revealing passage, 'is to live with men you have not chosen, most of whom arouse no natural sympathy within you; so that you are forced on to terms of intimacy without that touch of affection which reconciles and endears it to your soul.'[1] On Lacordaire with his apparent coldness and deep need for friendship, that emotionless intimacy must have jarred particularly. But he resisted his disinclination. Once he had conceived of the re-establishment of the Dominican order in France as part of the campaign initiated by *L'Avenir*, the consistency of his decision outweighed its discomforts, and he entered the life of a religious with a mind still ringing with the inspiration of Lamennais.

There was, however, an obvious contradiction. Why should a priest renowned for his liberalism and his sympathy for the aspirations of his century choose to revive an order which, with Dominic, had been implicated in the notorious Albigensian Crusade and, with Dominic's successors, had been so far responsible for the papal and mendicant Inquisition as to earn it the name of the 'Dominican Inquisition'? Such a record was not reassuring; but under Guéranger's persuasion Lacordaire at first overlooked the darker pages in the history of the order. He was drawn by the idea of the Friars Preacher, devoted to the complementary duties of penitence and apostleship. For these, which were after all the two needs of France, would be better fulfilled by the restoration of the Dominican order than by popular sermons in Notre-Dame. While sermons merely scratched the surface, the example of a band of monks could strike deep into the nation's life—could reach the sources of religion and replenish the wells of belief.

Those who knew Lacordaire only as a preacher and a polemist formed an inadequate idea of his personality. Had they seen him at closer quarters, they might have discovered an unexpected ingredient in a character habitually so serious and even grave. For his judgements were hasty to the point of irresponsibility; he had a gay certainty that was repeatedly belied by

[1] *Lettres à des jeunes gens*, p. 288. 'Monk' is here used loosely to mean *moine* or friar; the Dominicans, of course, are not a contemplative order.

events. One has only to turn over the pages of his correspondence to find countless examples; his letters abound in expressions of vague but emphatic optimism. Lacking any natural sense of criticism, he dealt constantly in surface judgements, dangerously simplifying the complexities of abstract thought and easily reclining on facile generalizations. 'I think all will go well in the end', he writes in December 1837, but for no better reason than that he hopes so. 'My book has the entire approval of Saint-Sulpice', he tells a friend in 1834, about his *Lettre sur le Saint-Siège*; adding without apparent irony, 'and the Abbé Carrière, their best theologian, has declared that the only passage open to criticism is an incidental phrase in which I compare the Pope and our Lord in their influence on the Church. Theologically the comparison seems to him excessive, which is true.' 'All the Dominicans who have read it', he writes about a new book in 1839, 'are pleased and consider its accuracy beyond reproach. There is a unanimous chorus of approval.' Moreover, if, as he thinks, all good men are agreed in praising him, it follows that criticism springs from an evil heart. Lacordaire repudiates his opponents with a serene self-righteousness; he makes no concessions, impugning both their honesty and their good faith. What is even more dangerous, he despises them intellectually. When, for example, a sermon he delivers at Metz in 1838 provokes rejoinders from Protestants and republicans, he cheerfully tells a correspondent: 'I have decided not to reply to all this, either in the pulpit or in writing, because it is not worth the trouble: the whole city is in my favour, and I have never had so large an audience as yesterday.' Now this is not forbearance, but self-confidence—the pride of the popular idol. It was Lacordaire's besetting fault to underestimate the strength of the opposition ranged against him and to exaggerate his own abilities; he imagined that difficulties and arguments were card-castles, to be overthrown with a puff of rhetoric.

Having decided on the Dominican order and obtained approval in Rome for his decision, he produced a *Mémoire pour le rétablissement en France de l'ordre des frères prêcheurs*. This, though frankly a piece of apologetic, is probably Lacordaire's best work and indeed the only one that can still be read with any degree of pleasure. He boldly repudiates much of the past —the wealth of convents and monasteries and their association with the nobility; and he denies that the Friars Preacher are a monastic order. Now here he shows a certain unconscious cunning. By 1840 the ideas of the Saint-Simonians, though not fully accepted, had permeated contemporary thought, and almost every writer conceded in some measure the social function of art; the workers, too, not being allowed to indulge in collective bargaining, were demanding the right to associate together freely, a right forbidden by law. Both these movements Lacordaire exploited. He presented the Dominicans as a community that would bring peace to society and support to the workers. 'No one can deny it,' he wrote: 'religious, agricultural and industrial societies are the only safeguards for the future against the continual recurrence of revolution. The human race will never return to the past; however heavy its burdens, it will never seek aid from ancient aristocratic regimes; but it will find the remedy for the scourge of individualism in voluntary societies based on labour and religion.'

On reading the *Mémoire* Mgr de Quélen overcame his surprise at seeing monks bracketed with trade unionists, and sent his congratulations to the author. These congratulations, however, referred to Lacordaire's dialectic rather than to his historical accuracy; for even Quélen must have been startled at the sixth chapter, on the Inquisition. Here Lacordaire met the question that had always stood in his path; but instead of grappling with it he glided skilfully by. He blandly denied that Dominic had ever played the part of inquisitor or invented the Inquisition; and with discreditable ingenuity he banished all cruelty and excess to the far side of the Pyrenees. 'This "wicked" court of justice', he explained sarcastically, 'is the Inquisition; not the Spanish Inquisition corrupted by the despotism of the kings of Spain and the peculiar character of the Spaniards; but the Inquisition as conceived by the Popes and perfected by them, after many exertions and endeavours, in the Roman Congregation of the Holy Office of 1542—the gentlest court of justice in the world, indeed the only one that after an existence of three hundred years has perhaps shed not a single drop of blood.' He did not add (perhaps he was unaware) that the Church, in its horror for bloodshed, handed over to the secular arm all victims for burning, excommunicating princes who refused the role of executioner. It was not Lacordaire's task to tell the whole truth; he was an advocate, pleading a cause with power and plausibility and striving to gain the assent of his readers. But if most of them yielded readily enough, Guéranger was more critical. 'No nobleman', he said, 'should disown his escutcheon.'[1]

In fact Lacordaire wavers unconvincingly whenever he considers the past as a whole. One moment he will reject, in an oratorical period, the whole idea of progress because it is a weapon in the hands of anticlericals:

'Aussi que disent les derniers adversaires, les adversaires présents de l'Eglise? Ils soutiennent que la raison de l'homme est un progrès continu où chaque nouvelle idée tue l'ancienne, où rien n'est stable et absolu, où tout est destiné à périr, sauf cette incroyable faculté qui fait vivre un moment ce qui doit mourir nécessairement. Ils confessent ainsi le néant de leurs espérances et celui de la raison, qui n'est qu'un passage à travers des sépulcres où elle laisse un peu de cendre.'[2]

But both idea and emotion seem to die away with the echoes of his voice, and a few years later we find him writing with equal sincerity: 'In the Middle Ages Christianity had already cured many evils, but it was young and human reason still undeveloped [*peu exercée*].'[3] What is this but the idea of progress? Unawares, without calculation, Lacordaire pursues the method of the advocate rather than of the philosopher, changing his ground according to the needs of the particular argument in which he is engaged. Moreover, he is even more prone than most critics, lecturers and polemists to assume omniscience and to exploit the inevitable ignorance of his public. In the *Mémoire*, for example, after painting his own ideal picture of the Inquisition, he calmly continues: 'These assertions may surprise those who believe in history as it has been written by Protestants and rationalists; but they will not surprise those who know that for the last three centuries history has been a gross and continuous falsehood, which has already been partly demolished by the scholars of France, Germany and England.'[4]

It is no doubt true that when the Romantics, fired with an interest in the past for its own sake, breathed new life into

---

[1] 'Un moine bénédictin', *Dom Guéranger, Abbé de Solesmes*, I, p. 250.
[2] Lacordaire, *Œuvres*, II, p. 43.
[3] *Correspondance avec Mme Swetchine*, p. 503.   [4] *Œuvres*, I, p. 96.

historical studies, one of the first tasks of the conscientious historian was to repair the tattered reputation of the Middle Ages and to defend them against the crude slurs of the eighteenth century. But no one had less right than Lacordaire to claim the support of research and scholarship. How far he stood from the relatively cautious and unprejudiced procedures of Thierry, Guizot, Barante or Michelet is clear from his *Vie de Saint Dominique*, which followed the *Mémoire*. It is a lengthy and tedious panegyric, unrelieved by the faintest suggestion of a critical spirit. With complacent credulity he recounts the wildest medieval legends as though they are established facts, assuming every story to be true because it accords with the prevailing tone of insipid piety. The work is rather less subtle than a child's first history book. But while almost every writer slips into this tone at some time or another, when his critical sense is asleep, Lacordaire never evades it. Yet he remained characteristically satisfied with the work for the rest of his life, and his friends were no harder to please. 'It is not only a masterpiece,' said Mme Swetchine, 'it is a miracle; for he is destined to perform miracles.' And Chateaubriand concurred: 'It is wonderfully beautiful: I know of no finer style.'

Had Lacordaire's shortcomings been merely personal, they would hardly be worth dwelling on; but they pervaded the whole movement which he hoped to lead. His popularity among laymen he owed to his modernity of outlook, his sympathy with the nineteenth century; and so far as it went, his sympathy was real enough. But his philosophy was ambiguous and vacillating, a compound of moods and velleities which lacked any solid theoretical basis; despite his reputation and his ambitions he was totally unable to reconcile his loyalty to the past and his love of the present. He was like a boy who was sometimes allowed out to play with his friends but was forced to return home instantly when summoned. No doubt his obedience was a high virtue, essential in a priest or a monk and rare in the rest of the world. But it was unrecognized by his playfellows and largely hidden from their eyes. As soon as they suspected this discrepancy in his attitude, they withdrew their friendship.

The discrepancy, however, existed not only in Lacordaire's loyalties but in his character. As an apologist he chose to show one side of his nature to the public; but there was another side, revealed only to his intimates, which would have scandalized his hearers in Notre-Dame. For in private life he was a thorough-going medievalist who insisted on employing every means of mortification known to the saints. Obsessed with the idea of penitence and the virtues inherent in voluntary suffering, he was ruthless to his own body. There was no more determined flagellant. Every day of his *conférences* he beat himself severely, and after becoming a Dominican, he regularly followed Mass with a visit to the cell of one of his friars, kissing his feet, asking for a heavy scourging, and, when it was over, remaining with his lips pressed to the scourger's feet. He liked to be slapped in the face, spat on, insulted. In the former Carmelite Church in Paris, which still bore bloodstains from the 1793 massacre, there was a sort of crypt or underground chapel, approached by a long corridor strewn with bones and death's-heads, and here Lacordaire often withdrew for his severer acts of penitence, especially during Lent and Holy Week. One Good Friday he erected a cross in the chapel and remained bound to it for three hours.[1]

We do not know sufficient about Lacordaire to draw any certain conclusions about the secret springs of this self-mortification, though his ferocity towards himself strengthens the suspicion that in private he was intensely ambitious. Nor does it concern us. It is enough that Lacordaire the flagellant and Lacordaire the liberal were uneasy allies, and none the less uneasy because he seemed strangely blind to his own self-contradictions. In one breath hailing the new age of science and social betterment, in the next demanding a penitential scourging, he personified the unresolved tension that thwarted every forward-looking Catholic. With his unfailing fidelity to Rome Lacordaire himself was not deeply perturbed about this conflict, chafing merely at the political conservatism of most of the faithful. But when even the religious in his charge shrank from what appeared a harsh and sterile penitence, it was clear that laymen would react with horror. In point of fact, the secret was well kept, and only after Lacordaire's death did his admirers learn how far he had imported medieval monastic discipline into the nineteenth century. But whether or not these practices were generally known, they were significant, for they cut to the root of Lacor-

[1] See Chocarne, II, pp. 58 ff., but compare II, p. 165.

daire's position as an apologist. If his primary appeal lay in his personality and if only a selected aspect of his personality was shown from the pulpit, he was deceiving his audience, however unconsciously. They left his sermons, feeling that they knew the whole man when they knew him only partially. Although Lacordaire always remained in their memories as an attractive, persuasive figure, his effectiveness as an orator suffered eventually from this censored edition of the man. For his audience was all the more shocked and repelled when they encountered elsewhere the full rigour of Catholic teaching and practice. Remembering the suavity of Lacordaire's tones, his friendly outlook on the modern world and the easy burden which he sought to lay on their shoulders, they felt abused. In fact, this was one of the main reasons why Lacordaire's movement, with all its power and promise, failed: sincere though he was, there was a radical distinction between the message which he uttered and the cause which he represented.

Receiving the Dominican habit in April 1839, Lacordaire retired to the convent of La Quercia at Viterbo for a year's novitiate before taking his final vows. In the meantime Mgr de Quélen had died, and his Vicar-General, by concealing his Gallicanism and thus gaining Ultramontane support, became Archbishop of Paris. Lacordaire immediately wrote for permission to preach in Notre-Dame, and late in 1840 he began his return to France. He wore the traditional white habit and black scapular, but, remembering that ten years earlier even the irregular clergy had been forced to go about Paris in secular dress, he packed a soutane for use should need arise. In fact, so innocuous did he find his countrymen that he gave the soutane to a ragged Spanish priest whom he met early on his journey. Monks, even if they were still widely distrusted as peculiar animals, had lost the sinister penumbra of evil that had once gathered round them; and when Lacordaire reached Paris, Affre, the new Archbishop, made no difficulty in allowing him to preach in his habit.

Lacordaire's sermon itself—on the 'Vocation of the French Nation'—though not one of his best, brought a huge crowd swarming into Notre-Dame. Among the ten thousand people packed inside the cathedral the journalists noted literary figures like Chateaubriand and Guizot, Berryer and Lamartine; preachers like Ravignan, Combalot and Dupanloup; the Ministers of Justice and of Religion and the Chancellor: ambassadors, peers of France and deputies; and the Archbishop of Paris, the Bishop of Meaux and the Papal Internuncio. The attendance was in itself a triumph; and when M. Martin du Nord, the then Chancellor, invited Lacordaire to a formal dinner in honour of the occasion, one of the guests who had been Chancellor under Charles X was heard to remark: 'How strangely the fortunes of this world revolve! Had I invited a Dominican to my table during my tenure of office, the place would have been burnt down the next day.'

Lacordaire, however, angered his opponents. True to his genius, he diluted exhortation with flattery, and immediately one critic was complaining that he had mentioned Napoleon without a hint of disapproval, and another was calling his sermon 'a proud harangue calculated to arouse national pride'. A 'revolutionary', a 'demagogue', he was denounced to Rome for attempting to revive Mennaisian ideas in the guise of the Dominican order. A certain Georges Dalcy, who had already published a pamphlet playing ingeniously on this theme, was powerfully reinforced by Metternich, who made representations to the Pope through an obliging cardinal in Rome. When, therefore, Lacordaire returned to Italy after two months in France, and assumed responsibility for the French novices, it was only a matter of weeks before he was struck at in a letter from the Cardinal Secretary of State, which ordered him peremptorily to remain in Rome while his companions were dispersed, half to La Quercia, and half to Bosco, near Alessandria. He was stunned with surprise. But however sharp his first movement of rebellion, his good sense did not desert him and he advised his companions to submit with no show of resentment. Bewildered about the origin of this new blow, reluctant to ascribe it to the Pope's credulity and suspicion, and yet blinded by his own optimism to the irreducible opposition that he would always stir up among legitimists and Gallicans in France, Lacordaire was ready enough to believe Mme Swetchine, who attributed it to the malevolence of the French Government. Perhaps this belief encouraged his docility; at any rate the Pope, who seems to have fallen for the idea that

Lacordaire was a dangerous revolutionary plotting disorder and heresy, was agreeably surprised to find him so tractable. In the event Lacordaire did not suffer; having chosen the Dominican order for alarmingly liberal reasons, he was bound to remain for ever an unorthodox and unreliable figure in the eyes of Rome, but at least by his willing submission he displayed a persistent loyalty to the Holy See and undermined the suspicion that he, like Lamennais, would end as a heretical demagogue.

But being deliberately cut off from the future Dominicans of France, Lacordaire was all the more free to pursue his career as an orator. In fact the period of separation was short, for in 1842, at the end of their novitiate, the two groups of Frenchmen were reunited at Bosco. Lacordaire's preaching, on the other hand, was to continue regularly until almost his death. The list of his stations over twenty years is long and impressive; it covers Paris and Metz, Bordeaux and Nancy, Grenoble, Lyons, Strasbourg and Liége, Toulon, Dijon, Toulouse and finally Sorèze. But of all these towns and cities, the one where he was most welcome and where his influence was widest, if not deepest, was Paris. In Paris he had first made his name, and though the other stations that he preached all over the country spurred on the religious revival and helped to dissipate the unpopularity of monks in general and of Dominicans in particular, Lacordaire rejoiced at Archbishop Affre's invitation to deliver a course of *conférences* in Paris during Advent 1843. Immediately, however, a difficulty arose. Affre, who was now more certain of his position as Archbishop and therefore more eager to assert his authority, stipulated that Lacordaire should wear a soutane instead of a Dominican habit. There were in fact two reasons. In the first place, the Archbishop, who grew more Gallican with every year that passed, welcomed the chance to assert his control over monks and their Ultramontane sympathies. In the second, considering the heated atmosphere that had been generated by the controversies of the past twelve months, he was unwilling to provoke any civil disturbance, for the king had already informed him, in a long and difficult audience, that if Lacordaire were allowed to preach, the Government would not provide a single soldier or National Guard to protect the cathedral and its dignitaries. But Lacordaire was adamant. He refused Affre's request, not once but repeatedly. Not till Affre had appealed to the Pope through the Nuncio, and the Master General of the Dominican Order had authorized Lacordaire to preach as a secular priest, was it finally settled that he should wear the canon's lace rochet and mozetta over his habit.

On 3rd December 1843 Lacordaire began what he was later to call 'the most dangerous and decisive of all my campaigns'. But in spite of his own anxiety and the Archbishop's nervousness it was immediately clear both that his eloquence had lost none of its old appeal and that there was no deep popular hostility towards the Dominicans. Discord he certainly provoked; but it was among the older members of the clergy and in the Faubourg Saint-Germain. His partisans in Notre-Dame heard the *moine*, the friar, as willingly as they had heard the priest. Every winter without interruption from 1843 till the *coup d'état* of 1851, he delivered seven or eight sermons in Paris, then moved to a provincial town to preach a course in Lent.

Lacordaire's main task, however, was no longer to preach. He was a religious, entrusted with the responsibility of establishing the Dominican order in France, and to this purpose he bent his main energies. In 1844, during the Lent station at Grenoble, he bought a convent, a rambling, dilapidated building straggling across a sunny plateau, once well known as the Chartreuse of Chalais; and the next year he obtained permission to transfer the French novitiate to the new site. Among the friars who joined him almost immediately was a certain Jandel, who now became Prior and Rector and was later to be appointed Master General of the whole order. Jandel was a shrewd, tidy, analytical mind who did not allow friendship to dim his judgement. Through his eyes we can watch Lacordaire as an administrator —the orator turned organizer—and the picture is not a flattering one.

In Italy, where the Frenchmen had observed the laxness of the Italian monks and their calm, complacent neglect of the Dominican constitutions, several had taken a vow 'never to co-operate actively in any arbitrary modification of their laws'. But Lacordaire signalled his arrival at Chalais by the announcement that he had requested the Master General to discharge them from this vow. They learnt the news with a shock, almost with resentment. It was not that Lacordaire was himself unexacting in his requirements: indeed far too often he impaired the

21044

health of his monks with irrational severities. But in spite of his energy and inspiration his companions felt deeply that regulations conceived by one man alone—even by Lacordaire— could not rival the established rules of the order. Jandel was particularly emphatic. 'It [Lacordaire's decision]', he wrote, 'reveals to us the true cause of our ills and sufferings since that time, the obstacle to the full realization of the magnificent prospects which lay before us, in fine (why should I not say it since I am deeply convinced of it?) the delay, involuntary without doubt but only too real, the indefinite delay to the accomplishment of the merciful designs of Providence for the regeneration of our order.'[1]

It was Lacordaire's great weakness to be a Romantic administrator. Though the religious in his charge were convinced that he had been specially chosen by Providence to restore the Dominicans to France (several of them even combined to draw up a memorandum of protest when he wished to lay down the burden of office), none the less they could not ignore his besetting faults. The ardent and impressionable nature that won him such popularity in the pulpit needed some check when it confronted the problems of day-to-day administration; and Lacordaire altogether lacked the curb of a critical, analytical mind. Unconsciously and benignly, he transferred his sensibility from the open fields of eloquence to the narrow paths of routine; and with unhappy results. The instability of temperament which had even been an asset when he applied it to understanding the hopes and fears of his generation, became a grave handicap when he turned it to the task of directing a community. Indeed Jandel found him almost impossible to work with. He was constantly plunging into contradictions of which he was unaware. One day he would support an idea; a week later he defended its opposite, and yet always in good faith and with conviction. During the early days of the novitiate, for example, he often spoke of the importance of the Frenchmen all keeping together, for in homogeneity lay success. But when they were dispersed and separated from his guidance, he explained that this was a great mercy of God: without dispersion they would never learn the traditions of the order, whose leaders would therefore have no confidence in their judgement. Lacordaire's

[1] R. Devas, *Ex Umbris*, pp. 33-4.

optimism was, as he himself realized, incorrigible: whatever happened was always for the best. His sanguine disposition purchased cheerfulness at the cost of truth.[1]

Moreover Lacordaire suffered from the self-imposed limitations of his curiosity, inflicting on the monks his own eccentric ideas about the past. It was one thing to delude oneself about the history of Saint Dominic; it was another to misconceive and misapply the history of the order. But that is in fact what Lacordaire did, knowing only the 1690 Constitutions, allowing himself large liberties in their interpretation, and ignoring the General Chapters that had followed. He might none the less have imposed his own spirit on the French province had it not been for the misfortunes that befell his first companions. Of the five men who had stood close to him when he first proposed the reintroduction of the Dominican order, only one, who lacked authority, remained his familiar. Three died in the space of seven years, and the fifth came to represent a different outlook and method. This fifth, who was Jandel and who had originally been drawn to the Dominicans by his personal affection for Lacordaire, endured a painful period of struggle with the man whom he had once revered as a paragon and now distrusted as a visionary. Yet it was typical of Lacordaire that, having by his unskilful opposition inadvertently assisted Jandel's nomination as Vicar-General of the order, he was afterwards convinced of his deliberate and decisive contribution to the appointment.

The future of the Dominican order in France, however, lay with Jandel and those of Jandel's turn of mind. It would be inaccurate and unfair to exaggerate the difference between the two men, but this small discrepancy exactly measures the extent of Lacordaire's originality, of his personal outlook. Had his originality been essential to the success of the undertaking, one would speak of his failure to leave behind a viable tradition. As it was, he lacked a personality distinct or strong enough to persist after his death. And his influence was as ephemeral elsewhere. Turning towards the Pope and against the leaders of the French Church, he lost whatever support he might have hoped for from Gallicans and legitimists. But though he aspired to become the leader of the second—and Ultramontane—section of clergy, he was hampered and frustrated by his deep emotional

[1] See Devas, *passim.*

liberalism and his former association with Lamennais. Even when he preached to the men of his own time, there were limits to his triumph, for his message concealed a basic inconsistency that ultimately weakened its impact and denied it the force to endure. Though Lacordaire was a leader, his followers marched towards a goal very different from his; and their victories were sometimes of a kind which he would have found it hard to applaud.

CHAPTER IX

Political Warfare

═══

During the decade that followed Louis Philippe's coming to power the political turmoil of the country subsided. Gradually the new regime gained strength and confidence, its stability enhancing its reputation and its reputation enhancing its stability. To this acceptance of the July Monarchy the Catholics themselves contributed, though perhaps involuntarily, by their works of charity. Charity is not dramatic in its effects; but the generosity and self-abnegation that were shown by social workers helped to convince the poor that the Church was not exclusively interested in titles and riches. The need was grave enough. When a new Prefect, taking up his duties at Lille Prefecture under Louis XVIII, had mildly asked the Charity Commissioners whether there were many poor, he was told 'More than twenty-three thousand'. The inquiry which he immediately set on foot showed that a third of the inhabitants of Lille were living in want and a sixth were maintained by the prefecture. His solution—the foundation of agricultural communities and the opening of workshops and workhouses—attracted few imitators. Alms-giving was almost entirely a private virtue. Even under the Empire, however, a number of religious societies had been established, and while some remained local communities, others expanded into congregations with branches throughout the country. This movement acquired impetus, and as the century wore on the number of congregations multiplied rapidly.[1] Meanwhile Ozanam founded the Société de Saint-Vincent-de-Paul, a group of laymen whose aims were to defend Christianity and to practise alms-giving. Numbering only eight

[1] For lists see L. Baunard, *Un siècle de l'Eglise de France*, pp. 279–80, 282.

members at its inception, it had gathered more than fifty by 1834, and eighteen years later there were two thousand in Paris alone.

Private charity, however, being variable in its scope and unequal in its incidence, could not cure the basic ills of society: moreover only a small minority of Catholics practised it to an appreciable extent. From about 1840 onwards the majority fixed their eyes on the political struggle that was developing between their new leaders and the Government. The immediate point at issue was education, an old battleground ever since Napoleon had reorganized the University as a body of lay teachers and given it control over the entire educational establishments in the country. This power the University retained under the Restoration: and although a bishop was admittedly made Grand Master, the religious observances which immediately invaded the curriculum were derided and disdained by the overwhelming majority of masters and pupils alike. Indeed many of the masters were flung into permanent conflict with the Church by their personal history; in 1815–16, for instance, the principal members of the staff of Rouen *collège* consisted of a former Capuchin, a former Oratorian, and three priests who had taken the heretical oath of loyalty to the Revolution—none of them men who could be relied on to teach sound doctrine.

Now many Catholic leaders, brought up like Lacordaire in a *collège* and converted in adult life, felt the inadequacy of religious instruction and feared the anticlericalism that was injected into children, like a routine inoculation, as soon as they passed into the hands of the University. Although in the days of *L'Avenir* Lacordaire and Montalembert had pleaded fervently for the abolition of the University monopoly, it was not surprising that in spite of their victories in the law courts they failed to persuade the liberals to abandon a control which was captured as recently as 1830. So far as primary education was concerned, Guizot's law of 1833 satisfied all but a few virulent Catholics. The problem and the prize, however, lay in secondary education. For the Chamber of Deputies was elected by two hundred thousand bourgeois, and everything depended on whether their education was secular or religious. If they could be won by the Church, political control of the country would pass to Catholics by about 1855. It was a glittering prospect, an opportunity which, if seized and held on to, might transform the history of Europe. Even if the electoral system changed, it would only change by an enlargement of the franchise. However one turned over the problem, however one conceived it and phrased it, it was clear that in France as in almost all other European countries the future belonged to the party which could indoctrinate the greatest number of children in the shortest possible time.

Not that the question was formulated so cynically. As in every large movement, there were a few men who grasped the real point at issue, and a great number who contented themselves with pious and inaccurate slogans. Conflict might indeed have been avoided had Guizot succeeded in forcing through his Bill for secondary education; but his government fell and the draft was shelved. After that, there were several false starts. In 1840 Villemain, the Minister of Public Instruction, put a number of new proposals before the Chamber, but they included certain restrictions on the little seminaries, and at the mere suggestion that recruits to the priesthood should be harried and coerced by a secular state, the bishops, who had hitherto stood aloof from a campaign that exploited the dangerous word 'freedom', made a solemn and resonant entry in unison—to such effect that the Government withdrew its proposals.

It was an emphatic Catholic victory; and the bishops, relishing this unusual experience, took the offensive. Led by the hoary and redoubtable Bishop of Chartres, they belaboured the University in sonorous episcopal prose. They accused it of 'a horrible carnage of souls' and of transforming children into 'unclean animals and wild beasts'. They tossed about insults at random. They invoked their duty as Christian Crusaders. It was all very exciting and all very harmless. But Montalembert, watching the dust rise from the battlefield, saw that if the French Church was to exploit its advantage, it needed warriors more skilful and adroit than the old Bishop of Chartres, who was trampling on friends and enemies indiscriminately like an enraged dinosaur. In fact, it needed laymen. French Catholics must start an agitation against secular education on the same scale as Cobden's agitation against the Corn Laws; they must form a party.

In two ways Montalembert gave a new twist to the Catholic campaign: not only did he organize a *parti catholique* but he claimed the independence of Catholic schools as one of the liberties implied in the Constitutional Charter. The latter was a doctrine he had learnt from Lamennais, and as it took root in the party, it helped to snap the links between Catholicism and the Bourbons. No doubt, as the past suggested and the future would prove, the Church of France stood to lose by too close an association with any political party; but by uniting Catholics in one aim, Montalembert made it difficult for them to indulge in sterile regrets for the old regime. Bishops could hardly praise liberty in one breath and Charles X in the next. Some of them, however, not only viewed with disquiet the entry of laymen into polemics, but said so forcibly. 'Laymen have no mission', said the Archbishop of Rouen; and again, 'Their best course is to pray while the bishops make requests'.[1]

Many bishops were at best lukewarm, but precisely when the temperature of discussion was beginning to fall, the indefatigable Villemain introduced a fresh Education Bill. This (and it was a considerable achievement) even made some progress in the legislature; but it contained a new condition by which no teacher could be a member of an unauthorized religious order. This disingenuous clause was directly aimed at the Jesuits, and rather than accept an imperfect Bill, the bishops once more sang their chorus of disapproval, and so vigorously that even their supporters were impressed.

By this time Montalembert had taken command of the movement. Under continuous pressure from Lacordaire, he had repudiated Lamennais in time to clear his name by absolute submission to Rome, and in the ten years that had since passed he had achieved authority as a speaker and maturity as a thinker. Maturity, that is, as far as he would ever possess it. For he was a quick-tempered enthusiast, temperamentally unsuited to the calculations of diplomacy. 'I am only a soldier', he said; 'a leader of the vanguard, at the very most.' An excellent man to carry a position by force, but a poor tactician and a worse strategist.

In fact the cooler heads among the Catholics were uneasy at the turn of events. Even Lacordaire, in spite of his enthusiasm about educational reform, was afraid that by the tone of his polemic Montalembert would alarm many who might other-

[1] Quoted by E. Veuillot, *Louis Veuillot*, I, p. 509.

wise be sympathetic. Ozanam sensibly remarked: 'I should not like a *party* to be Catholic, because then the *nation* could not be Catholic.'[1] And Affre, the Archbishop of Paris, discouraging his colleagues from public protests, urged them to proceed with discreet letters and private representations. But this was a policy that had been tried and had failed; and Affre looked not only foolish but ineffectual when one of his own private representations—a secret memoir addressed to the king—received the unwelcome publicity of a full reprint in *L'Univers*.

It was the more irritating because *L'Univers*, though a Catholic organ, was written and run by laymen; and no archbishop likes to be reproved by a member of his flock. But the days of undisputed episcopal pre-eminence were numbered; the party which Lacordaire had hoped to lead took its marching orders, not from the clergy, but from Montalembert and Veuillot. Of the two Veuillot was the stronger and the more resilient. Catholics who consoled themselves with the reflection that Montalembert was a nobleman, remained mute about the origins of his ally. For Veuillot was a peasant, and proud of his parentage. Born in 1813 to a cooper and a village girl, he had known the hard struggles that befall ambition when it is joined to poverty. But his early years as a lawyer's clerk and a provincial journalist had toughened his fibre and confirmed his buoyancy of character. By the time he reached Paris in his middle twenties he had proved his endurance and tested his adaptability. If, when he underwent conversion at Rome, it seemed that his career was broken, it was only for a moment. And in 1843, before he had yet celebrated his thirtieth birthday, he was established as the editor of *L'Univers* by a talent that eclipsed all rivals.

Veuillot was not disposed to concessions or compromises; he despised them as a sign of weakness. Having accepted Christianity absolutely and unconditionally without a prolonged inquiry into its history or doctrines, he also accepted the idea of a Catholic party. This sturdy, stocky peasant with his little eyes, thick lips, large nose and pock-marked face entirely lacked the subtlety that might have weakened his power as an antagonist. No one could invent a crueller insult or deliver it with a

[1] Quoted by P. Thureau-Dangin, *L'Eglise et l'Etat sous la monarchie de juillet*, p. 191.

more telling effect. Because of his elemental conviction of being in the right, there was nothing to check his violence, directed as it was both at Catholics and at their opponents. From the moment that battle was joined, he showed no mercy, almost unaware of the shrewdness of his blows. Insensitive by nature and brought up in a hard school, expecting no quarter and scarcely considering charity a virtue, he could make a lifelong enemy with a single sentence, and yet that sentence might be written without malice. Here, for instance, is his picture of Victor Cousin in the Chamber:

'Chez le docteur de l'éclecticisme, le rhéteur s'est montré beaucoup plus que l'homme politique, l'universitaire plus que le rhéteur, le courtisan plus que l'universitaire, le comédien plus que tout. Il y a eu des moments où, pour vanter l'Université, M. Cousin avait des larmes dans la voix, et il y en a eu d'autres, lorsqu'il parlait des Jésuites, où il s'éloignait avec horreur du verre d'eau sucrée, comme s'il avait craint que quelque main dévote n'y eût versé du poison.'

Or again, of the Duc de Broglie, a moderate Catholic:

'Contrairement à ses habitudes et contrairement aussi aux usages de la noble Chambre, M. de Broglie a apporté dans ses répliques beaucoup d'acrimonie. Cette dérogation à la morgue pédante et contente qui caractérise l'école doctrinaire, n'a pas servi l'éloquence de l'honorable rapporteur. La passion ne convient pas à ceux qui se sont fait une habitude de manier le sophisme.'

It was magnificent; but it hurt.

No doubt the Catholic campaign would have provoked stiff resistance even without the aggressiveness of Veuillot and Montalembert; but their insolent language and excessive claims, while rallying their supporters, lost them much sympathy and encouraged their opponents to undertake a counter-attack. Lacordaire, in one of his Pangloss moods, could still tell Mme Swetchine in June 1844: 'Have you noticed that it is the first time since the League that the Church of France is not divided by quarrels and schisms? Today we fall into one another's arms; the bishops talk of freedom and common law; the Press, the Charter, the modern world, are all accepted. . . .'[1] But his judgement would have been more secure had he recalled the

[1] *Correspondance avec Mme Swetchine*, p. 379.

Government's apprehension when he first entered the pulpit of
Notre-Dame as a Dominican six months earlier; for already the
opposition campaign was in full swing, and a much more perceptive observer was writing: 'When I think of the attitude to
religion shown by public opinion and the Press scarcely three
years ago, and compare it with the attitude today, I cannot help
seeing that the clergy must have committed huge blunders to
reach their present position. By violent personalities and exaggerated accusations they have contrived to spoil an excellent
cause. Instead of restricting themselves to common law and
claiming their elementary rights, they have revealed their
intention of dominating and even controlling all forms of
education.'[1]

By this excess of zeal over charity, the Catholic leaders forfeited much of the ground that could have been consolidated.
Eagerly inflating their demands as the opportunity of satisfying
them drew nearer, they forgot that success could only be
achieved if, to the public mind, it was ensured by reason and
justice. But reason and justice appeared to trouble them least.
The fact that many Protestants found little to criticize in the
educational structure itself indicated that behind the Catholic
claims there might lurk either a fear of rational teaching or a
plot to overthrow the Government. Political observers wondered
whether the regime would survive, and though Louis Philippe
might dismiss the whole business as a quarrel between pedants
and vestry-keepers, innocently asking whether M. de Montalembert intended to take orders, his throne ultimately depended on
the skill with which the situation was handled.

The anticlericals assaulted the Catholic flank, driving against
the Jesuits; for the Jesuits were convenient scapegoats, always
available in the absence of a grosser scandal. Reappearing in
France after the Restoration, they had never achieved official
recognition, and their unenviable reputation for ambition,
intrigue and corruption was a fair target for the enemies of the
Church. Victor Cousin as he spoke in the Chamber, drawing
away nervously from his glass of sugared water, was playing on
a well-known theme. Nor was the apprehension entirely simu-
lated, even by those within the fold. When Affre received the
Jesuits after his nomination as Archbishop, he told them

[1] A. de Tocqueville, *Œuvres et correspondances inédites*, II, pp. 121–3.

frankly: 'I do not know what you think of me, for it is very difficult to know the minds of Jesuits, but if I do not know now, I shall know within a month or a year; and if I find you are hostile, I shall—since you are here only as auxiliaries—ask you to relieve me of your assistance.'[1]

The Jesuits provided as useful an argument to the anti-clericals as did the Freemasons to the clericals. With Béranger reviling them in song, Eugène Sue traducing them in one of the most popular novels known to French literary history,[2] Ville-main and Mignet maligning them in parliamentary speeches, their reputation turned from grey to black. In 1843, too, both Michelet and Quinet, in their crowded lectures at the Collège de France, struck the order at its most vulnerable point by examin-ing its history with a critical method that was none the less effective for being highly tendentious. Indeed when Quinet's book on the Jesuits was published, even Affre was moved to censure it publicly. A Jesuit, in fact, became a myth, a figure of legendary evil and terrifying power, a nightmare apparition bent on crushing humanity. The black beasts of the thundering legion struck a chill into the bravest heart. Villemain, labouring under the heavy responsibility of his Education Bill, succumbed to a conviction that the Jesuits had marked him down for destruction and would not rest until his death. One day, crossing the Place de la Concorde with a friend, he stopped, pointed suddenly to a heap of paving-stones, and shouted: 'Do you see them? The Jesuits! the Jesuits! Let's run!' His subsequent resignation on grounds of insanity gave Guizot a welcome opportunity to withdraw the Bill.

Meanwhile Ravignan, the Jesuit preacher of Notre-Dame, who was second only to Lacordaire as an orator and his superior as a theologian, had dared to publish a defence of his order—probably the first occasion since the Revolution on which a Jesuit had publicly boasted of his allegiance. But while he attacked his enemies in public, in private Ravignan deplored his allies, realizing that he and his companions would pay the price—and pay it soon. He guessed correctly. On 2nd May 1845

---

[1] Quoted by Lecanuet, *Montalembert*, II, pp. 70–1, from *La Chronique catholique*, 31st May 1840.

[2] *Le Juif Errant*. It appeared as a serial in *Le Constitutionnel*, and earned its author a fortune. It is still read, though in abbreviated editions.

Thiers, who had been exploiting the situation in order to embarrass the Government, demanded in the Upper House that the laws against unauthorized congregations should be put into force; and the next day the Chamber voted their expulsion. Among the Catholics there was a flurry of indignation, and while Affre counselled submission, less cool-headed advisers urged the Jesuits to defend their rights. Guizot, the Prime Minister, kindly disposed though he was to the Catholics, saw that it would be political suicide to resist the Chamber's vote, but in order to soften the blow he dispatched to Rome a skilled emissary named Pellegrino Rossi to negotiate with the Pope. Guizot, who had in fact already been informed that the Vatican disapproved of *L'Univers* because there was not a single priest on the editorial board, expected from Rome a sympathetic understanding of his position. This he received. On July 6th it was announced that as a result of Rossi's mission the Pope had decided on the voluntary dispersal of the Jesuits in France. Their houses would be shut and their novitiates dissolved. But though for Montalembert and his friends this was a stunning blow, almost a betrayal, their indignation was premature; for Rossi and Gregory had come to an amiable arrangement whereby the Jesuits, though shutting their houses, remained as active as ever, scattered over the country in small discreet groups.

The dispersal of the Jesuits, by removing the most outstanding cause of offence, reduced the heat of the controversy; passion made way for argument. This was partly a tribute to Montalembert, for a general election loomed ahead and all parties were interested in securing the Catholic vote. But it was also due to another well-known figure, the Abbé Dupanloup, who had intervened with a pamphlet urging conciliation instead of aggression. Not only did he enjoy a great reputation as a teacher, but he was known to the public by his feat—impressive, if not altogether credible—in procuring the filial submission of Talleyrand on his deathbed. But Dupanloup's accession, though broadening the basis of the Catholic party, was distasteful to *L'Univers*, and Montalembert's talent was fully exerted in protecting him against a hail of criticism. 'If the Abbé Dupanloup had been born at the time of the Arian heresy', said one pamphleteer, 'he would probably have hurled reproaches at Saint

Athanasius and addressed bland words of conciliation to the courtiers and prelates who favoured the Arian sect.'[1]

But Dupanloup was to be proved right. Heartened by his support and strengthened by the formation of a Central Catholic Committee with branches throughout the country, Montalembert looked ahead cheerfully to the 1846 elections; and the results, when they came in, showed that no less than one hundred and forty-six of the candidates elected were pledged to the principle of liberty in education—understood, of course, in a Catholic sense. The Government, which had already suspended Quinet's lectures and suppressed the Council of the University, was not unmoved; and in yet another Education Bill, introduced the next year, it went some way towards meeting the minority's requirements.

The consequent slackening of tension was accelerated by additional circumstances. In Rome Gregory's death had brought to the Chair of Saint Peter Giovanni Mastai-Ferretti, henceforward Pius IX, a prelate whose notorious liberal sympathies had startled Metternich into a groan of apprehension. One of the new Pope's first acts was to urge on his polemists the need for charity. Secondly, the campaign led by Montalembert had drawn together as never before the separate groups and sections of the French Church in a unanimous demand for liberty of education, and we need not fall into Lacordaire's exaggerations to see that by his concentration on this single aim Montalembert had patched over many ancient rifts and differences. Thirdly, the particular purpose of the campaign was so successfully disguised with high-flown abstractions that many left-wing opponents of the July Monarchy felt an instinctive sympathy for priests and laymen who, day in, day out, spoke of liberty as the greatest of all civic gifts.

Indeed there is something ironical in the liberalism that apparently invaded the most unexpected backwaters of clerical opinion. Many Catholics raised their eyebrows when they saw Dupanloup, who had striven hard against *L'Avenir* and worked closely with Cardinal de Rohan, invoking 'the true and generous spirit of the French Revolution'. But what was Dupanloup beside the Archbishop of Bordeaux, asking for 'liberty for all';

[1] Quoted by P. Thureau-Dangin, *L'Eglise et l'Etat sous la monarchie de juillet*, pp. 434–5.

the Archbishop of Lyons, pleading for 'liberty as in Belgium';
the Archbishop of Tours, pressing for 'liberty for all, without
privilege or exception for any'; and the Bishop of Le Mans,
crying for 'liberty not only for us, but for everyone'? Even
L'Univers joined the refrain with its customary resonance, ex-
claiming 'Long live freedom of religion, freedom of the Press,
freedom of association! Long live the Charter!'; assuring its
readers that 'Catholics want and demand liberty for everyone';
and explaining, 'We wish our adversaries to have the freedom
to attack us and to use it as they will. This we say from the
depth of our hearts. We should no more dream of asking the
Government to suppress MM. Michelet and Quinet than of
asking God to take away free will because of the wicked in the
world.'[1]

Perhaps there was more sincerity in these claims than one
is prepared to allow at first sight; but if so, the sincerity was a
function of self-deceit, justifying a particular demand without
considering its implications. Had Lamennais written *L'Avenir*
in such an atmosphere, he would never have been driven out
of the Church; as it was, his ideas and perceptions spurred on
both the Catholic revival and its political exploitation. For the
Church at last seemed to have taken the measure of the century, adding its authority to the hopes of the rising generation.
Indeed the campaign for liberty prospered so well that in
January 1848 the Government even suppressed Michelet's
lectures.

As events were moving, it seemed that before long a reasonable compromise would give the country the educational system
which it needed; probably the new Bill, introduced in 1847,
would be remoulded and reshaped till it was entirely acceptable
to no party and yet accepted by all. Such was Guizot's hope;
but events took a different course. Almost accidentally, the
reformist demonstration that was planned to take place in
Paris on February 22nd turned into a revolt, and the revolt
unexpectedly developed into a revolution; so that on the evening
of February 24th, while old Louis Philippe wearily made his
way to Dreux, the doors of the Tuileries were flung open to the
world and crowds pressed through the royal chambers, sitting

[1] See, for instance, F. Lagrange, *Vie de Mgr Dupanloup*, I, pp. 347–8;
P. Thureau-Dangin, *op. cit.*, pp. 178–98; *L'Univers, passim.*

in chairs, prying into closets, lying in beds, tearing off souvenirs, stealing clothes, rejoicing in yet another change of regime.

But the Revolution had no quarrel with the Church, for was not the Church the foremost advocate of liberty? On the contrary, cries of *Vive la religion! Vive Jésus-Christ!* echoed through the streets. Priests making their way across Paris were helped past the barricades with encouraging shouts of *Vive la religion! Vivent les prêtres!*, and Affre, sensing the situation, allowed many churches to be turned into temporary hospitals for the victims of street-fighting. When the mob burst into the private chapel of the Tuileries, it was in no mood of destruction. 'You wish to be regenerated,' cried a student from the Ecole Polytechnique, waving an ivory figure of Christ above his head, 'do not forget that it can only be through Christ.' 'Yes, yes,' came the answer, '*he* is the master of us all.' And leading a band of insurrectionists and members of the National Guard, he carried the crucifix and sacred vessels out of the chapel and across Paris to the church of Saint-Roch, where they were solemnly delivered to the priest.[1]

It was a far cry to the sacking of Saint-Germain-l'Auxerrois.

[1] See *L'Ami de la Religion*, CXXXVI, 1848, p. 498.

PART TWO

Michon's Dilemma

CHAPTER I

The Use of Revolution

‘I admire Jesus Christ’, said the assassin Alibaud, shortly after his unsuccessful attempt to shoot Louis Philippe. ‘He was a republican like me, and he would probably have been a regicide too.’[1] The revolutionaries of 1848, if they repudiated Alibaud's method, were in full accord with his philosophy. They respected the Church. They honoured religion. They glorified the Trinity as devoutly as they invoked Lamennais and Leroux.

When, therefore, the clergy had overcome their first apprehension at the sudden disappearance of the Orleanist regime, they were astonished to find themselves popular and gratified to discover that their ministrations were in general demand. On the night of February 24th Veuillot and Montalembert sat late in the offices of *L'Univers*, elaborating an editorial which welcomed the new regime without committing them to its support. But nothing stales more quickly than political caution, and on the following morning Veuillot was defending his editorial before an indignant deputation of priests and laymen. By the 27th prudence was obsolete. On that day, amid a storm of clapping, Lacordaire mounted the pulpit of Notre-Dame and publicly thanked the Archbishop of Paris for his unprejudiced acceptance of the Republic. Meanwhile *L'Univers*, struggling to keep abreast of the tide of opinion, was asking its readers:

‘Who in France today thinks of defending the Monarchy? Who *can* think of it? France imagined that she was still royalist when already she was republican. Yesterday she was surprised; today she is surprised no longer.’

[1] Quoted by J. d'Alméras, *La Vie Parisienne sous la république de 1848*, p. 159.

The same note was echoed by more authoritative voices. While Affre informed the President of the Provisional Government that he was 'assured of the loyal assistance of the whole Parisian clergy', the Bishop of Langres advised his flock to adhere immediately to the Republic and Cardinal de Bonald was even heard to rejoice that Frenchmen had no longer cause to envy North America.

It seemed, in fact, that Lacordaire's aim had—almost miraculously—been achieved: who could perceive any conflict between the Church and the modern world when the Government asked for prayers, and priests throughout the country applauded the wisdom of the people? The isolated manifestations against the clergy that occurred at Lyons, Marseilles and Vincennes, fomented as they were by a handful of incendiaries, only served to emphasize the calm that prevailed elsewhere. In almost every city, town and village a tree of liberty was ceremonially planted and blessed.

'Frequently within the last three weeks', wrote the English Ambassador on April 1st with more than a touch of aristocratic disdain, 'have I strolled on foot into the populous and distant faubourgs, following with an observant eye, at a little distance, some of those strange processions carrying bare sickly poplars to plant in some most inappropriate spot as trees of liberty; the Curé being required to attend with his blessing, apparently to guard against open ridicule of that which was so purely absurd. The servants of the Church in gold-laced liveries with cocked hats and silk stockings, half lacqueys, half beadles, were the objects of intense admiration of the ragged crowd of attendant gamins, who would have mobbed them had they been seen behind a carriage.'[1]

Few of these trees of liberty were to survive into their third year, and their premature death was ascribed by anticlericals to poisoned holy-water. But in the spring of 1848 the buds burst gaily enough, like sudden hopes in a regenerated world.

Yet the enthusiasms, promises and acclamations of 1848 were like so much froth on a surface that still concealed the predatory monsters of the past. There was no agreement on the meaning of the Revolution or on the domestic policy of the Republic. The mere fact that Lamartine had formed a broadly based

[1] The Marquis of Normanby, *A Year of Revolution*, I, p. 279.

administration representing most of the groups who rejoiced at Louis Philippe's fall, disguised but did not dispel the sharp differences of outlook between its members. Perhaps there was never a more warm-hearted revolution than 1848: it was such a delightful surprise. But occurring almost accidentally and on its own impulsion, it caught the politicians unawares, plunging them into a new situation which everybody welcomed but no one understood. Experienced statesmen, like Lamartine himself, were inclined to see its causes as primarily political: Louis Philippe, they explained, had been dismissed for failing to extend the franchise to more than 200,000 property-owners, and the essential difference between the new Republic and the old constitutional monarchy lay in the democratic basis of the former; the immediate task was therefore to democratize the country—to give the vote to all male adults. It was a plausible argument. But there were other men in the Government— Louis Blanc, Ledru-Rollin, Albert the mechanic—who, having seen and suffered from penury and distress in industry, hailed the opportunity of introducing basic reforms in the social structure. The failure to introduce these reforms had, they explained with equal cogency, cost Louis Philippe his throne. As they pointed out, the corporations which once protected workers against unemployment, poverty and competition, had drifted towards bankruptcy under Louis XVI and been finally overthrown by the Great Revolution; and the few illegal associations that had since begun an unsteady existence were quite incapable of giving their members adequate support in the frequent stress of industrial crisis. Between these divergent views the Government attempted a compromise: it set up a permanent commission to study labour problems and it established National Workshops which represented a half-hearted approximation to the Socialist ideal of Louis Blanc. But the division between the two sections—those who were content with a political revolution and those who worked for a social revolution—was so deep that it was certain to end in a struggle for power.

The first conflict broke out over the elections. The Government was unanimous in granting universal male suffrage, but how would male suffrage be used? It was clear to Ledru-Rollin, the Minister of the Interior, that the illiterate peasants who constituted the vast majority of Frenchmen would either take

fright at tales of the Socialists' abolition of private property or
—if they were hesitant—succumb to the blandishments of the
local priests and gentry. In either case they would vote for the
right and Ledru-Rollin's party would lose. As the elections were
fixed for 9th April, he had to move quickly. He hastily arranged
for 'Commissioners of the Republic' to be sent round the country
to educate the nine million new electors in their radical duties;
and then, arguing speciously from the outbreaks of violence that
had already sprung from the conflict between bourgeois and
workers, he postponed election day till 23rd April—Easter
Sunday, thus dealing a calculated blow at churchgoers.

Priests had meanwhile assumed their civic responsibilities with
alacrity. Thirty-six, including four bishops, figured on the
electoral lists; and when the Government, controlled by its
more conservative members, appealed for the Church's help,
bishops throughout the country urged the faithful to record their
votes. Those who had formerly sympathized with Lamennais
felt free once more to develop their arguments. In Charente,
for instance, the Abbé Michon, honorary canon of Bordeaux and
of Angoulême, addressed an election manifesto to his fellow
priests, reviving the idea of the separation of Church and State,
an idea which had become almost improper since Lamennais's
apostasy. 'The union of Church and State', Michon stated
boldly, 'is good neither for religion nor for the government.
Vain attempts have been made to strengthen the throne by
means of the altar, and the altar by means of the throne. . . .
This has only led to political acrimony, to mutual distrust between people and clergy, in short to the abandonment of religion
and to indifference. I shall therefore vote for the separation of
Church and State. . . . It is a sad thing to suppose that our
religion can only subsist on Caesar's silver.'[1]

Meanwhile a letter in which Montalembert appealed to the
bishops to select suitable candidates for the Assembly met with
a widespread response. But while the clergy organized meetings
and distributed propaganda, Ledru-Rollin was not idle. He
weakened the conservatives by his choice of Easter Sunday as
election day. He handicapped the peasants by his insistence that
they must vote, not at the commune, but at the head town of the
canton. But in neither respect was he equal to the determina-

[1] *Profession de foi de l'abbé Michon*, 21st March 1848.

tion of the country priests. While many, indulging in a little political casuistry, explained to their flock that the duty of recording a vote took precedence over the duty of attending Mass, a large number overcame their personal difficulties by staggering the hours of service, so that they not only voted themselves but released their neighbours for the same purpose. Throughout France on that Easter Sunday 1848 the casual observer might have seen a compact and orderly band emerging from the village church, led by the priest and escorted by the local drummer, and marching away to the nearest polling booth, perhaps several miles distant.

As soon as it was announced that the almost unbelievable figure of 84 per cent of the electorate had gone to the polls, there could be no doubt of the result. In fact, out of 900 seats 700 were won by republicans of the centre, leaving the rest almost equally divided between legitimists and the left wing. Though Michon was defeated (for who could imagine the average priest supporting a candidate whose main proposal was separation?), three bishops and twenty priests were elected, among them Lacordaire. It was a surprise. In Paris and Toulon, where he had known that his name was on the lists, he had been defeated. But at Marseilles, which he had first visited a bare three months earlier, he was triumphantly returned—all the more triumphantly because his candidature had only been advanced at the last moment.

Lacordaire was indeed one of the few Catholics who were alive to the dangers and possibilities of the situation. However one may criticize his scholarship, learning or logic, there is no doubt that he felt the needs of the country more deeply and more intuitively than a professional politician like Montalembert. For the division in the Government was paralleled by a similar division among Catholics. Only a small minority acknowledged the existence of a real social problem. The clergy, coming as they did either from the aristocracy or from the peasantry, had no experience of industrial conditions, and even when they did not fear the workers, they failed to understand them. The bishops who had been appointed under Louis Philippe were, it is true, able and perceptive men—certainly far abler than the bishops appointed under the Restoration; but their training and environment blinded them to the facts.

They regarded industrial workers as a faction threatening the peace of the country and the safety of the Church. Affre, Archbishop of Paris, was an exception, realizing, however dimly, that the Church must develop a policy towards the victims of the social order; and with some insight he made use of laymen rather than priests in attempting to conciliate the proletariat. Veuillot, too, with his humble background and native shrewdness, saw the urgency of reform, proposing freedom of association for all workers without State intervention. But on the whole, Catholics, like liberals, accepted the *laissez-faire* theories of the mid-century economists, thinking that poverty and starvation were a necessary if regrettable part in a God-given social structure.[1]

On 15th April, however, just over a week before polling day, the first number of *L'Ere Nouvelle* appeared—a daily paper started under Archbishop Affre's patronage, with Lacordaire as editor in chief. Its career was as brief and dazzling as a meteorite. The administration Lacordaire shared with the Abbé Maret, a Gallican theologian of eccentric genius but undisputed authority, and among the regular contributors were the Comte de Coux, who had been an ally of Lamennais's seventeen years earlier, and Frédéric Ozanam, who had shocked Montalembert with his bold appeal, 'Passons aux barbares et suivons Pie IX'. *L'Ere Nouvelle* represented, in fact, the small but brilliant section of the French Church who perceived that political revolution was inadequate and impermanent unless it were reinforced by social reorganization. The whole policy of the paper was calculated to prove that a republic was the form of government best suited to Christianity. It was like a repetition of *L'Avenir*, but deprived of Lamennais and strengthened (almost unbelievably) by the Archbishop of Paris. Lacordaire, though he wrote rarely, was universally regarded as the paper's inspiration; and it clearly answered a demand. A subscription launched in its interest raised 11,000 francs in twenty-four hours, and the number of readers rose from five to ten thousand and then doubled again. This is an extraordinarily high figure when we consider that *L'Ami de la Religion* was selling under two thousand

[1] See particularly J. B. Duroselle, 'L'Attitude politique et sociale des catholiques français en 1848'. *Revue d'histoire de l'Eglise de France*, 1948, XXXV, pp. 44–62.

copies about this time and that *L'Univers*, which was generally regarded as the leading Catholic paper, sold no more than six thousand in 1845 and dropped to three thousand five hundred ten years later.[1] But most Catholics, observing that *L'Ere Nouvelle* dared to speak openly of 'Christian economy' and 'Christian socialism', reprobated Lacordaire's initiative. What use could Veuillot or Dupanloup find for such irresponsible catchwords? For once at least in their lives they saw eye to eye. Even Montalembert agreed, and while the columns of the paper were devoted day after day to earnest proposals for social legislation, he inveighed bitterly against the 'unworthy blandishments of that golden-tongued demagogue, Father Lacordaire'.

Like Michon, Lacordaire was on the crest of the wave in 1848. Unlike Michon, he remained there for some months, even convincing himself that the position was permanent. Public acclamation confirmed his illusion. Dressed in his Dominican habit, he was conspicuous among the new deputies when the Assembly, at its first meeting, emerged on to the peristyle of the Palais Bourbon to proclaim the Republic before the people and the National Guard; and in answer to the persistent shouts of the crowd he stepped down to the barrier, thrust his hands through the railings, and submitted to the kisses and caresses of a mixed band of bourgeois and urchins.

Taking his seat, he chose a position well to the left, on the top of what used to be called the Mountain, a few steps below his former master, Lamennais. But it was, as he later realized, a mistake to give so marked a token of adherence to the left and to commit himself so decisively to a struggle which he had not foreseen. For the Assembly, being predominantly conservative, not unnaturally proceeded with conservative measures, and as soon as this was recognized, disturbances broke out in Paris. Starting on 12th May, they culminated three days later, when the mob broke into the Palais Bourbon, told the Assembly that it was dissolved, and began to form a number of provisional governments in the different rooms of the palace. Throughout the hubbub Lacordaire remained coolly in his seat, convinced that there was little danger. Perhaps he was wrong. At any rate one workman was heard to say grimly to his comrade, with a

[1] See P. Thureau-Dangin, *L'Eglise et l'Etat sous la monarchie de juillet*, p. 211; Jean Maurain, *La Politique ecclésiastique du Second Empire*, p. 161.

glance at Lacordaire's long lean face and black hood: 'Do you
see that vulture there? I'd love to wring his neck.'

Veuillot, following the crowd into the Chamber, witnessed
some of those scenes that always give a touch of fantasy to the
drama of French politics. He saw, for instance, a disciple of the
Socialist Cabet, who, failing to obtain a hearing from any of
the numerous provisional governments, had desperately procured a large sheet of cardboard and was wandering through
each room in turn, pressing it to his chest and displaying the
simple legend:

SITOYENS
NOUBELIE PAS CABET

There was, however, little danger that this second attempt
at revolution would succeed, and the Assembly was soon cleared
by the National Guard. Ultimately it was the revolutionaries
who suffered, for the forces of order, alarmed at this new and
threatening outbreak of violence, closed their ranks and resolved
to crush all forms of Jacobinism; while men like Lacordaire,
who had pinned their hopes to the people, were dispirited and
shocked at so blatant an exhibition of illegality. It was clear
that a trial of strength was imminent between the two sections
that had formed the Provisional Government—the advocates of
social and of political revolution. But the Catholics of *L'Ere
Nouvelle*, however eagerly they desired a revision of social
conditions, could hardly support or condone any recourse to
mob rule, and Lacordaire, feeling himself caught in an impossible position, wrote on 18th May to his constituents, announcing his resignation from the Assembly. It was almost his last
excursion into politics.

Not till June, when the Government closed the National
Workshops which had been set up as a tangible guarantee of
the 'right to work', did the battle begin, and after three days
of bitter and bloody fighting the workers were decisively beaten.
The 1848 Revolution was thus given a definitive interpretation:
it was a political revolution. Prominent Socialists like Louis
Blanc, realizing their failure and anticipating the revenge of
the victors, hurriedly left the country in order to avoid deporta-
tion. Not only were they defeated but discredited. It was their
misfortune that one of the victims of the street-fighting was

Archbishop Affre, shot in front of a barricade as he was attempting to intercede. Although there was no evidence that he had been killed by the insurgents (indeed there was evidence to the contrary), it was obvious that, had there been no insurrection, Affre would not have died, and the insurgents were therefore blamed. His funeral was turned into a triumph for the Church. 'Seven hundred priests took part in it', wrote Allies. 'His body was borne uncovered. Everyone, especially the military, pressed to touch it so that the white gloves and stockings became quite black. An intense feeling had been excited by his sacrifice: people had never been so well disposed to the Church.'[1]

Two powers, in fact, emerged strengthened from the Days of June—the party of order and the Church: and not only strengthened but allied. For in the face of social revolution the bourgeoisie and the nobility revived their flagging devotions and courted the only organization that could teach meekness to the poor and contentment to the starving. It was a matter of convenience, not of conviction. 'The rich shopkeeping classes', Allies heard a month later, 'are universally unchristian; so that in repressing the last *émeute* of June, even the revolters behaved with more respect in the churches than the Garde Nationale sent to fight them.'[2]

Conversely, the majority of Catholics were only too anxious to co-operate with any forces that were strong enough to enforce order. Indeed Catholics themselves belonged to precisely those sections of society—peasantry, bourgeoisie, nobility—which stood to lose from any redistribution of property or wealth. Religion and conservatism were agreed in deploring any violent onslaught on the obtaining system, and few Catholics perceived that their own motives in opposing revolution ought ideally to be free from the selfish retentiveness that animated most of their compatriots. It was desperately hard to concede any virtue in a gang of working men behind a barricade; and even if not virtue, any justification. 'There is no middle term', said Montalembert. 'Today we must choose between Catholicism and Socialism.'

Veuillot concurred with his customary directness. 'There

[1] T. W. Allies, *Journal in France in 1845 and 1848*, p. 284.
[2] Allies, p. 237.

must necessarily be men who work hard and live in squalor', he wrote. 'Poverty is the law of part of society. It is a law of God which we must obey.' But unlike his friends he was disquieted by the Days of June, apprehensive of the party of order, sympathetic to the workers' needs. He saw that there were real causes for bitterness, that hatred could not be suppressed as easily as an insurrection. But he was isolated. Most Catholics, realizing that the straight course which they had plotted in the last years of Louis Philippe had led them to the edge of a precipice, and fearing that one false step would plunge them into anarchy, were politically at a loss. But whatever the route they chose, it must lead backwards, away from Socialism, away from danger, away from vertigo. Even Veuillot, if he was suspicious of the policy of the centre, was horrified by the policy of *L'Ere Nouvelle*, which meant disaster. And in concert with Dupanloup, he tried unsuccessfully to discredit and eliminate the paper.

But *L'Ere Nouvelle* was not to last for much longer, for it nourished hopes that now seemed baseless. Already Lacordaire, disillusioned by the violent passions of the sovereign people, had taken the chance offered by a change in proprietorship and withdrawn; and in the months that followed he was an unwilling, grudging spectator of the victory of conservatism, unable to welcome the authoritarian regime which was in the making, and equally unable to regret the mob rule to which it was an alternative. 'I admit', runs one of his letters, 'that I do not see clearly that there is necessarily more liberty, equality and fraternity in a democracy understood in that way [i.e. government *by* the people] than under a monarchy. There may be; there may not be. It is a question which for me, at any rate, is unresolved.'

The Republic, in fact, was already doomed. It was awaiting a strong man who, by destroying it, would relieve it of its inherent contradictions and uncertainties. That man arrived in Louis Napoleon. In mid-June he had been returned to the Assembly at a by-election, and though he prudently resigned, the threat that he represented was a growing one. Curiously enough, Veuillot was among the first to draw attention to it.

'Let us not be deceived', he wrote in *L'Univers* as soon as the news of Louis Napoleon's election was announced; 'if we wish to save the Republic, it is time, high time, to do more than shout "Long live the Republic!" There has been much talk of reaction: here it is! It comes not from the bourgeois—for they did not elect Louis Bonaparte—but from the people. If today Louis Bonaparte can—as seems possible—become a danger to the Republic, who is to blame?'

But by December, when Louis Napoleon was standing for the Presidency, Veuillot was less wary of his ambition, less attached to the republican ideal, quicker to acclaim a figurehead.

There were two points at issue for Catholics: would the candidates for the Presidency support freedom of education? and did they propose to restore the Pope to Rome? For Pius IX, who had begun his pontificate with such a hustle of liberalism, was enjoying leisure for second thoughts. The revolutionary wave of 1848, sweeping across Europe, had washed right up to the Vatican, and when his Prime Minister was stabbed on the steps of the Assembly[1] and he himself was obliged to flee to Gaeta, he reflected that his hopes had perhaps been too sanguine, and summoned Catholics to restore him to his Holy See. Now the Catholics of France, who were traditionally his most ardent supporters, did not belie their reputation, and Montalembert requested a firm statement of policy from Louis Napoleon and Cavaignac, the two principal contestants for the Presidency. It was a test of integrity. But while Cavaignac not only refused to stifle the new-born Roman Republic, but declined to commit himself on freedom of education, Louis Napoleon was less scrupulous. He gave satisfaction on both points. It is true that many Catholics wavered, that Veuillot, Dupanloup, Parisis were all somewhat less than enthusiastic, and that powerful figures like Ravignan and Sibour, the new Archbishop of Paris, sided with Cavaignac. But although the Catholic Committee decided against selecting an official candidate, Montalembert's enthusiasm was a conclusive asset for Louis Napoleon: it conferred respectability. In fact, Montalembert frivolously discharged a heavy responsibility. Led by family tradition and personal instinct to despise the people, shocked by the deistic humanitarianism of many republicans, imbued with current ideas on property and incapable of seeing any political

[1] It was Pellegrino Rossi, whom Guizot had sent to Rome as his ambassador in 1845.

future for the workers, he urged all Catholics to vote for the only man who would be able to steady an insecure government and was prepared to meet the Catholics in their main demands.[1] It was an enormous blunder, which he was bitterly to regret. It is true that the clergy did not support any one candidate and that Louis Napoleon's election was not their triumph. But that is the most that one can say in extenuation. For of its being a triumph there can be no doubt: Louis Napoleon received five million votes out of a total of seven million. Even more important, the Catholics, who had acclaimed the new Republic at its birth, were fatally committed against it before it was a year old, and in their anxiety to gain immediate political ends rapidly forfeited the friendship of all who cared for personal freedom, democratic government and social reform. The loss did not seem serious at the time, for democratic ideas were at a discount. But at a remove of a hundred years it assumed the proportions of a disaster.

[1] See André Trannoy, 'Les Responsabilités de Montalembert en 1848'. *Revue d'histoire de l'Eglise de France*, 1949, XXXV, pp. 177–206.

CHAPTER II

The Forces of Order and the Fruits of Power

F rom this point Catholics had no choice: although they appeared to preserve some semblance of free-will, it was illusory, sufficient merely to keep them contented while they were hurried on by events. They quickly claimed their two rewards. First, in the summer of 1849, a French expeditionary force overthrew the Roman Republic and set Pius IX back on his throne, where he was henceforward maintained by a French army. Secondly, negotiations were begun to realize at last the dream of free education. But the phrase 'freedom of education' disguised the Catholics' real aim. '"Freedom" is really used to designate rule', said Bismarck in one of his more urbane moods. 'By "freedom of speech" is meant the rule of speakers; by "freedom of the Press" is meant the predominant and preponderant influence of newspaper editors. Indeed, gentlemen —and I am not speaking as a sectarian—it happens often that "freedom of the Church" is taken as meaning the rule of the priests.' Freedom of education, in the France of 1849, meant freedom to expand and to gain control of the youth of the country.

The man in whose hands lay the task of preparing and promoting the bill was the Comte de Falloux, a sharp-nosed, almost feline royalist whose suave diplomacy earned the high tribute of Veuillot's mistrust. He had taken office with reluctance, on an explicit assurance from Thiers that the Cabinet would support his project.[1] The little bourgeois Thiers represented admirably those unbelievers who clung nervously to the

[1] Compare le Comte de Falloux, *Mémoires d'un royaliste*, I, pp. 39 ff; Eugène Veuillot, *Louis Veuillot*, II, p. 291.

Church as the guardian of necessary superstitions. Had he not declared in a recent book that the Church was a foundation-stone of society? Whether Christianity was true, he characteristically failed to inquire. When the bourgeoisie was in danger, he looked hurriedly and anxiously for some immediate bulwark against the twin forces of Socialism and Communism; and of this mood of profound and demoralized apprehension Catholics made the most, winning concessions that would have been bitterly contested two or more years earlier.

Not that Falloux lacked opposition, even from members of his own Church. As soon as he took office, he received a letter from Lacordaire, congratulating him, not on his appointment, but on his hesitations. 'It is probable', said Lacordaire, 'that your appointment will help to prepare the return of autocracy, through an Empire. I am certain that such a return would be disastrous to France, because it would only produce a sterile, inferior repetition of the past, and I fear to see your good name, and that of Catholics generally, compromised by an operation whose least misfortune would be not to attain its ends.' Lacordaire, true to his liberal instincts, sensed the peril of an alliance with the bourgeoisie, who were bent on maintaining their interests and on quelling the people. Ever since February 1848 his scorn for opportunism had stood him in good stead, reinforcing his political intuition and enabling him to look over the heads of his contemporaries to a time when the republicans, having gained power, would remember those who had helped or hindered them in the struggle.

But Falloux was also assailed on his other flank. He saw that any feasible Bill would involve a compromise with the University; sixty years had passed since the Church possessed a monopoly of education, and as a serious statesman he could not contemplate a reversion to the conditions of the *ancien régime*. In 1849, when only a minority of Frenchmen were Catholics, it would have been morally scandalous and politically suicidal to attempt to impose on the nation a denominational education to which it was sharply averse. But Veuillot took the other view; he attacked Falloux's project as 'an act of deceit, a sudden breakdown of reason and conscience, a pact with evil, a monstrous alliance between the ministers of Satan and those of Christ'. Confusing political questions with moral problems, he treated compromise as sin. And his case was plausible. If the Church were the only vessel of divinely revealed truth, without which mankind was damned, Catholics had an obvious duty to impart this truth to every child born into the world. It appears that in practice the forcible administration of dogma fails to produce secure convictions; but of the two points of view Veuillot's was the more logical, and he pressed it home with the incomparable power of his merciless pen.

In spite of his protestations in 1848—and no doubt they were sincere—Veuillot had no natural love of freedom. At any rate he despised the freedom of others. Freedom he thought of, not as an abstract idea, but as a particular condition benefiting his own party. He was plebeian without being democratic; Catholic in belief without being catholic in outlook. He could not feel that the Church would gain more from a republic than from a monarchy; whatever the form of government, his purpose was to exploit it in his own cause, not to defend its ideology. No doubt Protestants welcomed the Republic: had it not enabled them to hold a General Assembly of French Protestantism, the first since the days of persecution? But why should he, the baptized, illuminated, supremely Catholic Veuillot, defend a regime polluted with Socialism, humanitarianism, feminism and many other detestable abstractions? As for bargaining with the bourgeois representatives of such a regime—bargaining, too, on so sacred a matter as Catholic education—at the mere idea his invective began to flow. And so as the months passed in cautious negotiations, compromises and concessions, and the Bill took on its ultimate form, Veuillot grew at once more indifferent to the fate of the Republic and more hostile to that clear-minded, smooth-tongued politician who was responsible for the betrayal; and his wrath, spluttering through the columns of *L'Univers*, eventually brought forth a concise, satisfying and much repeated formula, 'Falloux *fallax*'.

The Loi Falloux was passed on 15th March 1850, some months after Louis Napoleon, irritated at the Pope's refusal to introduce any reforms in the Papal States, had dropped Falloux himself from the Cabinet. The law had all the characteristics of a compromise solution. It annoyed the partisans of both sides; it was illogical; and it worked. According to its provisions, education would henceforth be entrusted to two sorts of organizations—the state schools, which were in the hands of the University, and the 'free schools', which in practice meant schools run by religious associations. While politically it was a triumph for the party of order, establishing a form of education that would check and counterbalance the Communist-tainted schools of the State,[1] tactically it was a triumph for those who were now called Liberal Catholics—men like Dupanloup and Montalembert, whose religion did not prevent them from co-operating with other forces in the country. But to some this triumph appeared a defeat. It was bitterly attacked by Veuillot, who wrote immediately after the vote: 'It creates a dangerous and difficult situation for the Church; it strengthens the University and postpones, for a long time perhaps, that day of liberty whose dawn we thought to behold.' Indeed the Loi Falloux had its most important repercussions outside education; for by alienating Veuillot and his sympathizers, who had now earned the name of Intransigents, it dissolved the Catholic party for which Montalembert had worked so hard in the forties, and laid bare the deep rift that had only been papered over by an aggressive policy and the use of imprecise slogans.

If the split between Veuillot and Dupanloup grew daily wider, it was as nothing to the gulf that separated them both from the Catholics who had run *L'Ere Nouvelle*. For the bishops, who, taking alarm at its consistently democratic tone, forbade their clergy to read the paper, effectually undermined its circulation. To overcome its financial difficulties a certain Marquis de la Rochejaquelin offered to buy it, promising to make no changes in its staff or its policy; but once his fingers tightened round it, he summarily dismissed all contributors, so that as early as April 1849 *L'Ere Nouvelle* had virtually expired. Its day was over. Though a small and rather helpless Circle of Catholic Democracy, supported by a handful of working men, lingered on into 1851, the writing was on the wall. Democracy, whether Catholic or not, was due for the knife: Catholic democrats must cultivate other interests.

It was therefore fortunate for that uneasy and turbulent figure, the Abbé Michon, that he could escape from France;

[1] Particularly the *instituteurs*. See A. de Lamartine, *Le Conseiller du peuple*, 1849, pp. 220–1; A. Cobban, 'The Influence of the Clergy, April 1848.' *The English Historical Review*, 1942, LVII, pp. 334–44.

fortunate that he had won a reputation as a botanist. For Frédéric de Saulcy, an unusually able, exceptionally wealthy and abnormally presumptuous member of the Academy of Inscriptions, who had decided to lead a small scientific and archaeological expedition to the Near East, invited Michon to undertake the herbal of the journey, and Michon, promptly accepting, embarked at Trieste on 10th October 1850, glad to leave for a time a country that was sliding by its own weight towards a new Empire. It was more than ten years before Michon's moment was to come: in the meantime he furnished his arsenal.

The *coup d'état* of 2nd December shocked a few Catholics, surprised more, but secured general acceptance. It was not an unsatisfactory bargain to pay for the Loi Falloux with the liberty of one's opponents. Even Montalembert, startled as he was at the illegal enterprise of his protégé, hesitated for only a few days, and after persuading a group of deputies to sign a joint protest, announced his support for Louis Napoleon. 'Apart from the President', he wrote in *L'Univers*, 'I can see only the gaping void of a victorious Socialism. My choice is made. I am for authority against revolt, for conservation against destruction, for society against Socialism, for the possible liberty of good against the assured liberty of evil.' Veuillot, having long since abandoned his phrases about universal liberty, had been even more emphatic as early as December 5th:

'This is no time for choice, recrimination, deliberation. The Government must be supported. Its cause is that of social order.

'It must be supported today, when battle is joined, so that we can have the right of advising it later. Today, even more than before 2nd December, we say to the men of order: the President of the Republic is your General; do not forsake him; do not desert. If you fail to triumph with him, you will be conquered with him—and conquered for ever.'

Very few bishops withheld their approval, especially when a nation-wide plebiscite showed that the country was overwhelmingly in favour of this attack on its republican institutions. 'We are caught between the sword and the knife', wrote Mgr Pie; 'it is the inescapable dilemma of the moment. But', he added reassuringly, 'the sword frightens only the wicked, whereas the

knife threatens the good.' In Rome Pius IX made no secret of
his satisfaction at the virtual end of the Republic ('Heaven has
acquitted the Church's debt to France', he was reported to
have said), and if even *he* countenanced the *coup d'état*, why
should his supporters be more critical?

Only a handful cherished doubts about the moral superiority
of the sword over the knife. Sibour, who had succeeded Affre
as Archbishop of Paris, inherited a good deal of his predecessor's
Gallican liberalism, disliking Veuillot, distrusting Louis Napoleon, discriminating against Rome; and he tried mildly and
unsuccessfully to prevent the clergy from political indiscretions.
Dupanloup and the Jesuit Ravignan, who were less reserved,
both urged on Montalembert the dangers implicit in an ostenta-
tious acceptance of the Bonapartist regime; while Dupont des
Loges, Bishop of Metz, one of the shrewdest members of the
French episcopate, indulging his naturally caustic bent, wrote
to Pie the day after the *coup d'état*: 'At least let us hope we are not
asked for a *Te Deum* every time a conspiracy succeeds! What a
spectacle of meanness, cowardice, incompetence, blindness and
faction, the Lord sets before our eyes!'[1] And Lacordaire, seeing
deepest into the springs of power and neglecting the immediate
opportunities for Catholic gain, told a correspondent: 'The
violation of a country's constitution by military force is always
a great public calamity, preparing fresh troubles in the future
and the progressive decline of the civil order.'

Apart from the Catholic democrats of *L'Ere Nouvelle* and, to
a lesser extent, the amorphous group of Liberal Catholics, the
Church was guided by no political principle whatever except
its own direct advantage. Taught in the seminaries that they
owed obedience to any party or regime that happened to be in
power, the clergy were happy enough to acclaim the new
Government; for its enemies were their enemies, and its policy
promised to be their own. Any little matter of illegality was
hastily brushed over—justified no doubt by the urgent needs
of the country. Few priests—and they were growing old—felt
that only a Bourbon regime was pleasing in the sight of God;
but even fewer remembered the trees of liberty on to which,
four years earlier, they had sprinkled holy water with such
liberal, perhaps lethal, gestures.

[1] Félix Klein, *Vie de Mgr Dupont des Loges*, p. 82.

Meanwhile a similar reorientation was evident in Rome: Pius IX had attained discretion. In 1847, shortly after his election, a Jesuit general was reported to have said, 'This Pope is the scourge of the Capitol'. But his liberalism, his good intentions towards the people, his dismay at the flagrant misgovernment of the Papal States, were all manifestations of vague benevolence which never issued in a firm policy and could not survive the assault of popular discontent. Witty, charming, receptive, he fascinated his entourage; but he was dangerously aware of his wit, dangerously dependent on his charm, dangerously subject to his receptivity. He had all the inconsistent obstinacy of an impressionable man. 'I am a stone', he said; 'where I fall I lie.' Thus the sudden petrifaction which was liable to overtake his opinions was a natural expression of a character which enabled him to impose these opinions on others. His gentle inflexibility was abetted by his beautiful countenance and mellifluous voice; indeed few of the popes can have rivalled his natural eloquence and delivery. Moreover, his accession to the throne of Saint Peter had been greeted with such delight all over the world, especially by liberals like Ozanam and Montalembert, that he immediately attained a popularity and following which far outstripped whatever esteem had been won by that cautious old monk Gregory. When he was forced into exile, his popularity outside Italy increased rather than abated, and now that he was back in Rome, with all his liberalism forsworn, he enjoyed a prestige and sympathy that ensured him ready obedience and made it hard for his Catholic opponents to admit that they disagreed with his inspired prejudices.

As the helmsman of the Church he did not stray far from the course of his predecessor; but events seemed to conspire to his advantage, so that the goal of centralization was approached with ever-increasing momentum. He was known to be particularly sympathetic to the claims of the lower clergy against their bishops, and he gave nothing but encouragement to the Abbé André, their learned new champion, who eschewed the uncanonical excesses of the brothers Allignol. This sympathy in itself would have endeared Pius IX to the many priests who felt bitter at the autocracy of their superiors; and they saw him increasingly as the Pope who, in the fullness of time, would humble Gallican pride for ever.

Adulated by *L'Univers*, venerated by the clergy, Pius steadily turned his army against the ancient ramparts of nationalist and particularist feeling. A stronghold which resisted for thirty years was the Gallican liturgy, and its gradual capitulation caused passionate heart-burning even among Frenchmen who were out of sympathy with Gallican theology. But 'Gallican' liturgy was a misnomer: what passed under that name had in fact developed under Jansenist influence during the eighteenth century. Responding to a spirit of independent criticism, two-thirds of the French dioceses had manufactured their own breviaries, borrowing liberally from the Bible and shearing away the more startling legends about local saints. These breviaries, though perhaps Gallican in tone, had no relation with the ancient Gallican rites which had been superseded in the ninth century; on the contrary, while they preserved local features, they were essentially new creations, all deriving from one original source at Rome.[1]

Now it was confusing and unnecessary enough to have all these versions of one basic use, but confusion turned into chaos when the Concordat altered the ancient diocesan boundaries; for at one stroke of the pen half a dozen different breviaries, which had hitherto decently kept to their proper limits, came jostling into a single diocese, producing a gay but preposterous inconsistency. Rome had never approved of the eighteenth-century breviaries; now, with the lack of uniformity as an excuse and the growth of Ultramontanism as a means, she took her chance, urging the superior virtues—whether musical, devotional, historical or administrative—of the single liturgy. Gradually the French dioceses fell into line: first Langres in 1839, last Orleans in 1875.

No doubt common sense, convenience, tradition and learning were all on the side of Rome. The supporters of the Gallican uses had only one sound argument—the attachment of the people to their local rite; and as most rites dated from the eighteenth century, even this argument was not a strong one. With the Roman breviary, however, Roman ceremonial entered too, displacing local ceremonials which had undergone little change in the eighteenth century and were often older than

[1] See, for an excellent summary, R. E. Balfour, 'Notes on the History of the Breviary in France'. *The Journal of Theological Studies*, 1932, XXXIII, pp. 365–76.

the current Roman use. Now ceremonial, though the least important element in any rite, is the most conspicuous; a change in ceremonial cannot escape even the most heedless worshipper. It was made evident to Catholics all over France that the office was being standardized. Though the Gallicans raised a cry of innovation and were even widely believed, they did themselves no good: their case having no substance, they were bound to be defeated, and by publicizing their successive reverses they brought home to the people the steady, implacable advance of the Ultramontane party.

Veuillot's school enjoyed, in fact, an easy majority. Even those who had at first favoured the Loi Falloux turned increasingly against it when they realized how far it was a compromise measure. By the part he had played, Montalembert forfeited his position as the most influential Catholic politician, and he lost still further ground in 1852 when, emerging from his brief period of reaction, he repudiated Louis Napoleon and went into opposition. For the bishops, by contrast, flattered and fawned: almost all Catholics looked ahead joyfully to the Second Empire. 'Gentlemen,' said Mgr Parisis of Arras, the day before the crucial plebiscite, 'you must support this astonishing Prince who has dared to undertake the wellnigh supernatural task of saving France. Of him we can say what the Holy Scriptures say of divine wisdom: *Attingit a fine usque ad finem fortiter, et disponit omnia suaviter*: She reacheth from one end of the world to the other with full strength, and ordereth all things graciously.'[1]

When the people, encouraged by the bishops, had duly complied and voted heavily in favour of the Empire, clouds of incense rose to the new ruler of France, whose dynasty was now established by a curious mixture of hereditary right and popular suffrage. A strange specimen of the incense-burner is Salinis, Bishop of Amiens. Beginning life as a royalist, he had been converted in 1830 to the ideas of *L'Avenir*. Four years later he had returned to legitimism, though willing enough to solicit a bishopric from Louis Philippe. 1848 found him a republican, full of praise for the people. 'Democracy', he assured them in a public letter to his bishop, who had asked him to stand for the Assembly, 'is the movement given to the world by the Gospel.'

[1] Charles Guillemant, *Pierre-Louis Parisis*, III, p. 399.

But somehow the movement, despite its evangelical authority, was short-lived and Salinis had to seek another political creed. He was not long in finding it. Snugly ensconced in the episcopate, he reproved Dupanloup for expressing obsolete ideas about the relations between the Church and liberty. The Church, Salinis explained, cannot undertake any action in the world without encountering power—or Caesar; this encounter involves a choice between peace and war; but the Church cannot choose war; so when she meets Caesar, she goes to welcome him, offering peace. And asking, Salinis might have added, for a treaty of alliance.

Yet Salinis was an able man, and perhaps more sincere than he sounds. It was difficult for any priest without firm ideas of political morality not to welcome the new Government. In 1830 the Church as a whole had approved of Charles X's attempt to twist the constitution to his own ends; in 1851 it had uttered no protest at the *coup d'état*. Louis Napoleon's aims seemed so admirable that it was almost pedantic to criticize his methods. 'Les hommes noirs, ils me dégoûtent', he was reported to have said in private;[1] but he welcomed the eulogies of Veuillot and the awestruck invocations of the bishops, especially when they were so good as to win him votes. Indeed he even toyed with the idea of being crowned in Paris by the Pope; but Pius, advised by a cautious entourage, would only consent if Napoleon agreed to abrogate the Organic Articles and abolish civil marriage. And that was out of all proportion.

Still, Napoleon tried hard to unite imperialism with Catholicism, touring Brittany as a Christian Emperor and erecting the bishopric of Rennes into an archbishopric shortly after the prelate had addressed him as a second Charlemagne. His marriage to Eugénie de Montijo brought another, and charming, exponent of clerical views to the court. 'Sire,' said the obliging Parisis, addressing them shortly after their wedding, 'we admire you as a man, we venerate you as a Prince; but as the privileged minister of Providence in the salvation of France, we lovingly bless you.'[2]

---

[1] To Persigny, who told Falloux. See *Mémoires d'un royaliste*, II, p. 285. Maurain (*La Politique ecclésiastique du Second Empire*, p. 15) thinks the story may have been exaggerated in the telling.

[2] Charles Guillemant, *Pierre-Louis Parisis*, III, p. 400.

Now Article 26 of the 1852 Constitution entrusted the Senate (or Upper House) with the rather difficult task of protecting at one and the same time 'religion, morality, freedom of worship, the freedom of the individual' and several other equally admirable abstractions. In practice the regime protected religion and freedom of worship (the Protestants were given a system combining democracy with State control), while morality was neglected, and the freedom of the individual despised. But in the first years of the Second Empire no one enjoyed greater personal freedom than the bishops: they travelled to Rome and back, received and published the Pope's Bulls, organized synods and provincial councils—in short, acted virtually as they pleased. Meanwhile full pomp and ceremony adorned the religious processions that paraded gorgeously through the streets of city, town and village, and the Bonapartist officials who were usually in bored attendance even delivered speeches, like tired schoolmasters, admonishing the population to return to the faith of their ancestors. In some places *Tartuffe* was banned; over the whole country the works of Diderot and Voltaire were forbidden to colporteurs; and scandals touching priests or monks were puritanically stifled.

Financially, too, the Church benefited. The Budget des Cultes, by which its operations were largely defrayed, rose in seven years from $39\frac{1}{2}$ million francs to 46 million. When the property of the Orleans family was confiscated in 1852, the bishops who might have protested were silenced on learning that 5 million francs of the proceeds were to be transferred to the Church.[1] And with money went other forms of prosperity. The Government, while suspending all Sunday work in public yards and shutting taverns during services, made no difficulty about recognizing the new religious congregations, so that between 1852 and 1860 nine hundred and eighty-two were authorized—more than in the whole Restoration period. Moreover these congregations became rich: in a decade they acquired 9 million francs by gifts and 25 million by legacies, and the value of their property reached 105 million francs.

'The clergy think the Middle Ages have come back', wrote

[1] G. Weill (*Histoire du catholicisme libéral en France*, p. 111) says that no bishops protested; that is not so; about six or seven, including Dupanloup and Dupont des Loges, signified their unwillingness to accept any such gift.

the old Comte Horace de Viel-Castel, gliding about the wings with the atrabilious eye of another Saint-Simon; 'they are trying to recapture their once sovereign authority—a pretension which may lead to deplorable consequences. In most towns the prefects have neither sufficient authority nor intelligence to counterbalance the bishops, and in any case their position is much less settled, most of them scheming to get promotion. . . . The Bishop of Angoulême, a crafty, cunning prelate, more sly than his brother of Périgueux, thinks fit to deprive the clergy in his diocese of the pleasure of smoking. The whole episcopate, in brief, raises its power to the point of tyranny.'[1] While bishops revelled in their authority, congregations multiplied, monks and nuns became familiar figures, and Jesuits profited by school and confessional to gain with the bourgeoisie the influence that they had lost with kings. Was this not Lacordaire's triumph? For it was he, far more than Guéranger, who had brought back monks to France, and they were now established in every part of the country, preaching, building, teaching, accumulating wealth.

[1] Le Comte Horace de Viel-Castel, *Mémoires*, 14th July 1855.

CHAPTER III

Ultramontanes and Liberals

Yet Lacordaire felt no pride of achievement: though he had forged the weapons, they were put to a new use. True, in 1850 he was elected the first French Provincial of his Order, but two months earlier Jandel had become General, and Lacordaire's influence was on the decline. It waned both in the Church and in the country. He continued, of course, to preach, drawing congregations as huge as ever; but they came to see a famous man, to hear the greatest orator of the day, not to share in the vision of a religion that fitted the specifications of the century. After the *coup d'état* Lacordaire felt so cast down in spirit, so sharply at odds with the predominant party, that he resisted all the blandishments of Archbishop Sibour and never again occupied the pulpit of Notre-Dame. 'I realized', he said, 'that in virtue of my thought, my language, my past, I was a kind of freedom myself and it only remained for me to disappear like the others.' But he allowed himself one resonant protest. On 10th February 1853 he was invited to preach in Saint-Roch, the church where he had delivered that first sermon from which his friends departed thinking he would never make a preacher. Perhaps he bore that failure in mind: at any rate he redeemed it. He delivered an attack on Napoleon I so detailed, stinging and devastating that his congregation listened in a hushed silence, plunged, as one of them says, in 'an astonishment mingled with fear'. Would he be molested? Many thought so. Discreetly selective, *Le Moniteur*, which was the organ of the regime, published a brief account of the sermon and left it at that; but the Belgian papers, whose circulation benefited enormously from the censorship imposed on their French contemporaries, managed to obtain a shorthand version, which they reprinted in full and publicized widely. To this the French Government could hardly remain indifferent, and the Minister of Religion inquired of Sibour whether the report was accurate. But, as the Archbishop explained, it was only a shorthand version; and they *were* Belgian papers. So Lacordaire escaped all trouble. But he was not allowed to preach in Paris again.

Depressed at the state of the country, anxious about conflicts which, as he dimly foresaw, would follow the collapse of the Bonapartist regime, Lacordaire turned to education; for in education lay the one hope of creating a generation that would diagnose social maladies skilfully enough to cure them. Seeing that the normal rules of the order were too strict for practising teachers, he founded a Third Order; and in 1854 he took over a school at Sorèze, at the foot of the Black Mountain, and began to organize it according to his own severe but sensible ideas. Lacordaire's prospectus is reminiscent of Arnold's programme, and he was so successful that the number of pupils rapidly doubled. But as an educator he had no imitators or successors. His years at Sorèze represented, in fact, a retreat—the withdrawal of a beaten man from the political arena. He was gay enough in heart to bear no malice for the past, looking ahead to a time when his liberalism would be vindicated. But for the moment the monks who spread across the face of France stood for another philosophy: they came in Lacordaire's name, not in his spirit. Like most apologists, he had been too popular to be representative, and the truer exponents of his cause were less persuasive. In Rome he was looked on askance. He said himself that if he were to transcribe a passage from one of the Fathers and put his own name at the foot, he would be delated for heresy. When he was re-elected Provincial in 1858, Pius sniffed with disapproval. 'The day after my return to Rome', writes Besson, his Dominican friend, 'I had an interview with the Holy Father, who received me with his wonted paternal kindness. But prejudiced as he is against Father Lacordaire, he thought our election ill-advised, and gently reproached me with weakness, not realizing that I had really acted with thorough impartiality, and solely with a view to the welfare of the Province.'

MICHON

But while Lacordaire and a few kindred spirits turned against the Second Empire, there were Bonapartists who turned against the Church. Napoleon III's supporters needed a tool, not an ally. As a French historian has pointed out, the Second Empire was merely clerical, never Catholic: to gain political advantage Bonapartists would have collaborated as readily with Mohammedans as with Christians. Realizing that its main interest was to win a maximum of support with a minimum of concessions, the Government became both stubborn and dilatory when Catholic spokesmen pressed further claims. Indeed the anticlericals won back some ground; for by an administrative subtlety the Catholic majority of education committees was transformed into a minority. As for those other pious moves—the attempts to impose religious marriage and to enforce Sunday observance—they were scornfully rejected.

But it was too late. Three years earlier Sibour, Archbishop of Paris, was writing to Montalembert: 'The Ultramontane school was once a school of liberty; it has been turned into a school of slavery with two main objects: the idolatry of temporal power and the idolatry of spiritual power.' That is, temporal power as represented by Napoleon III, and spiritual power as represented by Pius IX. Of course Sibour, embracing more and more the traditional Gallicanism of the Paris Metropolitans, went much further than Lacordaire: so far indeed, that one reason for Lacordaire's leaving Paris and retiring to Sorèze was to escape from Sibour's orbit. Next to Lamennais Lacordaire had done as much as anyone to nurture Ultramontanism; he did not abjure it; it was the *political* ideas of the Ultramontanes he could not abide. Sibour's strictures, too, are less than just to Veuillot: it would soon become clear that when there was a conflict between Veuillot's two loyalties, when his idolatry for Pius IX clashed with his idolatry for Napoleon III, the second was nowhere—a temporary crutch that could be thrown away when it was no longer wanted. But whatever concessions and qualifications one may make, there is no doubt that the Ultramontanism of the Second Empire, controlled and guided by the strong hand of Veuillot, rigid, ruthless and despotic, had little in common with Ultramontanism as Lamennais and Lacordaire first conceived it, a popular appeal to the Holy Father against the Gallican autocracy of bishop and king. Ultramontanism had been purged of democracy, had become strong and arrogant. The number of parish priests who signed petitions against adopting the Roman liturgy even shows that Gallicanism, as it died, still achieved a few spasms of resistance.

How far Ultramontanism had gone not only in France but in all countries acknowledging the Roman Communion was shown by the promulgation of the dogma of the Immaculate Conception in 1854. It was a doctrine highly favoured by the Jesuits, hotly disputed by the Dominicans, and magisterially rejected by St. Bernard and Thomas Aquinas. In 1588 a group of Spanish Jesuits had produced a metal coffer containing a sheet of parchment and some leaden tablets which, they declared, proved decisively what had hitherto only been suspected: namely that the Apostle James had dwelt in Spain and that the doctrine of the Immaculate Conception enjoyed apostolic authority. The Dominicans had no difficulty in showing that these documents were forgeries, and clumsy ones, too. More than half a century later, Rome advancing with her customary rapidity, appointed a commission to examine the evidence, and in 1682, almost a hundred years after the coffer had been produced, Innocent XI declared the parchment and tablets to be human figments likely to corrupt the Catholic faith. But the doctrine did not perish; indeed the growth of the cult of Mary helped in its diffusion, and although successive popes long hesitated whether to encourage or suppress it, Gregory XVI's approval finally meant that it could make its way. But what of the forgeries? Here the teaching of a certain Perrone was useful, for he argued that the Granada tablets were irrelevant and that the doctrine could be regarded as part of the secret tradition of the Church.

Thus while Cavour was whittling away the power of the Church in Sardinia and plotting to unify Italy and overrun the Papal States, Pius, who believed fervently in this doctrine, was brooding on some act of signal piety towards the Virgin. His belief was fortified and his piety encouraged by a special dogmatic commission, which reported that Perrone's view was sound: the Immaculate Conception was, in fact, a part of secret tradition—a tradition so secret that it had escaped the notice of less subtle historians and philosophers. Pius therefore took his decision. After consulting all his bishops by letter, he summoned forty to Rome, where they heard the Bull and were allowed to make mild criticisms. As it had already been explained that the opportuneness of the dogma concerned the Pope alone, there was little need for delay. On 8th December 1854 the new dogma was solemnly proclaimed: a month later, after a number of embarrassing defects in phraseology had been discovered and removed, the Bull was published.

Now the Immaculate Conception became *de fide* on the Pope's own authority, without the support of a General Council. It was the first such occasion; yet there was negligible opposition. True, some German theologians protested; but the whole Roman Communion submitted almost without a murmur and in France, where such pliability would once have been regarded with horror, the bishops hastened to defer, some promulgating the Bull at once.[1] Montalembert and Dupanloup, who might have been expected to boggle at a doctrine so welcome to Veuillot and his party, were lyrical in their acclamations. Ultramontanism had won its first spectacular triumph. The only Gallican grumbles came not from ecclesiastics but from the lawyers of the Senate, who objected to the dogma and to the way in which it had been published: but even by them it was eventually received, though with the traditional reservation.

'There remains only the one Catholic Church', Montalembert had written two years earlier, 'more united, more obedient to its head, than at any other time in its history. Gallicanism, in particular, which has been the most formidable and deeply rooted of our errors, is at bay.'[2] Yet by a curious paradox Montalembert found himself driven by the extravagances of the Intransigents to form a group in which the last Gallicans took refuge. This group was known generically as the Liberal Catholics. It had no discipline, no single leader, no specific policy; it represented essentially an attitude of mind—the attitude of all Catholics who valued political liberty, refusing to believe that discord must necessarily exist between their religion and the broad principles that had been established in 1789 and bade fair to dominate the future. Among its adherents it

---

[1] For the resistance of Bordas-Demoulin, Laborde and Guettée, who later joined the Greek Orthodox Church, see Léon Séché, *Les Derniers Jansénistes*, III, pp. 24–6.

[2] *Les Intérêts catholiques au XIXᵉ siècle. Œuvres*, V, p. 35.

numbered liberals, Gallicans, Ultramontanes, democrats, legitimists, Orleanists, and a sprinkling of professional rebels. Most
bishops were in sympathy with its general idea, but for different
reasons. At first, indeed, the Liberal Catholics were agreed on
little except the urgent need to fight *L'Univers*, and anyone who
was at war with Veuillot, whatever the reason, tended to drift
into the opposite camp, there discovering, under the stress of
party warfare, that his liberalism was more systematic than he
had supposed.

The case of the Archbishop of Paris is interesting and illus-
trates the fluctuating motives of many bishops. By temperament
Sibour was cautious and slow, deeply in love with moderation
and unwilling to flirt with any alternative policy. As a tactician,
therefore, he frowned on *L'Univers*: he tried to launch a rival,
he warned Veuillot against excess, he incurred frequent lacera-
tion from Veuillot's columnists. More than tactics, however,
was at stake; for Sibour, with a grain of Gallicanism in his
theology, fostered liberal ideas for themselves, believing that
they were not only wiser but truer than the notions of *L'Univers*.
But the encouragement of liberal ideas does not always make a
liberal: and the reverse side of Gallicanism is shown in Sibour's
fury at the criticisms which a certain Abbé Combalot dared to
formulate against one of his pastoral charges. Sibour was
angry, not so much at being attacked, but at being attacked by
a mere priest; he gathered his archiepiscopal dignity around
him and insisted on an apology. Sibour, in fact, pursued liberal
aims with an illiberal method. One moment he spoke sincerely
of the national aspirations of the people; the next he brought all
the weight of his office to bear on some indiscreet priest or
layman. He delighted to reprove Veuillot for abusing some anticlerical journalist, but his own abuse was too pontifical, and
his own opinions too tepid, to win him more than a handful of
sycophants. Too often he appeared in the undignified posture of
a man pompously sitting on an unusually rickety fence.

Tepidity was not the vice of Dupanloup, who since his
nomination as Bishop of Orleans had spread his name all over
France as a passionate controversialist. Receiving Combalot's
pamphlet against Sibour, Dupanloup dismissed it angrily with
'You are raising the flag of presbyterianism'. But in spite of his
pride as a bishop, in spite of his legitimist past, he was essentially

more liberal than Sibour, more mindful of that spirit of 'pacification' which he had urged on his colleagues in 1845. Not that he was pacific in his methods. Born to a peasant girl seduced by a tailor, he became one of the noisiest, most active, most influential and hated of all the bishops in the Catholic world. He seemed to have discovered the secret of perpetual motion. With his tall figure, big head, aquiline nose, piercing eyes and flushed complexion, he stood out like a great sinister bird in salon, committee and pulpit. A brilliant catechist, a skilful spiritual director, a triumphant educationist, he leapt from one task to another with a vitality that astonished even his enemies. The man was a fountain of energy. He seemed to take breath only on his rare retreats. For the rest of the time he was fighting—fighting any opponent who cared to give battle, fighting with a combative ardour that often seemed disproportionate to the cause at stake.

'He is so certain of being right', said Emile Ollivier, 'that sometimes, to prove it, he ceases to tell the truth.' He is, remarks one of his old friends, 'a burning coal, fanned now by grace, now by nature'.[1] Consumed by the persistent need for action, fretted by his own impatience, Dupanloup none the less possessed the politician's craft and the tactician's skill. It was he who led the Catholics on the education commission; he who drew Thiers to the utmost limits of compromise; he who worked out the precise details of the Loi Falloux. And his success fomented the hatred of his enemies. 'M. Dupanloup has destroyed you, I say it with deep conviction', Montalembert was told by an acquaintance in 1849; while at the same time Combalot was writing to Veuillot: 'The Abbé Dupanloup is moving heaven and earth to trick the Pope, the Nuncio, the bishops, the clergy and the faithful. That is why he must no longer be spared. He needs not to be insulted, but unmasked. That man is doing enormous harm to the Catholic cause. Intrigue underlies all his actions.'[2]

In spite, too, of his lowly origins Dupanloup moved easily in high society. He had conducted the religious education of the Orleanist princes and emerged as a familiar figure in the salons of the Faubourg Saint-Germain. Such a background was hardly

[1] Quoted by F. Mourret, *Le Concile du Vatican*, pp. 62–3.
[2] E. Veuillot, *Louis Veuillot*, II, p. 384.

likely to endear him to Veuillot, whose robust nature was irked by the enervated urbanity of the *beau monde*. Moreover Dupanloup's penetrating mind had the civilized quality of tolerance. Famed though he was for his converts, he was shrewd enough to perceive where there was no real religion, and humane enough to say so. It was he, as Director of Saint-Nicolas-du-Chardonnet, who diagnosed Renan's troubles, not as intellectual temptations, but as a genuine loss of faith, and diverted him from the priest-hood—a decision for which Renan never ceased to be grateful. Later, while Veuillot was dismissing *Madame Bovary* as 'not filth or blood, but sanies', Dupanloup called it admirable, quietly adding: 'To realize its merit to the full you ought to have had my twenty years' experience as a provincial confessor.'

Dupanloup, then, was a predestined opponent of *L'Univers*. The real struggle broke out when a certain Abbé Gaume published *Le Ver rongeur*, a disputatious work in which he inveighed against the use of pagan classics in schools, arguing that they should be replaced by such Christian classics as the Early Fathers. Though winning the support of only a few bishops, Gaume was power-fully reinforced when Veuillot produced a series of violent articles in *L'Univers* against Dupanloup; for Dupanloup had based his teaching at Saint-Nicolas on Latin and Greek. Dupanloup was already angry; now he became furious: to be attacked by a layman! Forbidding all officials in his diocesan seminaries to read *L'Univers*, he drew up a declaration of policy and by his usual methods of passionate cajolery persuaded forty-six bishops to sign it. There were reverberations in every diocese and distant rumbles in Rome. At length, though Antonelli, the Cardinal Secretary of State, condemned Dupanloup's declaration, Veuillot was advised to curb his rhetoric.

The controversy, as the Government realized, was of no intrinsic importance.[1] Gaume put his case so badly that even an Intransigent like Guéranger was unwilling to support it. But though the battle was indecisive, it raised a great deal of dust and both inflamed tempers and sharpened the differences that were already apparent between Intransigents and Liberal Catholics. Once hostility between two schools of thought has reached such a pitch, it will always find occasion to express itself, and there is no need to examine in detail the various

[1] J. Maurain, *Le Saint-Siège et la France*, pp. 220–1.

pretexts that were seized on in the next five years by one side or the other in the hope of undermining its rival. A theological dictionary, a libellous sketch of Veuillot's life, a work of piety —they all provoked heated denunciations and clever innuendoes till the Pope must have become tired of the appeals that were constantly being referred to Rome, tired of recommending moderation to the impetuous members of the Church in France.

Thanks to Montalembert's initiative the Liberal Catholics acquired an organ of opinion—*Le Correspondant*. The censorship regulations would have made a newspaper too dangerous an undertaking, and they therefore bought this ailing fortnightly and restored it to vigour. In fact, they turned it into the most cultured and informed religious review in the country. With Albert de Broglie, Falloux, Dupanloup, Foisset and Auguste Cochin to help him, Montalembert had an editorial board of conspicuous ability, and he was assured of Lacordaire's approval. Though standing aloof from controversy, Lacordaire could hardly refuse to co-operate with a group that represented many of his ideas. He disagreed with Falloux's legitimism; he had often trounced Dupanloup's intrigues; he deplored Montalembert's adherence to Whig politics. Nevertheless he felt bound to join in.

Nor was *Le Correspondant* the Liberal Catholics' only means of obtaining a hearing and influencing the Government. Urbane and respectable, they were well regarded by intellectuals who had nothing but scorn for the Intransigents. As a result, they were elected one by one to the Academy till it became almost a Liberal Catholic club. Montalembert in 1850; Dupanloup in 1854; Falloux in 1856; Laprade in 1858, Lacordaire himself two years later; then Albert de Broglie, Louis de Carné, Gratry —there was no danger of the Liberal Catholic case going by default in the highest councils of the Empire. Pie and Gousset might have the ear of Rome, Parisis and Salinis might be in favour at the Tuileries; but the Liberal Catholics included so many men of intellectual ability and literary skill that however ineffectual they might be as theologians, however negligible in their influence on priests and prelates outside France, they carried formidable weight among cultivated laymen.

But to what did they owe their standing? Primarily to their gifts of oratory. Despite the excessive mutual admiration among the staff of *Le Correspondant*—and that indeed was one of the reasons for its ultimate failure—not one of these men was a scholar; only Gratry was a theologian, and he an erratic one. Dupanloup, for all his roaring reputation as an educationist, shocked Acton with his superficial half-learning. As for Lacordaire, he was described by a fellow-immortal as the most ignorant man in the Academy. There was no question of the Liberal Catholics rivalling the erudition of Döllinger and Hefele in Germany; no question even of their being liberal in theology. Clinging to a belief in political freedom, they never rationalized and systematized it, never brooded on the relations between faith and freedom of mind. In consequence they remained supremely indifferent to historical criticism and scientific inquiry, unaware that any problem existed, as ready as any Intransigents to stamp on independent examination of Church history or biblical texts.

As a talented, illogical, unorganized group, their function was to pester and harass the Intransigents, to preserve some flicker of respect for personal freedom—a flicker that would be slowly fanned under the Third Republic. Without realizing the uncertainty and insecurity of their position, they carried on a steady campaign against Veuillot. In 1856 it was Falloux's pamphlet (first published in *Le Correspondant*) on the Catholic party; and this was followed by an anthology, *L'Univers jugé par lui-même*, in which the choicest insults and excesses of the paper were sedulously collected and juxtaposed, with a virulent commentary. The author was known to be a certain Abbé Cognat, but Dupanloup and Sibour were obviously behind him. Egged on by the Ultramontane bishops and encouraged even by the Pope, who was reported to have said 'Let him stick to his path; I read *L'Univers* and like it', Veuillot brought an action against the anthologist, hoping to wound the powerful figures who lurked in the background. But he withdrew it under an unexpected stress. For on 31st January 1857 Sibour was dramatically stabbed to death in a Paris church by a half-crazed priest whom he had inhibited for immoral conduct and who blamed him for the dogma of the Immaculate Conception. It was an end not without irony; for Sibour was one of the few French bishops who had resisted the new dogma to the limits of discretion.

CHAPTER IV

The Rebel

⸎══════════════════════════════════════⸎

few years after Montalembert had announced that
Gallicanism was at bay, the Abbé Michon was declaring
in one of his voluminous pamphlets that 'the advance
of Gallican ideas is now so rapid that we do not fear to predict
a time when they will represent the general opinion of Europe'.[1]
As usual Michon was out of step; he had been out of step most
of his life. Like most of his contemporaries in the priesthood, he
was of humble birth—his father was a village tailor—and but
for the interest and encouragement of the local priest he might
never have learnt to read or write. But his natural precocity
and independence of mind were such that an outstanding career
at Angoulême *collège* was followed by an estimable one at
Saint-Sulpice. No doubt precocity and independence of mind
are both virtues which carry some spiritual danger, and Michon
may already have shown some hint of exasperation with the
hierarchy and its policy. At any rate, after his ordination in
1830, he failed to receive the openings to which his talents
entitled him: what, for a man of his gifts and ambitions, was
the drudgery of seminary teaching and the solitary labour of
parish work? Such tasks might occupy him for a year or two,
but hardly for ever. In fact even at this time they did not occupy
him entirely. Impelled by a native restlessness, he founded a
congregation for women at Angoulême, and the money which
was left over from this venture he devoted to a boys' school,
which flourished for a few months and then painfully disin-
tegrated over a number of years, taking with it all his means.
    Eighteen months with another cure of souls tired him of

[1] J. H. Michon, *Du progrès et de l'importance des idées gallicanes*, p. 19.

MICHON'S DILEMMA

parochial business and he resigned, hoping no doubt to catch
the Bishop's eye. Not that he took easily to discipline; he had a
habit of disobedience, a refractory nature which led him not
only to resist pressure from above but to explain his resistance
in pungent terms. He insisted on using his own mind. Chroni-
cally insolvent, he turned to local history—archaeology as it
was then called—and with his *Statistique monumentale de la Charente*
(1844) produced a work about his native district which, in spite
of its shortcomings, reflects a prolonged and careful study of
ancient monuments and is still waiting to be superseded. His
aim was purely objective—to record the antiquities of Charente.
But Michon was not made for objectivity, and as he wrote he
delivered glancing blows at medieval superstitions, at monks and
even popes. He was more at home in the pulpit, travelling up
and down the district, preaching strange, disturbing sermons,
enkindling rustic congregations and alarming his superiors.
What were his doctrines? They are not clear: they seem to
involve a Gallican form of Mennaisianism, an eccentric form
which rejects the authority of the Pope without accepting that
of the Bishop. But he was less concerned with ecclesiastical
controversy than with the task of preaching the Gospel, and
he did this with sufficient skill to become honorary canon of
Bordeaux and of Angoulême.

Like all liberals he was disillusioned at the turn of events after
the bright dawn of 1848; but he was saved by his hobbies.
It was still possible for the amateur to dabble in several sciences
at once; and Michon, driven by eager curiosity, put no check
on his interests. All his life he displayed a passion for factual
knowledge, even though he was hardly able to interpret the
facts at his disposal. He was one of the few priests of his time who
had a natural bent for the sciences and a general understanding
of empirical method. However short he was of money, he always
contrived to keep a broken-down horse and a flimsy conveyance;
and he used to go on long lonely expeditions about the countryside, furnished with a geological hammer or a botanical box,
taking exuberant notes, accumulating irrelevant specimens,
multiplying his diverse collections. Back home, he wrote learned
and inaccurate articles about archaeology, botany and numis-
matics. On rare occasions he even found time for theology.

When Saulcy invited Michon to join his party to the Holy

154

Land, he paid a conscious tribute to Michon's reputation as a botanist, at the same time giving him a chance to break away, at least for a few months, from the stultifying atmosphere of the declining Republic. But Michon did not depart without a twinge of regret. 'Before leaving my little patch of land', he wrote, 'I walked round it lovingly. Should I be allowed to see it again, to fill it with plants from the East, as I had already filled it with plants from the Pyrenees? Should I have the joy of building a second sepulchre, a second calvary, in memory of that Calvary and that Sepulchre where I should have bowed my head and celebrated the great mysteries? . . .'

Michon's outward trip was marked by one of those tantalizing encounters that escape all adequate record. When the party reached Constantinople, they met two young men just returning from an extended tour of Egypt, Palestine and Turkey and beginning the last lap of their journey through Greece and Italy. They were Maxime Du Camp and Gustave Flaubert, the first bent on reaching Paris and making his name, the second already dimly glimpsing the seductive features of Madame Bovary. 'We met M. de Saulcy,' Flaubert told his mother, 'a Member of the Institute and the Director of the Artillery Museum; he is travelling with Edouard Delessert, the son of the late Prefect of Police, and a bunch of others. Great cordiality from the start; we dropped the monsieur; questions of the grossest obscenity, jokes, puns, French wit at its best. . . . By next morning we were such friends that M. de Saulcy was patting me on the belly and saying "Ah! my old Flaubert!"'[1] Certainly Flaubert met Michon; he even recalled their encounter twenty-eight years later. But what passed between them is unrecorded. Did they have any private conversation together? Did their talk even turn on literature? These questions remain unanswered and unanswerable, and the two men said good-bye for ever, each unaware that he had met the agent of one of the greatest literary sensations of the next twenty years.

There is not much respect nowadays for Saulcy's work. Professor Albright says dryly that 'his enterprise exceeded his knowledge and his vanity exceeded both'; and when one realizes that he excavated in company with Michon, it is not surprising that their enthusiastic conclusions were premature, that they

[1] Flaubert, *Correspondance*, II, pp. 265–6.

decided the Tombs of the Kings belonged to the Kings of Judah (who lived five hundred years and more too early), and that they brought back to the Louvre what they took to be the sarcophagus of David. On the other hand, they were pioneers, among the earliest modern excavators in Palestine: they had to create a method and technique.

Not content, however, with his task as botanist and archaeologist, Michon had decided to investigate the situation of the Eastern Churches and to seek out means of attracting them back into the Roman Communion; and so when he was not filling his plant box or mapping antiquities, he was deep in converse with some Copt, Syrian or Jacobite. It was all very disheartening. He was at once too impressionable and too fair-minded to make a good disputant. In Greece he had been profoundly excited and soothed by the sight of the Acropolis; in Constantinople he was so struck by the minarets that they made him 'jealous for Christianity'. Now, in Palestine, he was either convinced by the arguments of the opposing sects or else persuaded that there was no real barrier to the unification of Christendom.

Meanwhile his scientific labours proceeded apace. Studying the bas-reliefs on the Parthenon, for instance, he discovered the microscopic vegetation which, he thought, gave the monuments of the ancient world their golden colouring; while on the mountains of Lebanon he gathered a fine harvest of (he says this proudly) caryophyllaceae, arabis, crocus and anemone. Sometimes his work entailed embarrassment. When a rumour spread that he had unearthed a fabulous hoard of treasure, the Pasha immediately sent a detachment of soldiers to turn over his excavations and ransack his luggage. But the embarrassment was not exclusively or primarily physical. The monks, whether of East or West, shocked him by their laziness, their petty hatreds, their indifference to the life of the people; and the Holy Sepulchre was even more dispiriting. 'Oh! how much happier it would be for the Christian pilgrim', he wrote, 'if he could look through a grill at his Saviour's tomb, rather than stand in front of a mass of inferior sculptures, under countless blazing lamps, seeing a sort of coffer of white marble which has been turned into an altar. I emerged with a heavy heart. . . . The monk took me into the chapel of the Latins, where a frag-

ment of the Crown of Thorns is kept. The archaeologist in me
was so weary of his disappointments that I would not expose the
naturalist to temptation. I did not ask to see the relic. . . . A
monk was praying in the chapel. I joined my heart to his.
There my faith no longer faltered; I no longer feared the pious
frauds and deliberate mistakes of men; I adored God—greater
than his temple, worthier of veneration than his tomb.'

That is the key to Michon's character—his fear of being
disabused, his distrust of the uncritical piety of his fellow priests.
Excitable and easily moved, he would be swept up to some peak
of emotion, his imagination aglow, his blood on fire, only to
discover that it was all an illusion and a cheat. Where a calmer
temperament would have inquired more carefully in the first
place and felt less bitterness in the second, Michon knew no
inhibitions; he hurled himself forward with the naïvety of an
essentially genuine nature, eagerly responding to imaginative
stimulus and recoiling with disgust if he found he had been
deceived. It was his misfortune and originality to combine deep
religious feeling with more than a smattering of the analytical
sciences; as a result, his profoundest, most intimate experience
of faith was flawed by the suspicion that it involved misconcep-
tions, inaccuracies. Every opinion, he found, had chinks through
which error came creeping. His mind, of course, was critical
rather than scholarly: he conceded no long apprenticeship to
the discipline of fact. But however inadequate his devious
searches for truth, they revealed to him a Sahara of self-
deception, credulity, trickery and sham, over which millions
of good and pious people daily travelled in perfect content.

For Michon once to see this was to inflame him against it;
he had all the impulsiveness, if not the absolutism, of Lamennais.
Just as he knew no emotional restraints, submitting entirely to
any cause or belief that won his allegiance, so he knew no
intellectual inhibitions, pursuing a particular idea beyond the
bounds of all reasonable possibility and belabouring his enemies
with any arguments, however gross or unfair, which happened
to lie at hand. When his *Journey* appeared in an English translation, a reviewer remarked that it 'can hardly be said to partake
of the antiquarian character at all. Indeed the author gives
scarcely any of the particulars of his visit to the Holy Land, but
confines himself chiefly to the present condition of Christianity

in the East, especially in reference to the prospect of a reunion of the two great branches of the Church; a subject on which we cannot but fear that he has allowed his zeal or enthusiasm to outrun his calmer judgement.'[1]

Michon always allowed his enthusiasm to outrun his calmer judgement. It was at once his virtue and his defect, betraying him into acrimonious struggles with his superiors, yet typifying a dogged courage. Nowadays it is almost impossible for us to disentangle the man's real character from the abuse and vilification his enemies heaped on him: if we are to believe them, he was nothing but a godless cynic, hiding in the cloth in order to wreak the greater harm upon the Church. Was it so? The answer must surely be that it was not; that he was as sincere and genuine in his faith as Veuillot. The fact that he was independent all his life, refusing to become the tool of any party, refusing to incur the responsibility of powerful supporters, is hardly a reason to accept the overwhelming weight of obloquy that has buried his memory. 'The day I left Jerusalem to begin my exploration of the Dead Sea basin,' relates Saulcy, 'my son left for Beirut with M. l'Abbé Michon, who preferred to forgo the most interesting part of our journey rather than leave a sick young man to face the roads of Syria in the company of a worthless dragoman and a few unreliable muleteers. On this occasion M. l'Abbé Michon gave me a token of friendship which I am happy to acknowledge here.'[2] And by the testimony of those who knew him, such acts of generosity were common.

But bishops saw another side to his character. 'M. Michon', said an acquaintance, 'was gentle by nature, but stubbornly so. He listened to everything calmly, attentively, respectfully; then did as he wished.' This stubborn gentleness was a rock against which more than one bishop struck in vain. For though Michon was sent to a small country parish immediately on his return, it did not satisfy him. The simple life and narrow interests palled; he grew tired of the monotonous progress of the seasons, the trivial wrangles of local politicians, the irksome authority of his bishop; he longed for action. He was sure that

[1] *Dublin Review*, 1853, XXXV, pp. 140–1.

[2] F. de Saulcy, 'Les Ruines de Masada', *Revue des Deux Mondes*, 1852, I, p. 402.

if a change was to be made it could only be from the centre, and so he resigned and returned to Paris and to trouble.

He had already been campaigning vehemently in two papers, *La Presse Religieuse* and *L'Européen*; but whereas the former enjoyed a fair success, weathering political and ecclesiastical storms, the latter was twice censured in two years and finally suppressed by the Government. Mgr Cousseau, Bishop of Angoulême (the same who forbade his clergy the pleasures of smoking), honoured Michon with particular attention, watching him, warning him, threatening him. And Michon was as blandly obstinate as ever; charmingly submissive, entirely unreliable.

'In January 1854', wrote the Bishop, 'I bade you cease all contributions to *La Presse Religieuse*, because I did not consider you fitted to defend the cause of religion in public controversy; you gave me your promise, yet a few months later, in your new paper *L'Européen*, you attacked the teachings of the Holy See, viz. the encyclical *Mirari* by Gregory XVI. After a personal interview in July 1855, you agreed to write and sign at my desk an act of submission and complete adhesion to the doctrine set forth in this encyclical: which has not prevented you attacking the same doctrine in your pamphlet on the "Split in the Catholic Party".'

Michon was indeed liberal in a sense that would have shocked the Liberal Catholics. Accepting the principles of 1789, he argued that the Church had no need whatever of the State and that separation and disestablishment were in true accord with the apostolic spirit. Politely acknowledging the representations of Cousseau, he continued to advance the most outrageous opinions in one pamphlet after another—outrageous, that is, to the complacent authoritarians of the Second Empire. What use had they for a priest who counselled abstention from politics; who urged the Church to reject the blandishments of Caesar; who threatened it with the bloodiest calamities if the principles of the Revolution were ignored? Incredibly, Michon escaped disciplinary action.[1] With his genius for intractable tractability he forestalled Cousseau's fulminations, yielding just

[1] Mgr Robiou, the Gallican Bishop of Coutances from 1836 to 1852, even recommended Michon's controversial technique. See Albert Houtin, *Un Dernier Gallican. Henri Bernier, chanoine d'Angers*, p. 466.

enough ground at the last moment to save him for another day. He displayed a patent, precipitate sincerity of purpose which won him the sympathy, if not the respect, of his superiors.

'I prefer to write to you about M. Michon, rather than send him a *celebret*', wrote the Cardinal Archbishop of Bordeaux to Cousseau in 1860. 'Please be satisfied with his canonical letters, which I have not withdrawn. The Archbishop of Paris allows him to say Mass, and has procured him a retiring pension. This man inspires me with an immense pity. No one has ever impugned his morals.'

So it went on: Michon leaping blindly forward into the pits of indiscipline and even heresy; clambering breathlessly out; tumbling back immediately; and each time risking permanent degradation and disgrace. He was the professional rebel, the predestined insurgent, the protestant Catholic.

DUPANLOUP

CHAPTER V

Philosophers and Politicians

I n the meantime the sciences were being rapidly systematized
and extended, till only a specialist could reach their fron-
tiers and subdue new territory. Lamarck classifying modern
and fossil shells; Cuvier reconstructing extinct beasts from fossils
and bones found near Paris; Lamarck, again, evolving the first
logical theory of evolution; Champollion unriddling the mystery
of hieroglyphs and founding Egyptology—all these men had
worked thirty years earlier, but the implications of their success
were just beginning to dawn on the new generation. Theological
knowledge had been static, allowing no scope to originality,
teaching the son exactly what his father had learnt, and his
grandfather before him. But here was a form of knowledge that
was new and exciting: a scientific fact, once established, was
(so it seemed) established for ever, leading on to another discovery and to another discovery still, so that one glimpsed a
vast and indeed endless concatenation of solid, proved, objective
truths, each eternally linked to its neighbour, the whole series
providing an unshakeable chain that would culminate in a complete understanding of the universe. Knowledge like this was
anything but static, but it was sure. How sure was startlingly
shown in 1846. Working independently on the perturbations of
the planet Uranus from its orbit and basing their calculations
on Newton's hypothesis of gravitational attraction, Le Verrier
in Paris and John Couch Adams in Cambridge both argued
that these perturbations were caused by another planet; and
they indicated its position. An astronomer in Berlin trained his
telescope on to the spot and there he discovered the missing
planet, Neptune. It was a resounding triumph for the mathema-

ticians; it seemed a supreme proof of Newton's theory; it stirred French opinion to an awestruck recognition of knowledge that appeared infallible. Just when Paris had ceased to be the scientific centre of the world, Frenchmen realized with a shock that their scientists had mastered the principles of the universe, had unveiled the powers that kept the stars in motion, had exchanged speculation for certitude. Or so it seemed. The prestige won by astronomy spread like a rash over the whole face of science till anyone calling himself a scientist was assured of an excited, an almost painfully obedient respect. Comte's Positivist philosophy, which upheld the concept of science as the basis for intellectual and social life, drew a swarm of new adherents from among the more advanced members of the community. Who could blame them? They saw a light and followed it.

Catholic philosophy, on the other hand, decried the power of reason and upheld tradition as a guide. The traditionalist teaching, which had been revived by Lamennais and pervaded the thought of most orthodox French philosophers, maintained that man's mind was virtually incapable of intellectual discovery without some form of revelation; by himself, unaided, he was blind and helpless, cut off from knowledge, abandoned to illusion and self-deceit. Almost all the Intransigents—and that meant most Catholic philosophers—preached this doctrine; for years it was defended by Bonnetty in the columns of his paper; and in its name Father Ventura declared that the entire thought of the past three centuries was null and void. But the traditionalists went too far. In their anxiety to reduce the human mind to complete dependence on faith they blundered into fideism, the error which denies any critical power to reason. Fideism had already been censured in Lamennais and Bautain, and in 1855 the Congregation of the Index extended its blame to Bonnetty, the most eminent exponent of traditionalist doctrines.

After this hammer blow one might have expected traditionalism to expire in silence, but condemnation had a curious and contrary effect. Now that tradition was no longer regarded as a necessary means of knowing primary truths, it descended to a lower level, becoming the insidious guarantor of all kinds of legends about the Church, past and present. What these legends were will appear later. For the time being it is enough that Gaume's influence, with his *Ver rongeur,* was increased rather than diminished and that anecdotal historians of early Christianity took new heart, discovering innumerable traditions with unimpeded zeal. Gaume himself was a bold and un-flagging metaphysician. Unperturbed by Dupanloup's fury and Dupanloup's protégés, encouraged by Veuillot's friendship, he devoted a 400-page treatise to holy water; and in another work, rising serenely above orthodox astronomers, he explained that the reason for the seven days of the week was that the Devil had marked them out as proper to the seven sub-devils who administered the seven deadly sins.

Not that the Liberal Catholics were inactive. They watched with a startled incredulity the manœuvres of their opponents, finding it hard to believe that even the Intransigents could jump back voluntarily into the Middle Ages. At a time when every thinking man knew of Le Verrier's forecast and its confirmation, it was small service to the Church to resurrect the dreariest medieval doctrines and treat them as passports to salvation. Bonnetty, of course, had his adversaries in the Liberal Catholic press, such as a Jesuit who had written so outspoken a commentary on *Mirari vos* that he dared not publish it. But Bonnetty was on any showing a worthy man with an incisive mind, and though his condemnation was a triumph for the Liberal Catholics (who rejoiced at any misfortune that overtook the Intransigents), negative triumphs were not enough: positive doctrines were needed. Maret, it is true, ransacked an immense library of theological writings to find arguments that would reconcile tradition and reason; but he was little known. Gratry, who was more in the public eye than Maret, attacked traditionalism in terms of philosophy rather than of faith; but he failed to persuade waverers. The real Liberal Catholic spokesman in matters of philosophy was Hugonin, who taught that in every exercise of human reason there was an element of the divine. Hugonin was a plausible theorist and a fluent writer; his conception of reason was exactly what was needed by Christian apologists. It was, therefore, all the more unfortunate that he, like Bonnetty, should be persuaded by his own plausibility and led to adopt an equally untenable position. He came under suspicion at Rome for rationalism, which is the opposite error to fideism, and before the Holy See would accept him as

Bishop of Bayeux, he was obliged to sign a retractation of his essential doctrines. By the reproof administered to Hugonin the Intransigents avenged their repulse over Bonnetty: honours were even.

These domestic quarrels were, however, growing out of date, for Positivism brought a new threat. Comte himself, the Positivist high priest, was authoritarian in his outlook, and though denying Christian dogma, wished to support the Church because the Church supported conservatism. 'All those who believe in God are to be begged to return to Catholicism in the name of morals and religion,' he told an English correspondent, 'while those who do not are, for the same reasons, to become Positivists.' Positivist or Catholic, the great thing was to have a religion; otherwise society crumbled. But Comte could not be responsible for his disciples: like Descartes he founded a movement which he would have abjured. Littré, the most eminent of his followers, accepted Comte's scientific outlook while deflecting the movement towards democracy; indeed under Littré's guidance Positivism became republican in spirit, and being republican, became anticlerical. Shocked at this aggressive iconoclasm which seemed to be gaining the young philosophers, the heirs of the spiritualist tradition turned towards the Church which they had once patronizingly tolerated; and old Victor Cousin, quivering slightly at the prospect of universal atheism, looked wistfully to Rome, wondering if some working agreement could be reached between Christianity and eclecticism. It was typical of the mood of the time that as soon as Cousin's overtures were noised about, he was furiously slashed by Mgr Pie, one of the most able Intransigents, and it needed all the tact of Sibour and Dupanloup to prevent his being condemned by the Index. The Intransigents were so proud of their eminence, so certain of their authority, that they repudiated unhesitatingly any offers of alliance from men who did not concur entirely with their politics, religion and philosophy. Either one went to the end of the road or one was not allowed to begin it. The Intransigents spent much time and trouble in turning potential friends into confirmed enemies.

It seems, in fact, that immediately the Catholics gained power, their moral and intellectual influence began to recede; at first the ebb was barely perceptible, a slight weakening in the force of the advancing wave, but as it continued, laying bare large tracts that had once been covered, it went with a rush that could hardly be withstood, and not till the water was very low did the tide begin to flow again. In literature, for instance, the great impulse given by *Le Génie du Christianisme* was spent. The first Romantics had been royalist and Catholic, finding in religion a sensuous, sentimental thrill which almost atoned for their lack of conviction. But they were now either dead or had turned away. Not religion but the national, democratic idea inspired Michelet; Hugo was excited by the people, by history, by spiritualism, by himself. While a few discredited provincial poetasters like Reboul and Brizeux still took Catholicism as their theme, the real aesthetes of the Second Empire were lukewarm or hostile to dogma of any kind. What did Leconte de Lisle, Flaubert or Renan care for the ancient teachings of the Church? Without being blind to religious feeling, they tried to refine it of all Christian associations—to refine it even of God.

Not that Chateaubriand's spirit was entirely dead: it survived in diabolism, the diabolism of Baudelaire, Barbey d'Aurevilly, Villiers de l'Isle-Adam. As Viatte has shown, the Romantic movement was pervaded with occult teachings; and though it is hard to take seriously the self-important priests of these secret doctrines, their influence did not wane with the Romantic decline, but persisted through the Second Empire, reaching its peak in the eccentric ambitions of the Symbolists. Probably the decay in Christian belief encouraged dilettanti to meddle in less reputable substitutes; for our natural human credulity seems always to need an object. At any rate substitutes were provided. While Hume, the famous Scotch medium, was delighting the Court with his virtuosity, persuading a table to speak in the name of Queen Hortense (she predicted a two-year war) and inducing an accordion to rise bodily from the ground and play without the assistance of a performer, other people of fashion were indulging in unscientific experiments with hypnotism. Moreover textbooks sold fast. The occult works of Eliphas Lévi enjoyed a popular vogue in the latter decade of the Second Empire,[1] and from them even the most desultory

[1] *Dogme et Rituel de la haute magie* (1856); *L'Histoire de la magie* (1860); *La Clef des grands mystères* (1861). His real name was Constant. Ordained as a deacon, he left the cloth in 1848.

reader gathered that by applying himself properly to esoteric mathematics there was a powerful hope of solving the mystery of the universe: certainly it could not be solved by mere religious or philosophic speculation.

In short, intellectuals repudiated Catholicism when they did not ignore it altogether. Faith was such a medieval affair. The existence of an isolated novelist like Feuillet, who even dared to use fiction as a vehicle for Catholic apologetic, only acted as a straight rule, showing how other intellectuals veered to right and left. Diabolists, occultists, hypnotists, Positivists, deists, atheists—they all swerved sharply away from the path of orthodoxy, seeking salvation, or at least satisfaction, on a less exacting route. To them indeed the orthodox path looked as narrow, as hard to negotiate, as a tightrope.

At the same time, however, as the intellectual leaders of the country were taking up positions flatly opposed to the Church, the Church was tightening its grip on education, preparing a generation which (it was hoped) would not only save its soul but vote in accordance with episcopal advice. When the Loi Falloux was originally passed, most of its opponents imagined that it would be a hollow victory, for the clergy would be unable to profit by its terms. But they were wrong. A year after the Bill became law, 257 new schools had been opened, and there was no slackening in the speed of the clerical advance. Between 1850 and 1866 the percentage of boys educated in Church primary schools rose from 15·7 to 20·9, and that of girls from 44·6 to 55·4. In secondary education the advance was even faster: by 1854 the number of pupils in the hands of the Church had overtaken those in charge of the State and was still going ahead.

This is the context for the controversy over Gaume's *Ver rongeur*. Foreseeing no check to their educational progress, the clericals were trying to work out a policy—the best means of conditioning youth to Catholic obedience and Catholic values. Was that policy to derive from the Liberal Catholics or the Intransigents? Should one prefer Gaume or Dupanloup? In the end, despite the Pope's qualifications and provisos, Gaume won. As one historian remarks, 'the law was voted to suit Falloux; it was applied to suit Veuillot'. Now however valuable the social cachet conferred by the Jesuits, however deep and wide their learning, they could not encourage any sympathy for modern ideas; and where even *they* failed, there were no Catholic educationists in France who could succeed. Two results followed: their more critical and independent pupils ultimately broke away from religious doctrine, turning instead to those modern ideas which had been presented as incompatible with faith; and their more pedestrian pupils accepted the authoritarian, obscurantist doctrines that were drummed into their heads, forming an inflammable, unreflective section of the populace which was to be the bane of the Third Republic. In 1858 a pupil in a little seminary was asked:

'Are you agreed on politics?'
'No! There are two sides, the Blues and the Whites.'
'Whites! What are they?'
'They are for Henry V.'
'And the Blues?'
'They are for the Emperor.'
'What about republicans?'
'There aren't any.'[1]

To find republicans one would have to look in a state school. In Church schools a republican meant Antichrist. Perhaps that is why the Catholic education movement failed. For fail it did. Certainly a more measured and sensible upbringing would have stood the Church in better stead after the collapse of the Second Empire, when cool heads and calm judgements were at a premium. As it was, the fervent prejudices and eager bigotries instilled by Catholic teachers sharpened national dissension and postponed compromise and reconciliation to a day that has only now dawned.

The Bonapartist priesthood produced some curious figures. One glimpses, for instance, the plump good-nature of Mgr Dubreuil, who began as chaplain at the Empress's school, and ended, by a natural progression, as Archbishop of Avignon. Unlike many of his colleagues, he refused to repudiate his patrons: on the contrary he could always be relied on to defend the dynasty. The prelates at the Vatican Council, engaged in exhausting discussions of primacy and infallibility, were surprised to see Mgr Dubreuil, flushed and earnest, rise from his

[1] Emile Faguet, *L'Anticléricalisme*, p. 183.

seat, and astonished to hear him solemnly intone the virtues of Napoleon I as a catechist.

Even priests who could not emulate Dubreuil's spaniel-like devotion felt more than satisfied with the regime, especially with its foreign policy. After all, was not the Crimean War ostensibly fought to keep the Holy Places from being appropriated by the Greek Church? The Church of France accordingly hailed it as a crusade against infidels and heretics. Less apparent but equally true was the fact that the Crimean War represented Cavour's first move in his attack on Austria—a crusade which the Church was to regard with much less favour.

But that trouble was still brewing. In 1858, while Cavour was yet plotting his campaign, the Mortara case exploded with a report that reverberated all over Europe. The Mortaras were a Boulogne family, Jews by race and creed. When one of the children fell dangerously ill, his nurse secretly arranged his baptism as a Christian. Unexpectedly he recovered; and the Holy Office, following the laws of the States and the doctrine of the Church, took him from his family and sent him to the Pope's dominions. He was (so the argument ran) a Christian and was entitled to Christian instruction. On logical grounds the Pope's case was unanswerable and he had no intention whatever of giving way. But the Church's action ran entirely counter to the current doctrine of personal liberty. Why was Mortara snatched from his parents? Because he was a Christian. Why was he a Christian? Because his nurse had him baptized when he was far too young to give consent. The Pope, in short, was presuming on a primary act of deception and force; because of a servant's duplicity he deprived two parents of their child. To Catholics, of course, the nurse was right, obeying a higher loyalty; but to non-Catholics—whether Protestants, Jews, atheists or deists— the Pope was upholding the theocratic ideals of the Middle Ages in defiance of modern conceptions. The entire business savoured of casuistry—casuistry, moreover, aggravated by the physical force at the casuists' disposal. It illuminated the authoritarian theory which Rome had never disavowed, and raised the whole question of temporal sovereignty, which had made Mortara's abduction possible.[1]

[1] Mortara was educated in Rome and became a monk. The recent Finaly case (1944 onwards) has followed a similar pattern.

The Mortara case prepared French opinion for the change Napoleon was meditating in his foreign policy. He was an unpredictable, coquettish politician. Narrowly escaping death from a bomb thrown by an Italian revolutionary, he warmed to the views of his would-be assassin. Baited with the hope of acquiring Nice and Savoy, he fell in with Cavour's plans for driving the Austrians out of Italy—fell in more deeply than he thought. For Cavour's aim was not merely to drive out the Austrians, but to unite Italy under the Sardinian King; and that meant overrunning the Papal States. Already Napoleon had troubled his clerical associates with ambiguities and vacillations in his policy; already Veuillot had referred to him a little uneasily as 'un Louis-Philippe perfectionné'; but these weaknesses were generally ascribed to the disloyalty of his executives. Now, however, it became distressingly clear that the new Charlemagne, the reincarnation of Saint Louis, the sword of the righteous, the defender of the Church, was flabby in conviction and fickle in policy. Was he only a Bonaparte after all? Straws came floating down the wind. There was a remark dropped to the Austrian Ambassador; then a pamphlet which was obviously blessed with official approval. Finally the Austrians launched an ultimatum and in a matter of days France was at war by the side of Sardinia.

Now by changing his foreign policy Napoleon upset the balance of forces at home. Catholics who had once eulogized his regime shed their enthusiasm like a coat that had gone out of fashion. The first to turn against him were the Liberal Catholics, for they were already in opposition and had no loyalties to strain. As they saw the war against Austria developing into a war against the Pope, they lashed the Government with all the invective that is usually provoked by the defence of a Christian cause. That Cavour might possibly be a better representative of Italian liberty than the Austrian Emperor troubled them not at all. As Liberal Catholics, they espoused the Pope's liberty—his liberty to be an absolute ruler in a corrupt realm—leaving the Italians to look after themselves.[1] Dupanloup wrote public letters deploring the war: Montalembert incurred prosecution. An isolated figure, who did not

---

[1] See, for example, Montalembert's article, 'Pie IX et la France en 1849 et en 1859'. *Œuvres*, V.

lament the war from the first, was Lacordaire. 'Whatever happened, whether good or bad,' he explained, 'I remained true
to my two separate convictions: independence and liberty of
Italy; preservation of the Pope's temporal power.'[1] When his
candidature to the Academy was mooted, his opponents pointed
to his uncertain attitude to the Pope's sovereignty. For the
Roman question was an infallible test of political conservatism,
and Protestant Guizot and atheist Thiers both objected to him
as not Roman enough to be reliable. But 'liberty of Italy and
temporal power'—even Lacordaire could not drive two such
dissimilar horses in harness for long; before many months he had
rallied to the main body of Catholic opinion. It needed the
irreducible, inexpugnable Michon to stand out permanently
against the assault of events, arguments, discipline and dogma.

It is true that Napoleon III had not suddenly become anticlerical; true that he kept a French army in Rome; true that
he hoped to preserve some temporal authority for the Pope.
But his queasy policy was easily upset. Despite the preliminaries
of Villafranca and the Treaty of Zürich the Papal dominions
could not be saved; for within a few months of the signing of
peace Garibaldi had liberated Sicily and landed on the main-
land. The Papal States rose in revolt against an administration
that had nothing to recommend it. By the end of 1860 Victor
Emmanuel's intervention meant that the Pope had lost not
only Romagna and the Legations, but the Marches and Umbria
as well, that his temporal sovereignty was confined to Rome,
and that even there his security depended on a French army of
occupation.

It was a fortunate chance for the Liberal Catholics that
Napoleon's sympathy with Italian nationalists set him against
the Pope. For long they had smarted at the Intransigents' claim
to be the only true servants of the Holy See; now they could
rush to the forefront of battle, overtaking and outstripping the
Intransigents, who were still entangled in nets of their own
weaving. But the Intransigents were not long delayed. Once
they perceived the trend and inevitable outcome of Napoleon's
policy, they hurriedly broke the bonds tying them to the
Bonapartist regime and joined Dupanloup in passionate protests. As for the Pope, he saw the temporal struggle in terms of

[1] *Lettres à des jeunes gens*, p. 396.

black and white. As soon as his armies were defeated, he resorted to transcendental weapons, issuing a Bull of excommunication against all those who were responsible for the loss of his territory; while Mgr Talbot, one of his confidants, padded softly round the Vatican, whispering to foreign diplomats that there was reliable evidence of Napoleon's league with the Devil.

But though the general concern of Catholics with the Papal States carried some promise of reconciliation between Liberals and Intransigents, it did nothing to recommend Catholicism to the average Frenchman. On the contrary, it alienated him still further. To anyone who looked at France without violent preconceptions it was clear that the Church was substantially, though not primarily, a political organization. Thanks to the Church's support the Second Empire had been secure for almost a decade, and in return the Government had conceded a number of clerical requests. But it now became evident that the Church had a foreign policy too. In the name of Christ the Government was urged to prop up the Papal States till the day of judgement; and it was not apparent, either that alliance with the Pope as a temporal sovereign was in the permanent interests of France, or (whatever might be true of divine justice) that human justice was best served by the maintenance of a ramshackle theocratic regime. Anyone, therefore, who sympathized with Italian aspirations for unity was liable to be bruised and battered by Catholic controversialists; and if he persisted in his attitude, found himself flung not only against the Pope, but against the Church and Catholicism. Could he be blamed for holding fast? There were, of course, no widespread defections in the French Church, but it became increasingly identified with the unintelligent, undiscriminating support of the old order. It lacked excitement, insight, imagination. It failed to recruit ambitious young men. It appealed not to the bold, but to the timid and the hide-bound. Those who had once responded to Lacordaire's oratory had second thoughts when they saw the Church ossifying in tradition instead of going out to meet the modern world; and the new generation did not listen to the preachers of Notre-Dame with the same delighted sense of revelation that had dawned upon their fathers.

The Church, however, was full of fighters. 'Wash thy hands, O Pilate', wrote the enraged Mgr Pie in what appeared to be an apostrophe of the Emperor; 'declare thyself guiltless of the blood of Christ.'[1] And immediate prosecution cooled his temper. In the meantime *L'Univers*, which had flouted the Government's warning by publishing an exasperated encyclical from the Pope, was finally suppressed. 'Caro Veuillot! Caro *Univers*!' said Pius with regret; for he had lost his doughtiest champion. Admittedly most of the staff were re-engaged by *Le Monde*, but with two all-important exceptions—Louis Veuillot and his brother Eugène. The Government had resolved to silence the most dangerous journalist of France: and Ultramontanes no longer heard the daily trumpet-call to war. While the Liberal Catholics exulted, regretting only that *L'Univers* had contrived to perish in such honourable circumstances, Veuillot, after looking round Paris in vain for a controversial opening, took the road to Rome, there to seek wisdom and consolation.

As Veuillot turned his back on Paris, the Imperial Government set on foot the changes that were symbolized by his departure. To sack Veuillot and to put Mgr Pie into the dock were indications of a careful campaign. At last—rather too late —the Government repented of its encouragement of Ultramontanism; the bishops whom it now nominated tended towards Gallicanism and resisted the encroachments of Rome. Nets were woven round the religious orders; their days of unlimited expansion were over. At the same time Catholic schools, which had once been regarded as bulwarks of society but were now turning out pupils who sided with Pie and Veuillot against Napoleon III and his ministers, had to meet increasing competition from state schools, where tamer political doctrines were taught. All over France the Church stumbled into difficulties. But these difficulties were not solely provided by the Government: on the contrary, there were sinister signs of a changing temper among the people.

[1] L. Baunard, *Histoire du Cardinal Pie*, II, pp. 112 ff.

CHAPTER VI

Patterns of Unbelief

In the midst of these disturbances Lacordaire died at Sorèze, despondent at the religious conflicts in France and Europe, utterly faithful to the Holy See, but torn by the stress of his two loyalties. Perhaps he was lucky to die when he did; he would have derived little consolation from the future policy of Pius IX. At any rate, the crowds who filed past his body and kissed his naked feet—one biographer says there were thirty thousand of them—already thought of him as a survivor from a past age, a specimen of the gay, buoyant liberalism of 1830, a lovable anachronism from the *Avenir* days, who had contrived to store up sufficient hope in the modern world to survive even the disillusion of the Second Empire.

Even his work for monks was in peril. Though surviving the deliberate indignities inflicted by the Government, they were threatened with a far worse evil—an insidious, mounting unpopularity. For this they were partly to blame themselves, but it would not have grown so fast without official sanction. The Government, in fact, slackened the reins on the anticlerical Press and took no steps to hush up scandals which would earlier have aroused no comment because they would have acquired no currency. A characteristic and notorious case was the Ratisbonne Affair of 1860. Ratisbonne had founded a female congregation in Paris, and among others he converted a Jewess named Anna Bluth, who hastened to instruct her seven brothers and sisters in the way of salvation. In 1854 the Bluth family left Paris for Cambrai, where Anna, now an obedient worker in the Catholic cause, became the mistress of a local canon called Mallet. Unfortunately, however, her parents, whose conversion had never been whole-hearted, decided to return to the Jewish religion, demanding the simultaneous restoration of five of their children who, as minors, were receiving a Catholic education. Of these children the boy was recovered without any difficulty; one girl was found hidden in a Belgian convent; another, also hidden in a convent, temporarily lost her reason; the third went mad for life; and the fourth disappeared altogether. What was worse, it transpired that Mallet, not content with Anna's favours, had tried to seduce two of her sisters.

No one would seriously suggest that Mallet was typical of the French priesthood, but unsavoury anecdotes of this kind did the Church much harm, alarming the bourgeoisie, disquieting parents, bringing conventual life into disrepute. Newspaper readers jumped to the conclusion that the madness of two of Anna's sisters was a result of being shut up in a convent. Probably they were wrong; but wrong or not, they hesitated before committing their children to such conditions. Priests, provided they were guilty of some gross misdemeanour, made headline news, and in the first months of 1861 case after case reached the courts of fraud, captation and immorality. Vice, of course, supplies much more interesting reading than virtue, particularly when it hides under virtue's mask. The public was fascinated by the sight of a Montpellier priest, who had been inhibited for adultery, protesting to Rome and impugning the morals of his bishop; and the Government, while stifling political criticism, was only too glad for the Church to become a butt, drawing off the fury and indignation which might otherwise have assailed the regime. In this way republicans were kept so busy with their anticlericalism that they could spare little time to be republican. It is none the less clear that scandals occurred with uncomfortable frequency. The most notorious cases concerned monks, particularly those engaged in teaching: assault and pederasty continually filled the columns, and increased the fortunes, of newspaper proprietors. Between 1861 and 1863 the percentage of public teachers found guilty of criminal offences was six times higher among members of congregations than among laymen. As a Catholic spokesman pointed out, the rapid extension of independent schools had over-stretched the capacity of the congregations to find suitable staff, with the result that all too many teachers without a real vocation had been admitted to the schools—men unable to sustain the high standards required of their calling.[1] Falloux, in fact, had been let down by his executives.

Now all these scandals were fuel to the anticlericals. It is significant that the word *anticlérical* first became current in 1859 and that *clérical* followed the next year as a term of abuse. Littré's brand of Positivism recruited scientists and republicans who would have been deterred by Comte's authoritarian philosophy. At one time, the republicans had been mainly Protestant, with scarcely a man in their ranks who did not believe in some kind of Deity. But now, with the acidulation of religious strife, Catholics moved further to the right and republicans to the left, so that Protestantism lost its hold and militant atheism gained control. 'Social reforms', said Littré curtly, 'can only be obtained by eliminating belief in God.'

Moreover the Press was heavily weighted against *L'Univers*. Between 1858 and 1864 several important papers began publication, with policies trained against the Church. *L'Opinion Nationale* is an example. Launched by Guéroult in 1859 with the support of Prince Napoleon and a number of left-wing Bonapartists, it was originally conceived of as a weapon against the *parti clérical*; but under the stress of daily controversy it turned against Catholicism in general, denouncing the congregations and the Jesuits, publicizing scandals, printing scientific articles in which Christianity was presented as demonstrably untrue. How far anticlericalism had gone within a few years is apparent from Augier's play *Le Fils de Giboyer* (1862), in which there is a famous, malicious portrait of Veuillot, or in Louise Gagneur's novel *La Croisade Noire* (1865), originally serialized in *Le Siècle*, where the author is at pains to annotate conversations and letters with such comments as *Historique* and *Textuel*.

As the conflict deepened, each side became more absolute in its claims and contentions: moderates were overruled or brushed away. While the anticlericals redoubled their attacks against bad logic, spurious history, superstition and hypocrisy, the clericals riposted with cries of naturalism or took heart by huddling in their new devotions. These devotions were hardly likely to placate the anticlericals. For one of the most conspicuous elements in nineteenth-century Catholicism is the

[1] J. Maurain, *La Politique ecclésiastique du Second Empire*, *passim*.

175

growing worship of the Virgin Mary, a process in which the dogma of the Immaculate Conception is only an episode. This renewed worship was accompanied, perhaps naturally, perhaps supernaturally, by a number of apparitions.

The French clergy had long been sceptical about miracles: had not miracles been used by the Jansenists to propagate error? But the Revolution and the Romantic movement both fostered a state of mind to which frequent divine intervention in the natural order was a not unwelcome idea, and from about 1815 onwards miracles occurred with regularity. While strange events were reported from Germany, incredible sights gladdened the faithful of France. There was the famous vision at Migne, a small village in Poitou: one evening at about five o'clock, just as a mission was ending, a cross about a hundred feet long suddenly appeared in the sky above the church and remained for about half an hour, so as to be seen by three thousand people. Then, as preposterously as it had come, it melted into the darkness.

But this was as nothing beside the apparitions of the Virgin Mary. In 1803, surrounded by angels, she had made herself visible to a country girl near Besançon. In 1830 she appeared three times to Sister Catherine Labouré in Paris, giving precise instructions for a medal to be struck which would confer special protection on the wearer. In 1846 she was seen by two children at La Salette. And twelve years later she deigned to appear to Bernadette in a dark grotto at Lourdes, announcing herself in the cryptic sentence, 'I am the Immaculate Conception'.

Two years before this the French bishops, meeting for the baptism of the Prince Imperial, had asked the Pope to make the Feast of the Most Pure Heart of Mary binding on the whole Church. But though there were few priests—and they mainly Gallicans—to oppose the brisk advance in Marian worship, many had doubts concerning the authenticity of each particular miracle. In spite of the swarms of pilgrims to La Salette and the profitable trade in water from the grotto, most of the lower clergy were sceptical, offering various plausible explanations. One of the children who was supposed to have seen the Virgin confessed to the saintly Curé d'Ars that he had lied; but later, under pressure, retracted. At the same time a woman whom two of the local clergy had accused of fraud sued them for libel, but was non-suited. At Lourdes, too, the malevolent whispered a tale about a well-known local lady who had arranged an illicit rendezvous in the grotto and on being surprised by Bernadette had saved her reputation by an impulsive feat of histrionics. But the malevolent and the sceptical failed to have their way: chapels were built, pilgrims thronged the highways, healing water sold fast, wonderful cures were announced. The miracles, in short, were accepted as authentic.

While the bishops as a body were ready enough to believe in such apparitions if sufficient evidence could be brought forward, the Intransigents went much further in their enthusiasm: with Dom Guéranger vigorously encouraging the cult of saints and of ancient relics and with Veuillot extolling each new miracle as though it supplied conclusive justification for the editorial policy of L'Univers, they chastised hesitation as sinful. The Liberal Catholics, on the other hand, were cautious: they suspected miracles and they hated agreement with Intransigents. Even so, it was Dupanloup's account of La Salette in a religious periodical that gave colour to the story.

To unbelievers, of course, each miracle was, if not divine, at least a godsend: it showed how deeply even the most intelligent spokesmen of the Church were tainted with medieval superstition and uncritical credulity. When priests themselves were suspicious and accused local women of personating the Virgin, anticlericals were all the more delighted: they had enough material for years of controversy. 'Wherever miracles are believed in', one of them wrote, 'miracles occur. Wherever they are no longer believed in—and that is where they are most needed—no one sees any. The Blessed Virgin appears at Lourdes, but not in Paris; she shows herself to Bernadette, but not to the Academy of Science.'[1]

It was the great weakness, the essential failure, of the Liberal Catholics not to understand the sincerity and earnestness that underlay disbelief. True, one of their shrewder members pointed out: 'In the nineteenth century atheists are learned and severe. . . . Ungodliness is banished from their speech; they can hardly be blamed if it is found at the basis of phenomena.'[2] But of such

[1] Guéroult, Etudes, p. 139. Quoted by G. Weill, Histoire de l'idée laïque, p. 135.
[2] L'Abbé Meignan in Le Correspondant, 25th March 1859, p. 432.

an avowal Falloux, Dupanloup, Montalembert, Broglie were none of them capable. Had they glimpsed the cogency of the historical and critical arguments brought against Christianity, their apologetic would have been stronger and their position in the Church more defensible. As it was, their appeal was purely emotional, a devout but inconsistent attempt to preach Catholic doctrine while practising bourgeois politics. Like Lacordaire, they ministered to the feelings of the nineteenth century; but lacking both his insight and the plebeian sympathies of Veuillot, they had no real grasp of the nation's needs, no real call on its gratitude. Michon, for all his vagaries, stood for a more percipient and discriminating attitude to the modern spirit.

In history, for instance, the Liberal Catholics were tirelessly inaccurate. Searching the past for lessons and morals that could be applied to the present, they abused texts, distorted evidence and defiantly repaired the most tattered reputations. With one eye on anticlerical historians, Falloux patched up the life of Pius V, the Papal Inquisitor, turning him into such an urbane and innocent character that even Lacordaire was shocked and indignant. Admittedly Falloux exceeded his brief: he forgot that he was a *Liberal* Catholic. A more normal pattern was supplied by *Saint Dominique*, in which Lacordaire, though conceding the existence of persecutors and tyrants, skilfully disengaged his own Dominican forces. Broglie's work, however, was even more pertinent. Studying the relations between the Church and the Roman Empire in the fourth century, he tried to show that much of Christianity derived from the pagan world; secular society was therefore not entirely wicked, and the Church, in the nineteenth century as in the fourth, could come to terms with it.

But though Liberal Catholic history was a useful weapon with which to belabour the Intransigents, it was too rhetorical to carry conviction. Montalembert, Broglie, Falloux all wrote well —almost too well; and the very relevance of their picture of the past made it suspect. Their work, like the work of their opponent Guéranger, was domestic in scope and transient in significance. If the history of Christianity was carefully scrutinized and discussed, it was not by Catholics. For the condemnation that had overwhelmed Richard Simon almost two hundred years earlier still hung over the head of any curious researcher who wished to remain within the Roman Communion: and wise men abstained. Since the Restoration the best minds in the French Church had concentrated on training teachers and priests, neglecting the narrow but vital field of higher education. From time to time a bishop deplored the lack of scholars; Affre had even founded the Ecole des Carmes to encourage learning and research. But the Ecole des Carmes, like the Sorbonne, bore the taint of Gallicanism, incurring the suspicion and dislike of Intransigents; and when a man like Meignan drew attention to the need for erudition at the highest level, his warnings fell on deaf ears. 'Scholars?' said the Cardinal Archbishop of Lyons jocosely. 'What do I want with them?'

As Michon pointed out as early as 1845, a school had arisen outside the Church that dealt continuously with the high questions of religion. 'One day', he said, 'religious history will judge the priesthood severely for not taking the opportunity of instructing a generation which thirsted for knowledge and was always ready to welcome genius.'[1] This school sprang up first in Germany, originating in the renaissance of philology. But no one in France seemed to care. Strauss was translated but ignored; the work of the Tübingen group was neglected; French atheists were still at the stage of dismissing Christ as a solar myth. Only when Le Réveil had revived Protestant interest in the Bible did France acquire scholars who examined and discussed biblical texts with a firm exegetical method; and those scholars were Protestants, publishing their conclusions in the Revue de Strasbourg, an organ of limited fame and influence. It took another eight years—till 1858, in fact—before a metropolitan paper was started to spread the early, tentative findings about biblical texts; and in the Revue Germanique the French public learnt for the first time that the Pentateuch had been composed by two authors, one Yahwistic and one Elohistic, and that the Fourth Gospel was less reliable as a narrative of fact than its three predecessors.

Even at its best, biblical exegesis is not a pastime: it demands learning, skill, discrimination. Had it not been for Renan, few Catholics would have heard of the new assaults on ancient assumptions, and fewer still would have taken heed. The learned reviews reached only a small public, distinguished perhaps, but unrepresentative, and it would have needed many years for the

[1] J. H. Michon, La Femme et la Famille dans le catholicisme, p. ix.

opinions of this minority to percolate through to the incurious, unlettered masses. In 1863 how many Frenchmen had heard of Garnier, Denis, Louis Ménard, Miron and Aubertin? But within a matter of weeks everyone knew Renan's name. *La Vie de Jésus* was half the size of an average novel and ten times as exciting. In graceful, easy language it reduced Christ to the level of a village illuminato. It was shrewd and critical enough to please the instructed; suave and polished enough to attract the ignorant; warm-hearted and idealistic enough to tempt the sober-minded. It enticed, charmed and persuaded. Even suspicious readers were lulled into acquiescence by its melodious prose.

Of course Renan started with an advantage: it was only a few months since his lectures at the Collège de France had been suspended for a reference to Jesus as 'an incomparable man'. But that temporary notoriety was eclipsed by his new-won, permanent fame. In two months 40,000 copies were sold, and the book maintained its popularity. Calling on a girl who occasionally condescended to read the daily papers, a well-known playwright was surprised to see a copy of *La Vie de Jésus* lying on a table in the lounge. 'What on earth do you hope to do with that?' he asked. 'You won't read it.' 'Of course not,' the girl replied, 'but I was told I ought to possess it.'[1] And so the success continued, through the last months of 1863, all through 1864, exhausting edition after edition, till by 1865 the sales touched 100,000 copies—a huge figure for the period.

It is typical of the elaborate tessellations of ecclesiastic politics under the Second Empire that Napoleon himself, though in conflict with a large section of the Church, was still bent on cutting a figure as a defender of the faith and wrote a public letter to the Bishop of Arras, deploring Renan's sacrilege. He only repeated what every bishop and priest in the country was saying: denunciations pelted from the pulpits. Indeed part of Renan's success he undoubtedly owed to his detractors, who by the fury of their indignation procured him the most unlikely readers. But some reply was needed. The Protestants, for their part, gave the book measured consideration, some praising it

[1] L. Halévy, *Carnets*, I, p. 26. How widely the book was read is shown by the fact that in July, almost immediately after publication, a working man sent Maret a vigorous, detailed denunciation. See G. Bazin, *Vie de Mgr Maret*, II, pp. 282–4.

in the *Revue Germanique*, some publishing cautious and scholarly analyses. Perhaps they were too friendly; certainly Athanase Coquerel, the leading figure of the liberal school, contrived to produce such an amiable refutation that he lost his Paris pastorship.

Meanwhile France waited for the Catholic reply—a systematic, fully documented disproof; and after months of waiting, with now a pamphlet and now a brochure to pass the time, it slowly dawned on Frenchmen that no full-scale reply was forthcoming. No one was qualified to undertake it. No doubt some Catholics agreed with the *Dublin Review*, which declared that 'this much-vaunted book has no such scientific value as to make it worthy even of serious refutation. It is an insult, not a blow, to the Catholic faith.'[1] But others were offended, even shaken, in their convictions; they needed someone to remove this stumbling-block from their path; otherwise they might pitch over it. The only man to grapple with the book systematically and courageously was Meignan, but even he knew too little about biblical criticism to overthrow Renan's arguments. Apart from Meignan there was merely incompetent bustle or chilling silence. The wheel had come full circle. It was not more than three years since Lacordaire had told a correspondent: 'I have always bothered little about controversy, being persuaded that the forthright exposition of Christianity destroys in advance all the objections that can be brought against it. Christianity is like an ancient monument stuck fast in the solid ground; and controversy is like the sand which the wind blows against its unshakeable bulk.'[2] The simile might hold good for a man with Lacordaire's faith; but to scorn the aid of analytical argument when dealing with doubters, inquirers and waverers was to indulge in a cloudy optimism that nearly spelt disaster. Because of neglect, incuriosity and airy self-confidence Christianity at last seemed breached; after nineteen centuries the ancient vessel had sprung a leak and the water came swirling in, spirting over the timbers, gushing into the hold, swamping the bilge, till the ship rode perilously low in the water.

[1] *Dublin Review*, 1864, Vol. II, No. IV (New Series), p. 417.
[2] *Lettres à des jeunes gens*, p. 418. One bishop thought that the best refutation of Renan was to publish a selection of Lacordaire's sermons.

CHAPTER VII

The Abbé ⋆ ⋆ ⋆

A few months after the publication of *La Vie de Jésus*
Michon set out again for the Holy Land with Saulcy's
second expedition—a venture as ambitious and as fruit-
less as the first. He did, it is true, collect some botanical and
archaeological debris which was divided between the Louvre
and Angoulême Museum, and he brought back a few jottings
which were eventually put together in a book on Christ and the
Gospels. But even before departing he cast his die.

As he looked back over his life, it must have seemed a desola-
tion. Not one of his projects had matured. At first there had
been so much promise—Saint-Sulpice and the hope of intellectual eminence; Angoulême and the sight of congregations trans-
ported by his eloquence (was he not the only preacher apart
from Lacordaire who could raise applause?); Paris and the
chance of moulding the whole life of the Church, of guiding
French Catholicism out of sterile deserts into a promised land.
And what had it all led to? Throughout his life he had been on
the brink of achievement, yet had achieved nothing: just as
the cup touched his lips it was knocked away. Instead of
advancement, bankruptcy; instead of eminence, persecution;
instead of influence, neglect. Had he thought only of himself,
of his own ambition, Michon might have accepted his fate and
lapsed into bitterness. After all, he was nearing sixty, distrusted,
discredited, discarded; there was no hope of capturing the
allegiance of the younger clergy or of supplanting Veuillot in
the affections of ordinary Catholics; if he spoke out, it was at
the risk of exacerbating and imperilling his declining years.

But Michon preserved the naïvety of the true believer. With

182

THE ABBÉ ***

every year that passed, the Catholic Church went further down a road which, he was convinced, led to superstition, deceit and ultimate perdition. He felt that he had a personal contribution of immense importance to make—felt that because of ill fortune and the forces ranged against him he had never been fairly heard. As he contemplated the anachronistic theologians of France and Italy at their work, and watched the Intransigents gaining power over parish priests, bishops, Press and people, and beheld the congregations spreading over France, carrying with them ancient and destructive doctrines, anger bubbled up within him till he was no longer master of himself. He determined to wage war, to have a final say. But he could not shut his eyes to the power of his opponents, who had hitherto rendered him harmless; and so, in accordance with his philosophy of religion which (it was another irregularity) scarcely admitted any distinction between priest and layman, he resolved to address not theologians alone but the whole reading public. In short, the Abbé Michon turned novelist.

'This book', says the preface to *Le Maudit* by L'Abbé ***, 'is a work of art; it is neither polemic nor history.' That it is not history is obvious enough; but it constitutes in fact one of the purest pieces of polemic of the century. The story, which sprawls over three lengthy volumes, concerns a young priest called Julio whose liberal sympathies earn him first the distrust and then the implacable hatred of the Jesuits; after bitter struggles, including a period of incarceration in Rome, he dies, passing on to his friends the duty of opposing the Jesuits.

Now if *Le Maudit* were merely another anticlerical novel, it would have contained little of interest for the readers of the Second Empire and nothing for us today. But Lacroix, the publisher of the Librairie Internationale, at once perceived the quality of the book—that is, its selling quality. For under the Second Empire the Librairie Internationale, with its translations of Grote, Buckle, Merivale, Bancroft, Motley, Prescott and Gervinius, had become almost a revolutionary centre: publishing works by Hugo, Michelet, Pelletan, Quinet, Simon and Proudhon—Lacroix had even served a six months' sentence for issuing Proudhon's annotated edition of the Gospels—the house was always in quest of new and scandalous books. When, therefore, a lean and paradoxically soft-spoken priest arrived

at these offices with the bulky manuscript of *Le Maudit* under
his arm, Lacroix ran his eye swiftly over it and hastened to do
business, promising to make every effort to promote its sales.
He was as good as his word. In the weeks before publishing day
he ensured by advertisements and posters that no one in France
with the slightest interest in current literature was ignorant of
the great event impending; the number of prospectuses was
variously estimated at between 100,000 and 500,000; and when
the book at last appeared on the stalls and in the shops, the
public rushed to buy it. What were the scandalous revelations
of the Abbé ***, his unanswerable charges against the Church?
Why was this novel hailed as a worthy successor to *Candide*?
Appetite, once whetted, had to be satisfied.

Though dated 1864, *Le Maudit* came out just before Christmas 1863, and with it Michon presented his compliments of the
season to the Intransigents. Scarcely had the first notices of the
book appeared than authority rumbled angrily: in the Senate
a cardinal denounced it as the most abominable of all the
religious books that were flooding the country, and on March
15th it was put on the Index.

'What', asked the critic of the *Revue des Deux Mondes*, 'is this
book which has caused uproar in the Senate almost before
publication—this book which, anathematized as it is, has
played so sudden and unexpected a role in the embroiled affairs
of France and Europe?' The question was easier to ask than to
answer. If the critics were honest, they could hardly pretend
that the book possessed any literary value. Facile, clumsy, long-
winded and melodramatic, it bore a marked kinship to the
garish novels of the popular lending libraries, the works of Sue,
Soulié and Ponson du Terrail. Yet there was more—a quality of
painful sincerity that set it apart from the average crude assaults
on religion. It was not a book one could pass over in silence;
despite its grotesque and preposterous faults the reader felt that,
buried under layers of wild fantasy and frenzied rhetoric, there
lurked a small hard core of true conviction, real passion.

Occasionally a critic like Zola could be found who dismissed
the book out of hand, declaring that the author, whether layman or priest, was either an unscrupulous impostor or a bare-
faced traitor. But the problem was not so easy. *Le Maudit*
revealed a remarkable familiarity with the trivial details and

petty intrigues of clerical life—a familiarity that would be exceptional, even in an abbé. According to the most favoured theory there were at least three authors, two of them priests. 'Such an uneven style', wrote that influential critic, Cuvillier-Fleury, 'does not belong to one man. There are several of them; some jump nimbly and boldly over the ditches and bogs; the rest fall in.'[1]

But who *was* the author? The question was asked on all sides and it was a serious one. Surely the Church authorities could not tolerate an apostate within their ranks without striving to unmask him? They certainly did their best. Long-faced gentlemen interviewed Lacroix, inveigling him into friendly conversation, setting ingenious traps; neighbours were questioned about his visitors, acquaintances cross-examined about his friends; *Le Maudit* was scrutinized from first page to last for some telltale indiscretion—and yet it all led nowhere. Though investigators narrowed their suspicion to a handful of eminent rebels, there was no one man on to whom responsibility could be pinned, and when Michon's name was mooted, a German periodical absolved him entirely, explaining that his views, though radical, were not sufficiently destructive to make him eligible.

Today, if that question is answered, another rises to take its place: was Michon disloyal? The answer depends on where his loyalty lay. If a priest's first duty is to the Church of which he is a member, the Church visible by whose organization he is bound, then Michon betrayed his duty. *Le Maudit* is an unflagging inculpation of almost every aspect of the Church's activity in the modern world. Michon assails congregations and missionaries, Ultramontanes and confessors, bishops and popes; he draws a lurid picture of deceit, obscurantism and stupidity. Following *Le Maudit* with a long series of similar novels in which passionate repetition cannot disguise the gradual parching of belief, he exploits his success with commercial acumen.[2] And there, unhappily, is the flaw, the vexing inconsistency. For if

---

[1] Cuvillier-Fleury, *Etudes et portraits*, p. 337.

[2] *La Religieuse* (1864); *Le Jésuite* (1865); *Le Moine* (1865); *Le Confesseur* (1866); *Les Mystiques* (1869); *Le Fils de prêtre* (posthumous: 1885). Among the replies were: P. Bélet, *La Religieuse selon l'auteur du Maudit* (1864); Mme E. Poujade, *Essai . . . à propos du Maudit de l'abbé **** (1864); Mme ***, *Le Vrai Maudit* (1866).

the power of *Le Maudit* lies in its sense of grievous wrong, its spirit of moral indignation, one feels that in its successors this basic and ultimately generous exasperation gives way to a discharge of personal bile—that the author is so intent on making out his case that he deliberately and consciously panders to his public, scandalizing them with anecdotes which he knows to be untrue. Given a man with Michon's temperament, it is just possible that *Le Maudit* is entirely sincere; but his later novels degenerate into a sedulous rehearsal of foolish prejudices.

Yet remembering Veuillot, Dupanloup, Montalembert and the current tone of Catholic argument, one cannot write him off as a hypocrite. He meant, profoundly and passionately, every word of his attack on the Church, but was carried away by the desire to justify and prove it. It is some tribute to his cogency and to his residual Christianity that even while the Ultramontanes were censuring his heresy, the freethinkers were reprobating his faith. If one casts away his indiscretions—his innuendoes against the modern form of confession (they were not unfounded), his criticism of sacerdotal celibacy, his deep-grained Gallicanism, which led him to acclaim Napoleon's Roman policy—there is much of value left. Perhaps his idea of the Church is wider than becomes a priest:

'All who adore God in spirit and in truth are Christian in our eyes, no matter in what climate, civilization or cult. Repeating the beautiful definition of the Church given by Saint Augustine, we say: The Church is humanity itself, *Ecclesia homines sunt*. Those who have faith and love are its members.'[1]

But his broad view of life has more to recommend it than the dark prescriptions of his bitterest enemies:

'Love is not, as they, with their brutish psychology, think, a corruption of our nature, but a pure and holy passion, set in our soul by the Creator, like friendship, gratitude, self-sacrifice. . . .'[2]

How far he was ahead of his time is evident in *Le Maudit*, where the hero defends geological theories about the age of the world against biblical authority and states specifically:

'The Bible is divine in the order of revealed truths, not in the order of scientific truths.'[3]

[1] *La Religieuse*, II, p. 91. [2] *Le Confesseur*, II, p. 47.
[3] *Le Maudit*, I, p. 362.

And this in 1863, just seven years before the Vatican Council confirmed the teaching of the Council of Trent about the Bible, declaring its historical veracity to be inseparable from its inspiration.

Le Maudit was a sensation rather than an influence. Ten large impressions were exhausted in a year; it spread all over Europe and was several times translated. To Lacroix's offices in Paris there flowed a turgid stream of correspondence, one-half ecstatic, the rest abusive. Wherever politics and literature were discussed, the implications of the book and its successors were analysed. Awarding it studied commendation, a writer in the *Quarterly Review*, who evidently possessed private sources of information, told his readers:

'Their author is a distinguished French Abbé, mixing with the religious and literary society of Paris, and who, though well known as the writer of these obnoxious volumes, has never afforded in his faith or conduct any mark at which the keen eye of religious jealousy could aim, so as to secure his long-coveted suspension from the ministry.'

Moreover, though the reader's first instinct was to dismiss much of the book as exaggerated and incredible, it contained sufficient truth to surprise and shock those who were not intimate with the less scrupulous techniques of modern Catholicism. As one English clergyman wrote during a visit to Italy:

'Much that one hears of the immorality of the Roman clergy in Italy is of too *scabreux* a nature to be further alluded to. The charge of spiritual tyranny and of extortion in the confessional I have heard, I think, brought home to them, by special instances, in a way to justify much that has been lately said of ecclesiastical cupidity, both in the French Senate and the pages of *Le Maudit*.'[1]

No doubt Michon enjoyed his celebrity: he had a spark of sardonic humour which enabled him to savour the anger and indignation of the Intransigents and to relish their feverish attempts to pierce the veil of anonymity. How pleasing to be in the ascendant for once. But although he escaped molestation —a Government report declared his books to be innocuous and not devoid of value—the conviction grew among his opponents that he was the real author, and several times he resorted to

[1] W. Talmadge, *Letters from Florence*, pp. 67–8.

dubious expedients in order to save his position. Driven into a corner, he wriggled and squirmed, never admitting his identity with 'l'Abbé aux trois étoiles', yet never quite denying it. In 1872, for instance, the Abbé Bonnetat declared in a Bordeaux court that Michon had written *Le Maudit*, and the case, seized on by *L'Univers* and prominently reported, drew forth the following letter:

Dear Sir,

It in no wise follows from M. Bonnetat's testimony that M. Mouls told him I was the author of *Le Maudit*. But even if M. Mouls had said anything of the kind to M. Bonnetat, it would be pure supposition. In fact, M. Mouls knows that I have never made any such statement.

Yours etc.

J. H. MICHON

An odd denial, commented *L'Univers*: why not ignore Mouls and Bonnetat and simply declare, 'I did not write it'?

Michon's oblique and curious tactics matched his bizarre and contradictory temperament. His strong face, with its petulant mouth and passionate eyes, affords us as true a guide to his real nature as his reckless, forceful, inconclusive books. There is scarcely a point on which he does not give himself the lie. He promises to write a work of art and produces a huge pamphlet in fictional form. Defending the Church against abuses and reconciling it to the contemporary world, he plays into the hands of the anticlericals, who are delighted by his charges and revelations. He declares himself to be a devout Catholic, whereas he ignores the essential Catholic virtue of obedience; a Christian advocate, he quotes the most scandalous cases from the courts; and while emphasizing that his shafts are aimed at institutions and not at men, he draws a gallery of recognizable caricatures, including an unspeakable journalist called Falot.

Now all these inconsistencies can be ascribed to Michon's discordant temperament, ever at war within itself, ever unable to set a single straight course; but though envenomed by his habit of mind, this conflict was perpetuated by the insoluble intellectual problem that bedevilled his life. Had he been blessed with Lacordaire's lack of analytical power and indifference to science, had he even possessed Lacordaire's submissiveness, he might have escaped distress and torment of soul. But he was just enough of a scientist to realize the deep fissure which was splitting knowledge into two separate parts—faith and fact; and neither part could he abjure. Born a Catholic, he wished to remain one—a Catholic of the Gallican brand, independent of the Pope, free to argue and speculate as conscience and curiosity prompted him. One may feel that Michon's proper home was in one of the Protestant churches; but for Protestantism he had nothing but scorn, convinced as he was, like many of his Catholic contemporaries, that the schism of Luther, Calvin and Henry VIII would not long survive and that the next hundred years would see, in particular, the Church of England obliterated by renascent Catholicism, with Protestant Churches all over the world dwindling into tiny, trivial, unconsidered sects. But if not Protestantism, what other communion? It is true that after the Vatican Council the Abbé Guettée, a learned Gallican whose history of the Church of France had won the approval of forty bishops before being put on the Index, broke away from Rome and became a priest in the Greek Orthodox Church. But even that was not for Michon. In spite of his yearly, even daily, vagaries he wished to remain where he had started, a priest in the French Church; and so his mutinous outbreaks, even to the end, are punctuated by brief periods of humility and compliance—periods just long enough to earn tolerance for the revolts that follow.

There is, however, one further aspect of Michon's career which cannot be passed over—his attitude to celibacy. When a priest turns novelist, the more successful his account of love, the more serious the doubts it casts on the genuineness of his vocation; and in a passage of one of his later novels an unguarded moment has perhaps stolen from Michon an involuntary confession. 'Frederick,' he says, 'consumed with love and jealousy, watched Raphael and Clementine with that bitter curiosity which leads us to seek out painful emotions.'[1] Is it autobiographical? Perhaps. Certainly the question of celibacy recurs again and again in his novels, not only in erring monks and priests, but in passionate appeals for the right to marry.

Now sacerdotal celibacy has always supplied the enemies of the Church with a welcome argument—never perhaps more

[1] *Les Mystiques*, p. 340.

used than during the nineteenth century. Not only was it
reinforced by the criminal cases that occurred at least every
decade—priests seducing, raping and murdering their penitents
or mistresses—but it gained strength from the almost universal
view of sex as a normal and inevitable outlet for a specific
impulse. Michelet, Quinet, Bouis and Gastineau were only a
few of the anticlerical scaremongers who traded on this belief,
warning their readers against the hideous temptations to which
confessors were a prey, and assuming that sooner or later every
priest broke his vow of chastity.[1] Moreover, although reliable
evidence is extremely hard to obtain and, even when obtained,
cannot be treated as representative, there is no doubt that a
good handful of priests were secretly married, often concealing
their wives as housekeepers.[2]

Michon, for his part, was not married, nor did any breath of
scandal ever touch his private life. But his advocacy of the
marriage of priests is so frequent and earnest that even the most
casual reader must suspect that more than a general principle
is at stake. Precisely where he stands is apparent from a letter
published after his death—a letter which reveals better than
any commentary the tormented personality hidden behind his
novels.

'All my life', he wrote, 'I have been sustained by attach-
ments which, because of a vow, must ask nothing of the senses;
and I have enjoyed relationships (all now ended in death)
which represented the most passionate love, the warmest inter-
mingling of souls, apart from the bliss of ultimate possession. . . .
Experience has proved—I am an example myself—that love as
passionate as anything conjured up by the imagination can last
for forty years without physical gratification. . . . No words can
tell the cost of this achievement, my endless struggles with
E. de V., the noble and beloved companion I have recently
lost. Often she said to me: "If we ever forgot ourselves, I know
how you would suffer." Only once in forty years did we share

[1] Thus J. Michelet, *Du Prêtre, de la Femme, de la Famille* (1845 and later
editions); C. Bouis, *Calottes et Soutanes* (1870); B. Gastineau, *Les Crimes des
prêtres et de l'Eglise* (1880).

[2] On the whole question see H. C. Lea, *History of Sacerdotal Celibacy* (1932);
Dolonne, *Le Clergé contemporain et le célibat* (1910)—to be treated with extreme
caution; J. McCabe, *Twelve Years in a Monastery* (1942); A. Houtin, *Un
Prêtre marié*, Charles Perraud (1908), and *Autour d'un prêtre marié* (1910).

the same wedding chamber—that chamber in which she used to sleep so peacefully—and that was the night after her death. . . .

'Today, after our final separation, I am consoled by the thought—and you will understand the exquisite pleasure it affords me—that I had the strange, exceptional good fortune not to sully her beautiful nature.

'And yet we were in the wrong; every day we violated a divine law, a law of nature.'[1]

And so the inconsistency runs right through his life; at each point the balance is tilted. The pathos of the priest who dares not look at the Crown of Thorns for fear of being disillusioned is repeated in the Catholic who hates Rome and in the celibate who believes in a married priesthood. With a kind of pre-destined malaise Michon picks out just those ideas which will set him against his vocation, turning him over upon himself, destroying faith by means of conviction. Blindly and helplessly, yet with a tenacious passion, he hammers out each note of discord, adding dissonance to dissonance, building up the chord octave after octave, till its clamant harshness cries out to be resolved and no resolution is possible. He remains a celibate Catholic priest with no faith in celibacy, Catholicism or the priesthood: he denies himself and somehow survives.

[1] A. Varinard, *J. -H. Michon, fondateur de la graphologie*, pp. 57–61.

CHAPTER VIII

Syllabus Errorum

I t is indeed a tragedy that Michon's talent—for that he had talent no one can doubt—should have dribbled away through this pathetically trivial outlet of anonymous fiction. In himself he is not important: he could never claim the influence and authority of Lacordaire or Veuillot. But he had sufficient awareness to separate him from the conventional run of priests, whether Gallican or Ultramontane—an awareness of social and intellectual tensions which inflamed his conscience, betraying him into error, rebellion, perhaps despair. That so much goodwill and earnestness should have been diverted into barren polemics and that the general public, when at last it was reached, should have been reached in *this* way, may be partly due to the inherent restlessness of Michon's mind, but principally results from the inextricable situation which had ensnared all French Catholics who were not Intransigents. For on this occasion, if Michon was out of step, he was in good company.

Taking heart at the advantage they had gained over the Roman question, the Liberal Catholics still hoped doggedly for a turn in the tide, and from 1859 they were relentless in their activities—Montalembert campaigning for political liberty, praising America and urging intervention in Poland, while the Abbé Godard, one of their lesser luminaries, obtained Rome's eventual approval for a brochure which linked extracts from the Fathers with the Declaration of the Rights of Man.

But they thirsted for a more conspicuous success, and in 1863 a Congress of Catholics was called at Malines in Belgium, to be attended by representatives from all over the world. It was a great opportunity; and though Montalembert, now a frail, sick man, hesitated when he was invited to address the Congress, his misgivings vanished as soon as he realized that his words would carry to every country, bringing an emphatic affirmation of all he had ever believed in. He delivered, in fact, two speeches, the first urging Catholics to accept the new democratic order, the second denying that the Church stood to lose by admitting liberty of conscience. These speeches represented, he said, his political testament.

But the prolonged and vociferous applause that greeted the orator in his invalid chair was short-lived: neither the Nuncio nor the English Catholics approved of his overbold doctrines, and a careful reading of the printed text suggested that his formulae were not only careless and unwise but might amount to heresy. Moreover he tactlessly published the speeches as *L'Eglise libre dans l'Etat libre*—a phrase of Cavour's—with a cheerful and incredible unawareness of the inevitable reaction in Rome. When, after prolonged discussions and representations, the Cardinal Secretary of State sent him a letter of measured blame, he was overwhelmed: it was virtually a condemnation of the cause to which he had given his life. Henceforward Dupanloup and his allies might speak at other congresses, expounding the principles of Liberal Catholicism with greater theological discretion, even rousing audiences to momentary enthusiasm: but the game was already lost.

Pius IX was indeed a very different man from the liberal-minded prelate who had ascended the throne of Saint Peter in 1846. Changeable but obstinate, he had long since shed his vague sympathy with reform movements, and from his tiny patch of land in the middle of Italy he looked out balefully upon his usurpers and despoilers. After the brief liberal exordium to his pontificate, he replaced his first confessor with a Jesuit, and every year he grew more hostile to the modern world, more convinced that its basic presuppositions were at odds with Christianity, more anxious to proclaim his disapproval. Ironically enough it was the Bishop of Perugia (later Leo XIII) who suggested in 1849 that the Pope should collect and condemn the worst errors of the time touching the Church, authority and the rights of property. But in all things Rome moves slowly and not till 1854 was a committee of theologians appointed to carry out the proposal. This committee might still have been sitting half a century later had not a French bishop issued a pastoral instruction formulating and condemning eighty-five propositions derived from contemporary writers. Pius read the pastoral instruction and liked it: he asked his committee to hasten its deliberations. Accordingly, when the bishops assembled in Rome in 1862 for a canonization, they were proudly shown this list of heresies and informed of its probable publication. Some—notably Dupanloup—were against the whole notion: most kept their own counsel.

If Pius still had hesitations, they were dispelled by three events: the Congress of Malines, which aroused him to the alarming modernity of many prominent Catholics; his own severe illness early in 1864, which set the diplomats speculating about the effects of his death and strengthened his desire to make a resonant protest before it was too late; and the Convention of September 15th in the same year, which provided for the gradual withdrawal of French troops from Rome and abandoned the Holy See to the protection, and the mercy, of the new Kingdom of Italy. He goaded on his theologians, arguing the urgency of action; and on December 8th the world received the famous encyclical *Quanta Cura*, together with its attendant Syllabus of Errors, the whole to be shortly followed by extracts from the Pope's own speeches.

The Encyclical itself, couched in the turgid and abusive Latin that seems habitual to most nineteenth-century popes, was obscure and unreadable, even when translated into French; and few Frenchmen troubled to peruse the version that appeared in their papers. But the Syllabus was another matter: it presented with stark lucidity those ideas—'bold, temerarious and perverse'—which, though almost universal, were in conflict with Catholic doctrine. Later commentators have, of course, made qualifications: they have said that the Syllabus, not bearing the Pope's signature, has no authority of its own, that it is not officially an act of the Pope and cannot be regarded as an infallible definition; they have glossed and diluted each condemnation till it is devoid of offence and seems almost to express a liberal outlook. But such was not Pius's intention, nor was anyone deluded as to his aims. For what does the uninstructed reader find if he looks through the list of condemned propositions? Many doctrines that are doubtless disruptive of stable society or dangerous to the Church and its teaching; but together with these doctrines, much that has become part of the humanist heritage of Europe. For instance:

'That every man is free to embrace and profess the religion he shall believe true, guided by the light of reason. . . . That the eternal salvation may (at least) be hoped for, of all those who are not at all in the true Church of Christ. . . . That the Church has not the power of availing herself of force, or of any direct or indirect temporal power. . . . That the Church ought to be separated from the State, and the State from the Church. . . . That in the present day, it is no longer necessary that the Catholic religion be held as the only religion of the State, to the exclusion of all other modes of worship. . . .That the Roman Pontiff can and ought to reconcile himself to, and agree with, progress, liberalism, and modern civilization.'[1]

This last proposition, directed as it was against Montalembert's confederates at Malines, extended its disciplinary effects much further, silencing and confounding all and any who had hoped for a reconciliation between the Pope and the modern world.

In France the Encyclical and Syllabus were greeted with stupefaction; apart from the Ultramontane section of clergy and their following of laymen, the country contemplated the Pope's action with as much surprise as if a knight in full armour had suddenly debouched on to a modern battlefield with a flourish of titles and trumpets, and ridden full-tilt at the nearest cannon. The Government, now fully conscious of the Gallican tradition behind it, allowed the papers to publish both documents unofficially, but refused permission for the bishops to read them from the pulpit. 'The vast majority of Catholics', the French Minister told his Ambassador at the Vatican, 'regard with mingled astonishment and disquiet the manifesto which the Holy Father has sent to the faithful. They see in the Encyclical nothing but an attempted apologia for the *ancien régime*.'

Considered dispassionately, neither the Encyclical nor the Syllabus adds anything to age-old Catholic doctrine: if the Church is the custodian of a revealed truth denied to all other organizations, compromise with philosophy, liberalism, pro-

[1] Translated by Henry Bettenson, *Documents of the Christian Church*, pp. 379–81.

MICHON'S DILEMMA

gress and every kind of extraneous idea is not only unnecessary, but must entail contamination and error. But dispassionate consideration was impossible. Though drawn up by theologians, these documents were immediately interpreted in a religio-political sense ('The parliamentary system', announced Veuillot, 'rests on a heretical principle') and the sententious pronouncements of the Pope, which had passed unnoticed when hidden in the lengthy allocutions of the Curia, took on a comfortless rigour now they were exhibited nude in the Syllabus and its appendix.

To do Pius justice, he was, in the words of the French Ambassador, 'a little astonished at the stir created by the Vatican manifesto in the Catholic world'. But his astonishment was nothing to the dismay of the Liberal Catholics. For a moment they even thought of relinquishing control of *Le Correspondant*. The Pope, as they saw, left impotently with the rump of his Papal States, longing for revenge, had presented the anticlericals with such an argument as they might not have found in centuries. On any showing the Syllabus was an enormous blunder, incompetently drafted, based on ignorance, published in pique—a blunder aggravated by the Pope's inability to foresee the probable consequences of his act.

At this juncture Dupanloup intervened brilliantly and persuasively: in January 1865, only a month after the appearance of *Quanta Cura*, he produced a pamphlet entitled *La Convention du 15 septembre et l'encyclique du 8 décembre*. Beginning with the Convention, which he disparaged at length in order to gain himself the Pope's preliminary commendation, he passed on to the Encyclical and Syllabus, explaining that they condemned only a *certain* progress, a *certain* civilization. His exposition was based on a distinction (which had been established only a year before) between thesis and hypothesis: the thesis being the ideal rule of the Church, and the hypothesis reflecting the conditions of this imperfect world; the thesis being the good, the hypothesis the lesser evil. Thus although the Church had never admitted heresy's right to exist, Protestants and even atheists were tolerated without being approved. Intolerance represented the thesis, tolerance the hypothesis; so that *Quanta Cura* and the Syllabus expressed a point of view which no one dreamed of putting into practice. As Cardinal Antonelli explained in the

Vatican, the thesis was the Pope's unflinching condemnation of
error, whereas the hypothesis was his toleration of synagogues
and Protestant chapels in Rome itself. Or as they said in Paris
after a close observation of the Nuncio's social life, 'The thesis
is to burn M. de Rothschild: the hypothesis is to dine with him'.

From the welcome accorded to Dupanloup's pamphlet—
34,000 copies sold in a few weeks and he received the felicita-
tions of no less than 630 bishops—it was clear that a great
number of Catholics and a majority of bishops were troubled in
mind and conscience about the rigid hostility with which Pius
faced the world. For no one could fail to recognize that the
documents published on December 8th, whether or not they
contained new doctrines or new interpretations, flagrantly and
aggressively defied the principles of forbearance and freedom
which, however imperfectly and uncertainly, animated nineteenth-century political theory. Pius did nothing to allay these
fears. He refused to encourage Antonelli's attenuation of the
Encyclical, and in writing Dupanloup a congratulory brief
about his pamphlet, he concluded with a thrust of malice:

'We therefore express to you the gratitude of our soul, persuaded by the zeal with which you have continued to defend
the cause of religion and truth that you will explain to your
people the true sense of our letters with a diligence and exacti-
tude all the greater because of the vigour with which you have
refuted the erroneous interpretations they have received.'

If there was one man who rejoiced at Pius's acts, it was
Veuillot, who had been in Rome most of the winter and striven
hard to discredit and refute Dupanloup. It is hard to know
which he relished more, the clear-cut condemnations of the
Syllabus or the harsh, inflexible language in which they were
couched. Replying to Dupanloup in an enormous pamphlet,
he trounced all victims of the 'liberal illusion' and adjured his
readers:

'We must all gather round the Sovereign Pontiff, follow unflinching his inspired commands, affirm with him the truths
which alone can save our souls and the world. . . . Let us hurl
ourselves into obedience. Obedience will give us the solidity of
stone, and on this stone, *hanc petram*, truth will set her triumphant foot.'

The Vatican Council loomed ahead.

PART THREE

Veuillot's Triumph

CHAPTER I

The Priest

⬥⬥══════════════════════════════════════⬥⬥

It is the pride and the weakness of social history that it deals in generalities. The individual who, standing alone, appears insignificant and puny, acquires a conspicuous importance when he is joined to a group: he becomes a trend, a movement, a tide of opinion. But at the same time as he takes on this influence and power, he ceases to be himself: his individuality, that which divides and distinguishes him from tens of thousands of other men, slips through the chinks of the generalization, and his essential nature is obliterated by the mere exercise of the plural. Thus to speak of priests in the mass is to neglect the priest in the particular: his personal, inalienable emotions fall through the mesh, leaving only an outline of behaviour, a conventional graph, a mensurable approximation to the norm where only the norm is calibrated.

An account of the past that does not relate every detail of every happening and of each individual biography is inevitably a summary and a simplification—a summary of events and a simplification of character. However necessary it may be to the understanding of processes of change and to the apprehension of patterns of behaviour, it represents something less than the truth, a half-truth perhaps, a quarter-truth more probably. By neglecting some events and telescoping others it may achieve its own degree of clarity, justifying its cavalier disregard for much that is relevant, but its validity depends on the recognition that it is only a selection, an intellectual convenience, a fallible sifting of accumulated material.

The danger of being misled by the nature of generalization is never more acute than in dealing with religion; for perennial doctrines and age-long customs confer a homogeneity on religious history—a homogeneity which is spurious outside a narrow compass. Because the same beliefs are taught in the same phraseology in the same church with only slight variations from century to century, it is easy to conclude that the priest's role in the community remains unaltered. Because Christmas and Easter recur with the regularity of seed-time and harvest, it is a facile assumption that the Christian Church is as immutable as the Christian festivals. Because the passage of a thousand years brings as little variation to the shape of the cross as to that of the ploughshare, one readily infers that its workings are as fixed as its design. But all these suppositions are false: the soutane and the chasuble are merely vestments, cloaking men that differ and change and develop. Mutability, variability and adaptation represent the rule and not the exception.

If, then, we pause in the year 1865 and look for a priest who will in himself sum up all the priests of France, we shall be disappointed. He does not exist: more than that, he cannot even be postulated. In each parish there is a man of a different age, a different background, a different temperament, perhaps even a different theology. To erect him into a type is at once a naïvety and an insult. Some of these priests (one plunges immediately into the plural and the individuals glide through the mesh) are Gallicans, some republicans, a few even Socialists. At the risk of inevitable inaccuracy, however, it is possible to be more precise. For with a fairly high death-rate among the clergy (whose life-span is usually longer than that of any other section of the community) few priests lived much beyond sixty, and the average age of the priesthood would fluctuate around forty. Let us take this priest of forty. Born in 1825 he has grown up amid the agitations of the *parti catholique*. Springing from peasant stock, he looks back on Louis Philippe as a bourgeois enemy of religion. In his youth he welcomed the February Revolution, but in middle age he deplores it. Indeed he has come to regard revolution with horror and republicanism with fear. He is happy to know that the Second Empire recognizes the place of religion and protects its ministers. Not that he admits any dynastic ties. His schooling by the *parti catholique* and his reading of Veuillot (for Veuillot's pamphlets still compensate in part for the silence of *L'Univers*) have taught him to exalt the political interest of

Catholicism above the ambitions of any royal clique. Napoleon III, he realizes, is not a Christian Emperor; and, dependent as he is on his peasant upbringing and his seminary training, he would prefer to see a Bourbon on the throne. But as the Bourbon pretender is far removed in exile, he accepts the Second Empire as an efficient agent of right-wing politics and as the regime most beneficial to the Church. Politics he conceives of inevitably in terms of personalities. In his village (for in 1865 most priests were country priests) the rich bourgeois stands for Louis Philippe, the *seigneur* for the Bourbons, and the school-teacher—if there is a state school—for atheism and republican-ism and Satan; while Napoleon III's regime is represented by the *maire*, a bourgeois not unfriendly to the ceremonies and causes of religion. Indeed the priest's congregation consists of all those forces in the community—peasants, landowners, a sprinkling of bourgeois—who are content with the present political and social order and tolerate, when they do not approve, Napoleon III's efforts in restoring stability to the country.

Within this narrow horizon the priest moves contentedly, conducting the offices with little realization of the social con-flicts and perils that beset his church. Weaned on the acid intolerance of Veuillot, he has witnessed enough disorder to detest and denounce it. Relying on the nobility for financial support, he leans on them also for political guidance. At election time he pursues the course suggested by *L'Univers*, urging his penitents to follow his example. His arguments are all the more powerful in that, if we exclude the nobility, he is probably one of the half-dozen literate men of the village. He can talk theology, read Latin.

Not that his opinions, if we test him with questions, will appear either original or enlightened. No doubt he bears an occasional grudge against his bishop and perhaps against his other superiors in the ecclesiastical hierarchy. But the adulation which he refuses to the bishop he accords in full measure to the Pope. For Pius is his lord, his master, his ideal. In all times of personal distress he looks to Rome for understanding and relief, and when the Pope himself must submit to humiliation and wrong at the hands of the modern world, the heart of the priest overflows with indignation and pity. The Pope is all-good, all-wise, all-comprehending: he is entitled to implicit obedience and loyalty. About the leaders of the French Church the priest is less decided. Veuillot, of course, possesses such political insight and power of expression that one can safely overlook his lay position. Dupanloup, on the other hand, bishop though he is, seems an ambiguous character, so formidable as to be suspect. Lacordaire? Certainly a great orator, but tainted by his early association with Lamennais: strange that Mgr Gerbet, Mgr Salinis, Dom Guéranger, Mgr Donnet should rise to such eminence, while Lacordaire, with no darker stain on his past, should remain in relative impotence. As for Michon, he is a public danger, a hothead, a renegade, perhaps even an apostate.

But the priest, though quick with his judgements, is slow with his explanations. Were he to expound the doctrine behind the Syllabus, complete with thesis and hypothesis, his wits would be sorely tried. Dealing with simple people, he administers simple ideas: and their lucidity is sometimes a danger. He leads, as even his enemies admit, an honest life of unassuming piety, into whose narrow confines doubt, despair and rationalism seldom stray. He has long since cast behind him the otiose studies of his seminary days; no intellectual curiosity disturbs the calm assurance of his faith. If the name of Renan has reached his ears, it is through the columns of *L'Univers*, through the chaffing of some cabaret anticlerical or through his bishop's pastoral charge; but he would as soon enter the gates of hell as open a page of *La Vie de Jésus*. True, he looks askance on the excessive zeal of the *missionnaires* as they lead revivalist meetings across the country; but his distrust springs in part from the traditional rivalry between irregular and regular clergy. Having discarded the Gallican, Jansenist rationalism of the eighteenth century, he is not sceptical by nature. No one welcomes more than he the growing cult of Mary and the saints. He would approve the spirit if not the expression of the letter one of his colleagues has addressed to the author of *Le Maudit*:

'Accursed priest, execrable, infamous, excommunicated apostate! Long live God! Long live Jesus our Saviour! Long live his Church! Death to traitors!'

Dealing with a priest of this kind, anticlericals had a simple task: they neglected his virtues and magnified his defects. It was indeed unfortunate for the Catholic cause that after the decline of *L'Ami de la Religion* there was no organ of opinion reaching the parish clergy which counselled moderation in belief and discretion in behaviour. All the weight of *L'Univers* and then *Le Monde*, all the authority of the Pope, were thrown on to one side of the scales, and apart from the limited operations of the Liberal Catholics and a rare and timid bleat from the bishops there was no counterpoise.

Intransigence swept the country, acquiring epidemic proportions. The doctrine of traditionalism, which had been condemned in Bonnetty's writings, now emerged in a less reputable but more seductive form. It was argued that according to tradition and legend the founders of Christianity in many parts of France had been apostolic figures. There was nothing but legend to support this contention—no documents, no memorials, no evidence of any kind. But the mere word 'tradition' seemed to carry with it an ancient authenticity, successfully disguising the novelty of the teaching which it was employed to justify. By a curious reversal of normal historical procedure the onus of disproof appeared to lie with the opponents of the legendary school, and the doctrine of apostolicity, though winning a negligible number of adherents from archaeologists and historians, so far imposed itself on the French Church that by about 1885, when Duchesne had the temerity to teach that Saint Sabinian, the first Bishop of Sens, was not one of Christ's seventy-two disciples, the reigning Archbishop of Sens attempted to deprive him of his professorship. Even today these spurious doctrines still command widespread belief among the French clergy and faithful.[1]

The priests of the Second Empire were on the whole glad to accept and disseminate a teaching which conferred additional authority on their Church. Unaccustomed to sift evidence, they regarded hesitation as a defect in faith. Their willing credulity would have done them less harm had it been more discriminating; but to many outside and even inside the Church it forfeited a large measure of its merit when it was directed at swallowing discreditable, faintly ludicrous and even obscene

[1] See A. Houtin, *La Controverse de l'apostolicité des églises en France au XIXe siècle, passim*; M. de la Bedoyere, *The Life of Baron von Hügel*, pp. 48–9; V. Carrière, 'Pour refaire la "Gallia Christiana"', *Revue d'histoire de l'Eglise de France*, 1933, XIX, p. 211.

anecdotes and traditions. There was, for example, the unfortunate affair of the Abbey of Charroux. In 1855 some Ursulines, while carrying out repairs on the ancient fabric, discovered two reliquaries which, on being opened, revealed decayed and unwholesome fragments. One of these reliquaries was confidently declared to contain a relic from the Circumcision, and the Bishop of Poitiers, somewhat embarrassed by this unexpected find, decreed its public display every seven years. The jubilation of the local Intransigents was answered by the delighted mockery of the anticlericals: it was left to the moderates, and to men like Michon, to deplore this impassioned discovery of irrelevant debris.[1]

In such an atmosphere a firm faith was the best defence against good taste and sound reason: indeed taste and reason were hard to reconcile with a religion whose loudest exponents were its most credulous publicists. Possessing faith, one renounced common sense; or pursuing reason, one abjured Catholicism. For us, who survey the Second Empire at the comfortable remove of almost a century, it seems strange and barely credible that to the mass of Frenchmen the articles of faith should have appeared to entail the acceptance of medieval eccentricity and modern superstition. But only a small minority were sufficiently independent and critical to winnow the chaff from the grain: the rest accepted or rejected chaff and grain together. Throughout the Second Empire there was a steady, unflagging growth of anticlericalism: even at a time when the Church was slowly recruiting new members, its opponents were rapidly gaining adherents from the ranks of those who had hitherto been vaguely deist or entirely indifferent. From about 1860 this movement acquired a new momentum. Fostered by the differences between the Government and the Church, strengthened by the greater freedom accorded to antireligious literature, encouraged by the stupefaction that greeted the Syllabus, it took hold of the youth of the country and linked republicanism with unbelief. Jean Macé founded his League of Education to secularize the mind of the nation; the International Society of Freethinkers was formed, enlisting members who undertook to have no priests at birth (if they had been baptized,

[1] J. H. Michon, *Le Moine*, especially p. 196. A. Houtin, *La Controverse de l'apostolicité*, pp. 98–9.

the matter could unfortunately not be rectified), no priests at marriage and no priests at death. And did not Ranc, a well-known freethinker, even hesitate to join the Freemasons because they acknowledged the Great Architect?

It was, in fact, through Masonry that these ideas were spread across the country, for the lodges were among the few meeting-places of the Second Empire where opinions could be freely expressed and exchanged. Not that Masonry had always been sympathetic to republic and revolution: the Great Revolution of 1789 dealt it a stunning blow from which it barely recovered. But it preserved a tradition of free thought and independent inquiry which had already earned it a long series of papal condemnations. Run by members of the bourgeoisie, it breathed a spirit of sceptical complacency and scientific optimism. For sixty years it had led a vegetable life of more or less harmless ritualism and radical orthodoxy; but now, under the impulsion of new members to whom fraternity was more than a conventional phrase, it moved sharply to the left and in spite of its protection by Napoleon III bred secret aspirations for a republican government. Massol was already urging that all mention of the existence of God or the immortality of the soul should be expunged from the constitutions. In townships, communes and villages all over France proselytes were sought: doctors, chemists (the descendants of Homais), shopkeepers, schoolteachers, excited each other with the vision of a new era of liberty, equality and fraternity, using their business and professional connections to gather fresh recruits and to inspire them with a new spirit of secular self-confidence. Tolerance became intolerant: indifferentism was obligatory. More and more understood freedom in the sense of the journalist who wrote, 'Freedom of religion has been proclaimed in Spain; all the convents are suppressed'.

Now freedom is indivisible: either it is generally shared or it does not exist. True freedom cannot be relative, conditional, or hedged with safeguards. If a man in any society appears to enjoy freedom while his neighbour suffers from checks and restraints, his freedom is a sham and a deceit; for freedom entails the existence of a free society. It cannot be the privilege or the monopoly of a few without denying its own philosophical basis. It is true that from time to time political, social and economic conditions occur in which one class, favoured by the conjunction of circumstances, appears to benefit from an accidental freedom; but unless there exists a political idea to reinforce, establish and spread this condition, it is only temporary, succumbing to the onslaught of social strife and historical change. Noblemen cannot be free while their vassals are in servitude; the Church cannot be free while its enemies are denied all power of self-expression; workers cannot be free while they insist on a closed shop.

It was because both the enemies and the defenders of Catholicism failed to realize the absolute implications of freedom that they were unable to clothe their views in an acceptable and permanent form. Each side invoked freedom when they were in danger and ignored it when they were in power. The bishops of Louis Philippe, aspiring to a greater control over education, had displayed a most unepiscopal concern for universal freedom; but as soon as Napoleon III was safely installed at the Tuileries and the clerical interest was reasonably assured, the chorus modulated into another key. Freedom had been a mere expression, a polemical weapon for the embarrassment of the July Monarchy. Now it was enveloped with a prudish silence. When Montalembert's small group attempted to revive it, they were denounced for a gross infringement of the decencies of organized religion.

One would think that the republicans, with the great tradition of liberty, equality, and fraternity behind them, would have perceived more readily the general application of the revolutionary idea. And so, in fact, for a few weeks in 1848, they did. But the alliance of the Church with the Second Empire, and the growth of an aggressively secular philosophy among its opponents, led republicans to conceive of freedom as a means of subverting the Catholic faith. It was not the mere prospect of freedom that excited them, but the freedom to secularize education, to expel monks and nuns, to humiliate bishops.

True freedom is neither a device in controversy nor a means of oppression, but until both parties understood that simple truth, there was no hope of pacification in religious strife. Peace, when it came, would demand from Catholics the recognition that Catholicism was the religion of only a minority of

Frenchmen; while radicals would have to concede that Catholics had always filled, and would continue to fill, a vital place in the nation's history. In the meantime the anticlericalism of café and cabaret found a moderate and able exponent among the Emperor's Ministers. Duruy, who held the portfolio of Education, was himself an avowed freethinker, but he differed from his more voluble supporters in possessing a shrewd grasp of general principles and a keen perception of future political contingencies. Probably he is the most skilful and far-sighted Minister of Education France has ever had. He realized at once the inevitability of universal suffrage and the resultant duty of the State to provide universal education. Moreover he saw that education must be given without charge. If Napoleon's timid opposition prevented Duruy from achieving the full measure of the reforms on which his mind was set, his work is none the less impressive. He multiplied the State primary schools and relaxed the conditions of payment. He reintroduced into the curriculum such subjects as philosophy and contemporary history which Napoleon I had cautiously eliminated sixty years earlier. He created—to the adjectival horror of Dupanloup, the scandal of the Pope, the remonstrances of eighty bishops—a secular framework of secondary education for girls which, though approved by so conservative a woman as the Empress Eugénie, was suspiciously shunned by the large majority of bourgeois families.

Duruy was one day to appear as a figure of shining white against the black and sinister silhouette of Jules Ferry, but in the 1860's his proposals were too dangerous and far-reaching not to arouse the Emperor's distrust. Napoleon, in fact, was drawing nearer to the Church: while the Italian episode receded into a discreditable but ever fainter past, the theological merits of order were once more hymned. The charming and ebullient Prince Napoleon fell from favour after an anticlerical indiscretion at Ajaccio: the shrewd and worldly Duc de Morny burnt his papers and curtly died. A little wearily, Napoleon abandoned himself to the conservatism of Rouher and the clericalism of Walewsky. Withdrawing his army from Rome in accordance with the Convention of 1864, he permitted its replacement by a considerable number of volunteers. The arrival of these troops, openly recruited on French soil, not unnaturally threw the Italians into a fury of resentment: every regular soldier who left

Rome was apparently met by a volunteer soldier travelling in the opposite direction. The Italian Government, smarting at what it considered a guileless and outrageous fraud, resolved on the equally disingenuous measure of allowing Garibaldi to organize a force of volunteers on the frontier and to launch an attack on Rome. But Napoleon, who habitually showed hesitancy when decision was called for, now showed decision when a more cautious policy would have been wise. He ordered a regular army back to Rome and thus put new heart into the Pope's defenders. On 3rd November 1867 Garibaldi's forces were met by papal troops outside Mentana and convincingly defeated. It was not a heavy engagement and no more than two hundred French troops were involved. But the presence of the French and their much publicized use of *chassepots* cost France the possible sympathy and aid of Italy in her own hour of peril and distress three years later. 'The assistance which the French troops have afforded the Papal troops against the pseudo-Garibaldians', Veuillot wrote in the meantime, 'is an act of loyalty and honour on which the Government must be congratulated. France has proved true, not only to her engagement, but to her vocation.' France's vocation being, of course, to act as underwriter to the security of the Pope's dominions. Veuillot was asking for the destiny of Rome to hang for ever, like a great question-mark, between France and Italy.

CHAPTER II

The Journalist

Veuillot's opinion was the more powerful because the Government had allowed *L'Univers* to recommence publication. With the return of *L'Univers* the great publicist strode once more onto the stage. Seven years of silence had done nothing to soften his blows or to fluff his pen: he remained true to his own absolutism. His silence indeed had always been relative, for his period of retirement had enabled him to produce a pile of combative pamphlets, ranging in subject from the genius of Pius IX to the wickedness of Molière. As incapable of repose as Dupanloup, Veuillot had seared his enemies in a volume of verse and flayed them in several volumes of prose. But with the familiar columns of his beloved paper once more at his disposal, he regained the power and authority which had made of him the most considered layman in the Catholic world. The mild flutings of *Le Monde* seemed almost ludicrous now that the trumpet tongue of *L'Univers* resounded again across the country. Who were Du Lac and his associates beside the great Veuillot?

Veuillot's presence was in fact a necessary condition for Catholic self-respect. He alone had the genius to turn the tables on the mockers and sneerers of the anticlerical Press—to laugh at them in tones as derisive and destructive as the voice of Voltaire. Where a journalist of less talent would have explained and defended and protested and perhaps allowed himself a little snigger of contempt, Veuillot rushed into the fray with a roar of delight, seeking out his opponents with a furious gusto, curling his lip at their puny resistance, toppling over their careful sophisms with a great shout of scorn. He treated controversy as a kind of physical exercise: his day was not complete without some brush with the enemy. From the offices of *L'Univers* he seemed to scan the country with eager anxiety, longing to catch some anticlerical with his head unprotected, or some Liberal Catholic incautiously bending. A victim once marked meant a pleasure in store. Veuillot fell on him in a fury of indignation, intoning fearful threats, cackling derisive laughter. His prose, at full flood, has a Rabelaisian tang to reinforce its natural directness. To deal a blow he gladly sacrifices elegance for power. He allows himself jokes, puns and brutalities that reveal the Loiret peasant, rolling round his mouth the simple words of old France, savouring their earthy vigour.

But if one met this stocky, pock-marked, pig-eyed journalist in private life, one was conquered by his charm. His contemporaries are unanimous in their tributes. His amiability, says Pontmartin, obliterated all memory of his ferociousness. 'No one', says Sainte-Beuve, 'could meet and talk with him often without recognizing that this celebrated ogre who attracted—and cultivated—so much hatred, was endowed with many private and sociable qualities.' 'You could not enter into relations with him', writes another acquaintance, 'without being both charmed by his urbanity and dominated by the majesty of his character.'[1] Veuillot plodded across the room with the sturdy determination of a labourer following the plough and peered myopically into the faces of his guests. (So weak were his eyes as a result of his prolonged night-work both as a clerk and as a journalist that sometimes, unable to write or to read, he left his offices and walked around the streets of Paris, avoiding sun and light, composing verse to occupy his mind.) But if his soft, rather husky voice and provincial accent blunted the edge of his formidable reputation, there was nothing provincial about his opinions or soft about his character. Like the Papal Nuncio he practised the hypothesis in society: putting down his pen, he dropped his hatreds and became an easy, fluent companion, a witty and amusing host. In his house in the rue du Bac, he entertained guests of every shade of opinion, from acrimonious Intransigents to caustic rationalists. Strangers who came expecting to meet a daunting swashbuckler were sur-

[1] A. de Pontmartin, *Souvenirs d'un vieux critique*, 6e série, p. 74; Sainte-Beuve, *Nouveaux Lundis*, I, p. 68; *Le Monde Illustré*, 14th April 1883, p. 230.

prised, and even a little disappointed, at his gentility of manners and charm of conversation.

Veuillot had, in fact, a consistent toughness of fibre. He was sufficiently strong to be independent of his own rhetoric. All the indignation and anger of *L'Univers*, despite their impassioned sincerity, could not dispel the calm which lay in his heart—deep and wide as the ocean, cooling his ardour, replenishing his courage, assuaging his resentment with the consciousness of an inexhaustible inspiration and refreshment. Behind all the bustle of charge and counter-charge he remained quiet in his centre. It is true that he propelled his insults like shuttlecocks and played with his innuendoes like bubbles of soap. But he felt that the essence of his opponents was never really involved in his personalities: however sarcastically he might inveigh against 'Monseigneur Félix', however ruthlessly he might harass 'Falloux *fallax*', there was a point beyond which his attacks could not reach, a point where the real Dupanloup and the real Falloux could take refuge. Veuillot was under the disarming impression that in attacking people he was attacking ideas, that the private personalities of his victims were never in question, that his blows were levelled at the public figures who were known by the same names. When he launched a campaign against Dupanloup, his shafts were directed at the Bishop of Orleans who wrote pamphlets, supported *Le Correspondant* and occasionally resented offensive remarks in *L'Univers*. Veuillot bore no grudge against the man to whom these incidentals were attached: in some ways he rather admired him. Indulging rarely in the luxury of resentment, he attributed a similar abstinence to his opponents and never admitted that he had given ground for permanent offence. At the censure, abuse and calumny that showered upon him, he remained naïvely indignant, explaining them as the products of malevolence and hatred. He was himself bereft of malice. Why should not his opponents be bereft of spleen? But it was too much to ask. When Dupanloup opened the pages of *L'Univers* at some incisive and acrimonious attack on his political ideas, his ecclesiastical policy and his theological orthodoxy, it failed to occur to his unimaginative mind that the Dupanloup who was mentioned in the article was not precisely the Dupanloup who read it. Nor did he hesitate to identify the Veuillot who edited

L'Univers with the Veuillot whom he met—and avoided—in society.

But the closer one comes to Veuillot the man, the more approachable does he seem. As a publicist he is so excessive as to be a liability: as a polemist he is so talented as to be intolerable. But in the narrow domain of the family he emerges as a fond brother, a devoted husband, an adoring father. He exemplifies all the admirable but irritating domesticity of French life. His correspondence, which his devotees rather optimistically set up to rival the correspondence of Flaubert and Voltaire, shows him occupied, from day to day and from year to year, with his duties as a Catholic and his obligations as a *père de famille*. Once the hurdle of conversion is crossed, he swerves neither to right nor to left, but pursues a steady, faithful course, marching on with proud confidence that the heavens above him are aglow and that their light will not fail.

Veuillot, who as a young man had fought two duels in twenty-four hours and incurred debts of more than 5,000 francs, carried over into Catholicism the same bellicose attitude towards his enemies. Duels he still fought with the enemies of the Church, but he used a deadlier weapon than the pistol or the rapier. Debts he still acknowledged, but they were paid to charity. His prose retained the bite of Voltaire while his private life took on the placid inevitability of Joseph Prud'homme. Or at least he strove to make it placid. He married at thirty-two 'a sweet creature', he says, 'who will never be troubled by the itch to read or write. She finds her happiness in prayer, her duty in serving me, her relaxation in mending old clothes.' Not, one might imagine, the ideal wife for an intellectual like Veuillot. But when she died, Veuillot was deeply moved, nor did he ever replace her. In their seven years of married life she fulfilled her domestic duties to the extent of bearing him six daughters, and he lost them one by one. Four died—three in the space of two months under circumstances so distressing that Veuillot's memory always bore the scar; one married; one took the veil. Thus when he was old and sick and needed consolation and encouragement, nothing remained to him of his marriage. He was left with only his sister Elise, an Ultramontane Gorgon, a stern, skinny creature whose devotion to her brother was expressed by a frigid efficiency in running his household, and under whose rough, affectionate, but barely tolerable rule he was condemned to spend his sad declining years.

Yet under the impact of calamity Veuillot did not flinch. The faith which his enemies described as an insincere pose sustained him, kept him rigid and resilient. 'There is no joy in the world', he wrote in his darkest moment, 'that I would willingly exchange for my immense grief.' And again, when his last daughter died: 'How great are the miracles God works for us and how little gratitude we show! What mercy to vouchsafe us the deepest peace in the greatest pain!'

Of such avowals he would have been incapable without a sure conviction that his articles in *L'Univers* played an important part in the divine purpose. It is true that he based his conviction on the repeated approval of Pius IX, for to Veuillot the Pope often seemed rather more than a man. But even to his own untutored gaze the achievement was respectable: he looked at his work, and behold, it was very good.

'The truth is', he wrote towards the end of his life, 'that if I judge by the light of human reason, I have played the role of a dupe. I have defended capital without ever possessing a penny's worth of savings, defended property without owning an inch of land; defended aristocracy—I who have scarcely met more than a couple of aristocrats; defended royalty in a century which has not seen and will never see a king. All these things I have defended out of love of the people and love of freedom; and I enjoy such a reputation as an enemy of the people and of freedom that at the first good opportunity I shall find myself strung up on a lamp-post. Yet my thought is straight and logical; but I have placed too much belief in duty and spoken of it too often. That is my only consolation when I consider, alas, all the things I have left undone. . . .'

It was, in fact, Veuillot's immense advantage to see one clear duty like a full moon hanging in an empty sky; and it was his immense virtue to remain unflinchingly loyal to it. He was not dazzled or bewildered by the flashing of innumerable will-o'-the-wisps, all equally bright, all equally seductive. There was one light alone to illuminate his firmament, a light whose radiance neither dimmed nor faltered, but remained shining for ever with a serene unearthly splendour.

His recognition of a single duty released all the forces of his personality and charged them with a tireless power. Fatigue and boredom remained strangers to him until at last his over-taxed body began to break up. Sitting in his office, he performed functions that would more naturally have been shared by half a dozen men. From early morning to late at night he was riveted to his desk, analysing rival papers, reading correspondence, glancing at books, receiving and welcoming visitors, planning the next number of *L'Univers*, allocating work to his staff, correcting proofs, and then writing the articles that bore his signature.

From his devotion to duty, too, he drew the firmness and vigour of his style. He wrote as a man who has never known the meaning of doubt.

'A journalist's talent', he said, 'is shown in swiftness, colour, and, above all, clarity. He has only a single sheet of paper and sixty minutes in which to explain the point at issue, refute an adversary and set out his own opinion. If he uses a word that does not get to the heart of the matter, if he utters a sentence that is not immediately understood, he has failed in his job. He must be quick, clear and simple. A journalist's pen enjoys all the privileges of untrammelled conversation, and he must make use of them. But without ostentation. Let him fear eloquence above all things. At the most he can salute her on the cheek if she comes to meet him. . . .'

These were his own principles. He shot as straight as an arrow for the centre of the target. He ignored qualifications, abjured hesitations, trampled on prevarications. His prose, for all its hidden skill, has the plain structure that comes of a passion for truth. It is as direct as a punch on the nose. But its plainness and lucidity are deeply embedded in the tradition of the language. Perhaps no one has written a more *French* French than Veuillot. If he loved Rabelais and Saint-Simon, he had studied Le Sage and La Bruyère—had given to his style a mould which would receive the homeliest metaphor without any loss of tone or elegance. His prose is in constant movement, its metaphors biting, its rhythms shifting, its arguments clicking into place. In terms of English it combines the simplicity of Shaw, the structure of Dryden, and the colour of D. H. Lawrence.

But is a plain prose the right vehicle for theological arguments? Had Veuillot been no more than a political columnist, chalking a long run of points against his adversaries, his methods would call for admiration even if his doctrines carried no conviction. And a political columnist of course he was. But at the same time he aspired to be a Christian advocate and a theological controversialist, explaining the faith to unbelievers and correcting the vagaries of his fellow Catholics; and in these duties his methods, however efficient, were often an embarrassment. The point is not an academic one. For Veuillot not only spoke for himself but for a generation of priests, and the echoes of his work went on reverberating long after his death, down the distorting caverns of *La Libre Parole* and *L'Action Française*. He created a tradition of aggressive apologetics, of sarcastic theology, whose success was to hang like a millstone round the necks of his less pious, less submissive, less talented retinue. Veuillot prepared the way for Drumont and Maurras, both of whom he would have repudiated. Indeed, the Catholic Press is still haunted by the figure of its most brilliant and most injurious representative.

No doubt plain prose and plain thought have their place in the exposition of basic doctrines, but when they are used in argument, their effect is to destroy the essential subtleties of distinction and to reduce reasonable statements to crudity, while their direct emotional appeal turns easily to anger and abuse. This is always true, whatever the circumstances; but it applies particularly to Veuillot, for his straightforward style reflects a natural bluntness of thought. Moreover this bluntness is made the more conspicuous and uncompromising by two circumstances: the professional omniscience of the journalist, which leads him as a purveyor of information to write as though he is master of every detail and intricacy of his subject; and Veuillot's own aggressiveness of faith. He is not merely combative in argument, but combative in belief. He seems to regard each new item in the list of Catholic devotion as a challenge to his power of assimilation. When he has swallowed the camel, he devours the gnat. In his own phrase he 'hurls himself into obedience', treating orthodoxy as an athletic exercise in which the capacity for belief is daily stretched and extended. There is not an episode in the history of the Roman Church which he is not prepared to defend and proclaim. The Inquisition? A divine institution. The dragonnades? An excellent means of converting the faithless. The Massacre of Saint Bartholomew's Day? A justifiable measure of rigour. Every great scandal in the Church's history he examines and approves. Calas, he thinks, was rightly executed. As for the persecution of Protestants in general:

'For my own part, I will say it clearly and frankly, before I explain my views in detail: if there is anything to be regretted in the whole affair, it is that John Huss was not burned sooner and that Luther was not burned at all; that at the beginning of the Reformation there was not a prince in Europe with enough piety and statesmanship to undertake a Crusade against the countries that had been infected. John Huss's heresy caused the death of 300,000 men, Luther's has destroyed millions, and the list of victims is still not closed.'

The vigour with which Veuillot defended untenable positions was a direct reason for the growth of superstitious intolerance among his followers—an intolerance which gradually pervaded the whole of the French Church. He was that most dangerous kind of apologist—the man who does not know how much can safely be conceded to his opponent, the man who, in all good faith and loyalty, takes over with his religion every trivial impurity and dishonesty, exerting his talent to surround with high battlements the worthless constructions of those who lack half his power or merit. He sedulously cultivated intellectual hebetude. Not only did he trust in the liquefaction of the blood of Saint Januarius and in the appearance of the Virgin at Lourdes: he even believed in the miraculous translation of the Santa Casa to Loreto. As Schérer once said, Veuillot would have believed that Jonah swallowed the whale.

CHAPTER III

The Liberals and the Council

Through almost the entire pontificate of Pius IX the Liberal Catholics were faced with a difficult and indeed insoluble problem: how to remain true to their liberalism without appearing disobedient to the Pope? Occasionally the wind would veer in their favour: whenever temporal sovereignty was in question, Dupanloup sprang into voluble eminence. But the policy of Pius was consistently directed at the encouragement and strengthening of Intransigence both in politics and theology; with the result that Veuillot and his school could pose as the favoured and devoted children of the Holy See.

No doubt it would become clear under Leo XIII that the Intransigents were conspicuous more for their self-righteousness than for their obedience, but for the time being no flaws could be perceived in their Ultramontane ardour. Indeed, so close were their relations with the Vatican that many observers blamed them for much of Pius's political unwisdom.

'The French clergy', Circourt told Nassau Senior, 'is accused of being Ultramontane. It would be more true if the Pope were called Cismontane. Since our occupation of Rome his whole policy, ecclesiastical as well as civil, has originated in France. Our bishops and our clergy are his advisers; they are the public whose applause he courts. It is an unfortunate change. The experience of nearly two thousand years had gradually elaborated in Rome a policy of caution and reserve and patience, suited to a power peculiarly founded on opinion. Our violent bigoted clergy, ignorant of the world, ignorant of any country except France, and of France except their own neighbourhoods, ignorant of history, ignorant indeed of human nature, are driving him to an aggressive intemperate interference in Germany, in England, indeed, in Italy, which is shaking his spiritual influence, and must precipitate the fall of his temporal power.'[1]

It is an overcharged but veracious picture.

Although, therefore, theory did not demand that an Ultramontane should be an Intransigent, in practice the Liberal Catholics were forced into the arms of the few remaining Gallicans; and as the Second Empire grew more liberal, both forces, seeking further support, drew nearer to Napoleon III. Liberal Catholics, who included many of the eminent figures of Church and State, perceived in the political development of the regime some promise that control of the country would eventually pass into their hands and that they could defeat the morose imprecations of the Syllabus by showing them to be unfounded. Gratry, in his *discours de réception* at the Academy, lucidly defended Liberalism; Hyacinthe raised echoes of Lacordaire from the pulpit of Notre-Dame; and Maret, the Gallican Socialist, revenged himself for the distrust of Rome by becoming theological adviser to the Emperor and to the Minister of Religion. Even the Jesuits, who were so often accused of obscurantism, ran a periodical which was at constant variance with Veuillot. No wonder the Liberal Catholics were not disquieted at the future; no wonder they awaited with confidence a progress that seemed inevitable; no wonder their less responsible members, striving to keep abreast of events, committed embarrassing indiscretions. Did not Gratry and Hyacinthe join Protestants and freethinkers in the Ligue de la paix? Did not Michon, in spite of reproof, remain obstinately attached to a society formed by Catholics, Protestants and Jews to undertake a new translation of the Bible?

But it is time to make the acquaintance of the most sinuous and skilful ecclesiastical opponent of papal power, 'a man [as even Manning admits] of great culture and intellectual gifts', the last inheritor of Bossuet's tradition, who was to see his cause irremediably defeated and was himself to fall to the bullets of a firing squad. From the moment in January 1863 when he became Archbishop of Paris, Mgr Darboy stood out as the leader of the antipapal movement in France. Darboy in the

---

[1] Nassau Senior, *Conversations with M. Thiers, M. Guizot, etc.*, I, pp. 357–8.

Senate, defending the Organic Articles; Darboy in his pastoral charge, minimizing the Syllabus; Darboy in Paris, defying the decrees of the Congregation of the Council in Rome; Darboy in his palace, slipping a letter of papal reprimand into his files and failing to reply; Darboy in private, saying that the Church was run like a market-stall—at almost every juncture in the tortuous relations between France and Rome he was present, discreetly and efficiently impeding the progress of Pius and his devotees.

Yet politically Darboy was not a liberal; distrusting the people, he hated any threat of anarchy. In spite of his origins (he was the son of a humble tradesman) his attitude was one of haughty independence towards all the powers of the realm. 'I will take anything from his lips,' said Napoleon III, 'for it comes from a man who has never flattered me.' And he was equally respected further to the left. 'Come!' Sainte-Beuve wrote to the Princess Mathilde on the day of Darboy's promotion, 'the right Archbishop is nominated: things are not entirely black.' He appears as a lonely figure, remote alike from Dupanloup's bustle and Veuillot's ardour; a man who inhabited a cool region of intellectual appraisal, of check and counter-check. Do not struggle if you cannot win, was his motto: do not threaten if you cannot conquer. Suffering from chronic ill-health, he devoted all his skill to the cause of moderation. Proudly, unobsequiously, he strove to enlist the Emperor's support for the Church, without committing the Church to support of the Empire. In Rome, his concessions were regarded with horror. Did he not conduct the burial service for Marshal Magnan, the Grand Master of French Freemasonry—a service at which (so rumour said) the Masonic emblems were displayed on the catafalque? Did the Pope not accuse him of Febronianism? Even without such deviations his gracious and urbane personality would have failed to arouse enthusiasm among the mass of French Catholics, whose taste was for noisier and more flamboyant prelates. Darboy's influence, by contrast, was exercised in private—in committee, council and chamber. There he was heard with deference; there his calm dignity was better prized. It was clear to his small circle of intimate friends that he, rather than the journalists and the bishops in the public eye, understood and practised many virtues that were forgotten in the stress of theological self-righteousness. The virtue of for-bearance, for example. He could resist the temptation to triumph, could abstain from the pleasure of inflicting a *coup de grâce*. When poor Hyacinthe, after months of self-questioning and hesitation, at last decided to leave the Church, Darboy was one of the few Catholic leaders who did not heap on him re-proaches and contumely. 'No,' said Darboy, 'Father Hyacinthe must be suffering deeply at this moment; and it is wrong to trample on those who suffer.'

But impressively as he rises above the trivialities of sectarian warfare, Darboy was marked by his own provincialism—the provincialism of an assumed class. He possessed none of Affre's hesitant insight into the social problem. It is typical of the intellectual complexities of Catholic politics that such an in-sight was granted to Veuillot, the popular leader of an absolutist party. Veuillot's social awareness was limited: he thought—and was he entirely wrong?—in terms of duties rather than of rights. But at least, within the limits of a philosophy that was to become increasingly unacceptable to the working class, he saw the deep need for wealth to be spread more evenly through society, so that the poor man benefited from the rich man's success. When the Bishop of Geneva delivered a sermon insisting on the obliga-tions imposed by wealth, Veuillot sprang to his support, accus-ing the rich of indifference and the poor of envy, and arguing that charity, which demanded generosity of the giver and humility of the recipient, was the Christian way of redressing the balance. Both Bishop and journalist may have been irritated by the reproach of Socialism which was immediately cast in their faces: but at least they were not dishonoured.

Veuillot, however, was soon to have an opportunity of proving his allegiance to absolutist ideals, for in 1868 Pius, who the previous year had announced his intention of holding an oecu-menical council, issued a Bull of Indiction fixing 8th December 1869 as the date of assembly. It was not a new idea. Pius had conceived it at the beginning of his reign and already in 1864 he consulted a group of cardinals about the advisability of such a step. Not all his prelates were in favour. The Liberal Catholics, who—it seems almost incredible in retrospect—had at first wel-comed the project because the Pope was apparently yielding to the opponents of his autocratic power, became increasingly uneasy as rumours circulated about the probable aim of the Council. Was its function to achieve some *modus vivendi* with the modern world or did the Pope cherish some more sinister purpose—a purpose spelling disaster for the Liberal Catholics? By 1868 Dupanloup's apprehensions had so far crystallized that he wrote to the Pope, asking that the Council should not be long delayed: for delay, as he forbore to remark, could only strengthen the Intransigents and create an atmosphere in which folly and excess, spreading with fungoid rapidity, would cast their spores far and wide in the Catholic world.

This is not the place to recount the history of the Vatican Council, a history which has been admirably told by Mourret in French and Dom Cuthbert Butler in English. But its significance is so deep and far-reaching that we must rapidly survey the pattern of events and observe the principal actors in one of the crucial conflicts of the century.

There is little doubt that by 1869 papal infallibility was tacitly accepted by the vast majority of Catholic theologians all over the world. That a doctrine which had always aroused the fiercest passions among the doctors of the Church—it had even been denied by the Council of Constance and the Pragmatic Sanction of Bourges—should have earned general belief among laity and priesthood alike, was some measure of the rot which had undermined the great Catholic bastions of antipapal theory. The progress of the doctrine and the decline of opposition were both, as we have seen, the results of political change rather than of theological illumination: indeed Napoleon has more right than Bellarmine to be regarded as the begetter of the Vatican Council. But sincerity of belief bears little relation to security of doctrine; too often they are violently at odds; and only in the backwaters of opinion did there lurk a few old Gallicans, like quarrelsome pike, still ready to do battle against their ancient enemies. Even Dupanloup, when he took his doctorate of divinity in 1842, chose for his thesis 'The Infallibility of the Roman Pontiff'. And where Dupanloup approved, the Intransigents were ecstatic.

Pius himself was an ardent believer in the infallibility attaching to his office. Flattered by his entourage, adulated by the faithful, he grew vainer and more autocratic with each succeeding year. As his worldly dominions receded and his physical powers declined, he consoled himself with the steady inflation of his spiritual authority. The promulgation of the dogma of the Immaculate Conception in 1854 was already an exercise in the plenitude of his rights: the Syllabus of 1864 was a proof of his attitude of barren obstruction towards the modern world. Incited—if he needed further incitement—by the Jesuits of Rome, who were traditionally the most strenuous advocates of papal infallibility, he convinced himself that the definition of this dogma would comfort the faithful, discipline the rebellious, and bring heretics and unbelievers streaming into a Church whose authority was miraculously exempt from the contaminations of error.

Not that the question of infallibility was the only business before the Council. True, an inspired article had appeared in the *Civiltà Cattolica*, forecasting that the assembly of bishops would be short and would end with a declaration of infallibility by acclamation; but the article was greeted with such an outcry of indignant protest that the Cardinal Secretary of State disclaimed it and the Pope privately explained that the paper did not express the opinion of the Holy See. Moreover, the Pope also flattered his leisure with visions of a reunited Christendom. He hoped that his reign would be known to history as the greatest pontificate of modern times, in which the work of the Council of Trent was completed, the great schism healed, and the Protestants gathered into the fold: all, of course, under the inspired direction of Pius IX. In the event the three great streams of Christendom, instead of converging, flowed still further apart. The Protestants, though they received no invitations to the Council, rationally expounded the causes for their abstention. Perhaps some hoped to attend; certainly they received no encouragement. To a Scottish Presbyterian who inquired on what conditions Protestants could take part, Manning replied that they must follow the example of the prodigal son: when they reached Rome, theologians would be waiting to convert them by argument. At the same time the letter addressed to the Eastern Churches was prematurely released to the Press, and the Patriarch of Constantinople, who would in any case have found its terms unacceptable, handed back the unopened envelope to the Vicar Apostolic, intimating that its contents

PIUS IX

were hardly less deplorable than the method by which they had been communicated.

By the time, therefore, that the Council opened, all prospect of reunion had vanished. In any case it had been a foolish hope, a typical illusion. Considering the general history of papal politics in the nineteenth century, the lamentable administration of the States, the huge blunders and miscalculations of the popes and their advisers, their sweeping ignorance of the ideas and forces at work in the world, it is barely credible that Rome, in the eyes of Protestants and freethinkers, should have preserved a reputation for serpent-like cunning and Machiavellian craft, or that the old men who inhabited the Vatican should have continued to enjoy from their adherents a respect which even the Caesars might have envied. Apart from the stubborn fortitude of Pius VII and the brilliant diplomacy of Leo XIII the popes, whatever their private virtues and their personal shrewdness, displayed a fundamental incompetence in dealing with the political situation. And not only were they incompetent but uninformed. Hampered by their sovereignty over half Italy, they confused their position as temporal rulers with their position as spiritual leaders. They interpreted a threat to their earthly dominions as a threat to their heavenly power. Blundering through the darkness of the modern world, they groped blindly for some guiding rail which would protect them from disaster. It is a crowning irony that their good fortunate outweighed their lack of skill, that the genius of Napoleon accidentally confirmed the popes in a power which seventeen centuries of Vatican politics had been unable to achieve, and that the initial loss of that temporal sovereignty to which Pius clung with such bitter tenacity ultimately established the Pope in a position of supreme moral and spiritual authority over the whole Roman Communion.

But good fortune—Pius refused to contemplate so pagan a notion. He relied instead on his Cardinal Secretary of State, Giacomo Antonelli, a man who had inexplicably earned a European reputation for political penetration and adroitness. He was, in fact, devoid both of principles and of acumen: he was unable to understand the plainest lesson of the past or to foresee the simplest probabilities of the future. Springing from an old robber family of Sonnino, he inherited the wide mouth, sharp eye and pointed nose of his ancestors: he also inherited their greed. Decorated with a cardinal's hat as early as 1847, he used his position at the Pope's right hand to accumulate a large fortune on his own account and to add to it ancillary fortunes for his relatives. This unusual prelate fiddled with the papal finances and rigged the corn trade. Cavour, announcing his abortive plan for the settlement of the Roman Question in 1860, refrained from mentioning a secret arrangement whereby Antonelli was to be compensated with three million lire and his numerous brothers were to retain their eminent positions. What Antonelli lacked in political insight or theological subtlety, he made up for in acquisitive instinct. Living in his sumptuous apartments in Rome, he displayed a taste for the magnificent which was reminiscent of the Borgias. His flashing jewels, his gorgeous clothes, his fragrant roses and exquisite camellias all bespoke a personality which would have been more at home in the Renaissance than in the nineteenth century. Nothing about him was ordinary except his mind. When he died in 1876, his illegitimate daughter, lured on by that portion of his fortune which had so far escaped her clutches, began a lawsuit which was rich in scandalous revelations. 'Do not speak to me any more about him', said Pius IX wearily when his name was mentioned.

But in 1869 Antonelli still enjoyed the Pope's confidence. It is true, as Catholic apologists sometimes point out, that he was only in minor orders; but that fact did nothing to limit his authority and influence. In his hands lay the preparations for the Council; in his hands, too, the task of defending them. When it was remarked that, contrary to precedent, the Catholic sovereigns had not received invitations, it fell to Antonelli to explain (with a certain pious disapproval) that the King of Italy lay under the ban of excommunication. And he, rather than the Pope, had to ward off the danger of intervention by the European Governments—a project assiduously canvassed by Bavaria.

For it was clear to the opponents of the doctrine of papal infallibility that once the Council had met, there was every likelihood of the dogma being approved. All their talents were turned to the task of excluding the subject before December 8th. Döllinger's articles in the *Allgemeine Zeitung* of Augsburg; his resultant book, *The Pope and the Council*, in which, as Butler concedes, 'a perhaps unique knowledge of medieval and modern church history' was directed against the conception of a political papacy; the 'Laymen's Address' from Coblenz; the pastoral letter from the German bishops at Fulda; Dupanloup's secret interview with Napoleon III; Darboy's expressed opinion that both good sense and history protested against the promulgation of the dogma—there was an almost hysterical burst of activity. Nor were the Intransigents idle. *L'Univers*, in particular, organized a great petition from priests and laity in favour of infallibility, and as the hour of the Council's opening drew nearer, Veuillot surpassed himself in his expressions of delighted anticipation.

Dupanloup, whose forebodings grew steadily darker, suddenly lost his temper. In an *Avertissement adressé à M. L. Veuillot*, published in November 1869, he launched a shattering attack on Veuillot's utterances in the course of the previous ten months, quoting chapter and verse in a way which did credit to the industry of his secretaries even if it sowed doubts about his own fairness of mind. Not that there was no ground for complaint. Dupanloup took particular exception to an article entitled 'Liberals and Monkeys', in which it was explained that the most liberal monkeys were those which lacked tails. For those with a tail 'belong to the moderate party. . . . They always bear their tails raised to heaven, as though to bear witness to the uprightness of their intentions, their love for order, monarchy and true religion, and their sincere wish for conciliation with all except the Jesuits.' Veuillot, while pointing out that the quotation originally appeared in the *Civiltà Cattolica* and not *L'Univers*, refused to disavow the parallel; nor did he abjure his indiscriminate imputation of disloyalty, ignorance and heresy to his political opponents. But it was, of course, his theological extravagance which exposed him to the greatest censure and most infuriated Dupanloup. What bishop could observe with equanimity the rapturous—and wellnigh blasphemous—expressions of devotion to the Pope which issued, for example, in this new version of the Nones hymn where PIUS replaces DEUS?

> *Rerum* PIUS, *tenax vigor,*
> *Immotus in te permanens,*
> *Da verba vitae, quae regant*
> *Agnos, oves et saeculum.*

Such follies Veuillot did not write, but he encouraged and printed them. Dupanloup had every justification for his stinging reproach:

'I especially accuse your excess in doctrine, your deplorable taste for dealing with vexing questions and for propounding violent and dangerous solutions. I accuse *you* of accusing, insulting and calumniating your brothers in the faith. None more than you deserves the phrase of Holy Scripture: *Accusator fratrum!*

'Above all I reproach you with making the Church a partner in your violence, by your unbelievable presumption in expounding as her doctrine your most personal ideas.'[1]

Dupanloup, however, was a less efficient controversialist than Veuillot because of his temperamental inability to restrain his indignation. He preached moderation at the top of his voice. The Bishop in full cry sounds a wilder, more dangerous leader than the journalist at full stretch. Where Veuillot is amusing, Dupanloup is merely angry; he delights his friends—his *avertissement* was as popular as a novel—without converting his enemies. How much deadlier are Veuillot's thrusts can be seen from an unfortunate incident that occurred shortly before the opening of the Council. Father Hyacinthe, whom Darboy had installed in the pulpit of Notre-Dame, had long been striving to sustain his tottering faith; but his own will to believe, the entreaties of his friends, and the foreseeable results of his defection were not strong enough to retain him in the Carmelite order. At the same time as he left it, he forsook the Church. The scandal was great. While Montalembert composed a letter of acid remonstrance, the Intransigents gleefully hailed his departure as though it were a victory.

'Deprived of that religious habit which he discards on the path of modern thought', wrote Veuillot, 'Father Hyacinthe will soon learn, if not the error of his heart, at least the error of his vanity. He derived a certain renown from his habit, which he treated as finery rather than as armour; but "Monsieur Loyson" will be a thing of small account. He can be sure that his last resonant phrase has been spoken. It is all over; the wind drives away the empty cloud. . . .'

[1] Dupanloup's pamphlet is conveniently reprinted, with Veuillot's brief replies, in the second volume of Veuillot's *Rome pendant le Concile*.

Such prose, easy reading as it was, gained far wider approval than the tacit abstention of Darboy.

Meanwhile, as the preparations for the Council advanced, the Freemasons organized an Anti-Council to open at Naples on December 8th, and the Protestants launched appeals for a society which supported Evangelical Churches in Catholic lands. It was clear that among the Catholic bishops themselves there would be three main bodies of opinion. Firstly, the heavy majority of infallibilists; secondly the anti-infallibilists—or opportunists, as they were more properly called; and thirdly, a small independent group whose cautious policy was to be dictated by events. The first body could count on the vociferous applause of *L'Univers*; the third had no following at all; and the second, though representing many scholars, theologians and statesmen, was only supported by small islands of opinion among the laity. For the opponents of the dogma were in a difficult position. If they declared their disbelief in a doctrine which commanded general consent, they would be obliged either to recant or to leave the Church. Moreover, the mere fact of their declaring their disbelief would probably advance the promulgation of the dogma by angering the infallibilist bishops and shocking their hesitant colleagues. What then should be their course of action? They must find a means of opposing without opposing: they must somehow block the dogma and yet appear to support it.

The solution which commended itself was to attack the dogma as inopportune: whether true or not, its promulgation at this point of time would retard the progress of the Church. Apart, therefore, from a few Gallicans like Maret who were cast in the ancient mould, no bishop at the Council dared to assail the dogma of papal infallibility itself. Meanwhile, outside the Vatican, Friedrich, Acton and Döllinger employed all the theologian's skill, the historian's knowledge and the pamphleteer's art to prevent the impending declaration; in France Gratry raised the question of Pope Honorius, who had undoubtedly been guilty of heresy, and Michon, following Gratry's lead, published an open letter to Antonelli, in which he appealed for delay. 'By deciding the question', he wrote, 'you lose some Catholics . . ., you sadden many; you create a deep schism, hidden though it may be in the depths of conscience; you profoundly weaken the Church; and the Easterners and Protestants are for a long time to come alienated from Rome.'[1]

But the bishops who were greeted in Rome on December 8th by the smooth eloquence of Pius IX and the vulpine craft of Antonelli indulged in no such luxuries of doubt. Almost to a man they declared their acceptance of the dogma. Who shall say whether in the privacy of his own mind each cherished a true belief in papal infallibility or merely took exercise in the Catholic virtue of submission? Their biographers, writing after the event, are naturally convinced of their prospective orthodoxy. Darboy, Dupanloup, Rauscher—of course they all believed in the dogma before it was promulgated, of course they all agreed with the overwhelming verdict of the Church.

And yet one has suspicions. Through the mutterings of the committees and the deliberations of the Fathers one hears a thin sharp cry that seems to echo a hidden torment of soul.

Perhaps Michon was right when he hinted at secret doubts; perhaps even in the Vatican itself one could find men with unavowed misgivings. Against the triumphant Ultramontanism of Manning in Rome must be set the nagging fears of Newman in England. Not that Newman expected any strain on his faith; but, as he wrote to his diocesan in a letter that was divulged and became famous: 'When has definition of doctrine *de Fide* been a luxury of devotion, and not a stern painful necessity? Why should an aggressive, insolent faction be allowed to "make the heart of the just to mourn, whom the Lord hath not made sorrowful"? Why can't we be let alone, when we have pursued peace and thought no evil?'[2] In the Vatican itself there is the old Bishop of Evreux, with (in his own phrase) 'tears in his heart', learning from the Secretary General of his see: 'I cannot find a single Catholic layman who does not fear the definition; belief in the new dogma would be a great sacrifice for the Church to demand.'[3] Beside the Bishop of Evreux there is Dupanloup, anxiously confiding to his diary: 'I am writing to M. Ollivier

[1] J. H. Michon, *La grande crise du catholicisme*. Lettre à S.E. le cardinal Antonelli, p. 25.

[2] Quoted by Butler, *The Vatican Council*, I, p. 213.

[3] Mgr Devoucoux. Lettres d'un évêque français pendant le Concile du Vatican, publiées par R. Batiffol. *Revue d'histoire de l'Eglise de France*, 1927, XIII, p. 207.

[i.e. the French Premier]. One must do what one can. But all depends on God.'[1] And with Dupanloup there is the Bishop of Kerry, sombrely admitting: 'The loss of souls who are near and dear to me, the fear of schism, and of secret heresy, make me miserable night and day.'[2] Nor can one forget that letter of Mme Augustus Craven: 'A poor woman, a saintly woman, tried by all manner of misfortune—English, Catholic, fervent and well-informed—who has long been ill, told my husband a few days ago that she was beseeching God to let her die before the promulgation of the dogma, so that she could be saved.'[3] How many more good Catholics were in this anguished dilemma?

Some of the bishops, at least, could hope to evade the problem in the same manner, for many of them were advanced in years and the programme of the Council put a heavy strain on their natural frailty. The procession into St. Peter's which marked the opening ceremony began at 8.30 in the morning, and the final prayers were not said till 3.30 in the afternoon— an unbroken stretch of seven hours which was not alleviated by the heavy rain that fell on Rome all day, or by the total lack of arrangements to drive the old men home. It was not surprising that by the middle of February the number of fatal casualties had risen to ten or that many more were seriously ill. But whether it rained or shone, whether the bishops lived or died, the fragile and obstinate old Pope was still there to urge on his cohorts with a remorseless energy, the indefatigable Antonelli always at his elbow to pit his Levantine cleverness against the opposition intrigues.

Butler considers that the only serious blot on the Council's proceedings was the selection of the crucial deputation *de Fide*; for the inopportunists had only one representative, and he was included by accident, having changed his mind since arriving in Rome. Acton, by contrast, regards the whole episode of the Council as an indelible stain on the history of the Church; but he agrees with Butler in ascribing particular importance to the partisan selection of this deputation. The disingenuous trickery by which the inopportunists were excluded turned the minority into an opposition. Had it not been for this step (Manning was

[1] Quoted by Mourret, *Le Concile du Vatican*, p. 257.
[2] Quoted by Butler, II, p. 28.
[3] Quoted from the archives of Saint-Sulpice by Mourret, p. 128.

apparently responsible), the dogma of papal infallibility would have gained easy acceptance. But it gave the signal for battle to be joined, and though the issue was never seriously in doubt, the Ultramontanes were obliged to wait till July 1870 before they could register their final and definitive triumph.

The French bishops were as prominent as the fame of the French Church demanded. Among the most ardent of Manning's associates was Mgr Pie, Bishop of Poitiers, whose red hair and majestic presence admirably matched his fiery temper and legitimist politics. It came as a surprise to learn that he was the son of a village cobbler. But if his origins were as humble as Dupanloup's, he was better able to curb his impatience, and it must be said to his honour that throughout the proceedings he remained aloof from extraconciliar agitations. Of such detachment Dupanloup was incapable. He multiplied his pamphlets and his warnings; he excited French opinion by his organ *Le Français*; he was constantly closeted with the leaders of the minority. But while Dupanloup, now storming, now wheedling, occupied the centre of the stage, drawing on to himself the bilious hatred of the infallibilists and the frantic applause of the inopportunists, the real leader of the minority was to be seen in the cold, almost marmoreal figure of Darboy. With unflagging courage and unfailing skill he played his meagre cards and watched trick after trick being captured by his opponents. It was Darboy who promoted that insidious but convincing pamphlet, *Ce qui se passe au Concile*; it was Darboy who secretly appealed for Napoleon III's intervention; it was Darboy who saw that the game was finally lost.

But of all the visitors to Rome, the man who exerted the strongest pressure on the outside world was Veuillot. Living near Monte Pincio, he established himself as the Pope's most reliable mouthpiece. At his headquarters the leaders of the infallibilist party were often to be seen—Manning with his tall figure and ascetic features, Pie with his high colour and daunting presence. Veuillot was always best informed of what was passing in the Council, always most familiar with what scheme was next afoot. Despite his selfconscious but sincere protestations that he was no more than a lay journalist, he had the ear of the theologians; he knew what was planned in their secret conclaves. It was his habit to send daily communiqués to *L'Univers*, announcing the dispositions of the enemy, rejoicing in their defeats, calculating their losses; and it fell to his lot to scotch the eccentric and sometimes dangerous rumours that agitated Rome. Was it not even whispered, then denied, then reasserted, then denied again, that a Wallachian spy in the pay of the Italian Government was caught trying to enter the Council disguised as a bishop? Over many such a story—and some of them were true—Veuillot laughed himself hoarse.

His dispatches to *L'Univers* gave a brilliant but one-sided picture of the ponderous advance of the Council to its appointed goal. To every argument he had an answer; for every opponent he had an epithet. The only inopportunist to whom he showed mercy was Darboy; and even there political reasons were paramount, for Darboy was the Emperor's correspondent in Rome. But even Veuillot, despite his genius for distorting arguments and mishandling facts, endured his uncomfortable moments, and one of these occurred on March 12th, when Montalembert, after a final flare of defiant liberalism, was at last released from his struggles by death. What should one say? Veuillot hesitated. Whatever his shortcomings Montalembert was one of the most gifted and devoted servants of whom the modern Church of France could boast; he had been Veuillot's comrade and Lacordaire's friend. Surely he could not be dismissed as a mere lackey of liberalism? The problem was solved by the example of Pius, who remarked when the news was announced: 'A man has died who rendered great services to the Church. . . . But he had one great enemy—pride.' And Veuillot, viewing with the eyes of his master the man who had dared to speak of the 'idol in the Vatican', composed an ingenious obituary in which his regret at Montalembert's death was nicely balanced against his grief for Montalembert's aberrations. But Veuillot's was too ardent a nature to suppress altogether his affection and admiration: the words in which he spoke of his vanished opponent were more generous than the grudging tributes of the Pope.

'His hostility', he wrote, 'has brought us to the cruellest situation of all: we are denied the consolation of praising and mourning him as he deserved. But that necessity cannot withhold our respect, our happy memories, our prayers, our hopes, and one day we shall bear witness to him as he now bears witness to us.'

But the central figure of the Council around whom prelates and journalists, diplomats and theologians, ceaselessly revolved was Pius himself, the man in whose office the miraculous virtue of infallibility was apparently latent. His enemies did not fail to point out the excesses of his eulogists. 'He is Christ on earth', said Mgr de Ségur. 'He is the third visible presence of Christ amongst us', cried Father Faber. These praises were not lacking in effect. Pius, who at the opening of the Council had severely stressed his own neutrality, dropped the mask as the proceedings were more and more protracted. Soon the pamphleteers were unfavourably comparing his attitude to the studied correctness of Pius IV at the Council of Trent. Of his own infallibility Pius entertained no shadow of doubt; and as the Council dragged on through the spring and summer of 1870, he made it plain that those who hindered its promulgation were not only incurring his displeasure but forfeiting their prospects of subsequent advancement. While Dupanloup saw all hope of the purple recede and vanish, anyone who wrote a book against the inopportunists could expect a brief of unstinted praise. Ramière, a nonentity who specialized in abuse of Dupanloup and Gratry, twice received the public congratulations of the Pope. Guéranger, who attacked Maret, was informed by the Pope (speaking of course as a private doctor):

'The adversaries of infallibility are men who, while boasting of their standing as Catholics, show themselves to be entirely imbued with corrupt principles: they reiterate cavils, calumnies and sophisms in order to lower the authority of the supreme head whom Christ has set above the Church and whose prerogatives they fear.'

Altogether it was a discreditable performance by a vain old man who gave ear to none but his own sycophants. What is more surprising than his breathless enthusiasm for his own dignity is the ease with which he convinced his supporters that only true doctrine was at stake. They were so dazzled by the honour of an interview that they did not pause to contemplate the divine being who received them. Elise Veuillot describes with rapture an audience to which she accompanied Louis and his two daughters:

"'I receive people [said the Pope] who ask me to have infallibility proclaimed and who inquire when the proclamation will take place. I reply, 'I cannot have infallibility proclaimed. That is the task of the Holy Spirit. He will do it.'" "The Bishops do not know when infallibility will be proclaimed. But the Pope knows, Holy Father," I said firmly. The Holy Father looked on me with such a smile and so affectionately that I repeated: "The Pope knows." Then his smile grew broader.'[1]

It is curious but typical that such an anecdote could be told and repeated without the faintest hint of criticism.

Pius's temper rose as the year wore on. He supported any of the lower clergy who protested against their inopportunist bishops; he dismissed the learned keeper of the papal archives under suspicion of abetting the opposition; he grew impatient at the delay of the Holy Spirit. In June, when Cardinal Guidi, the erudite Archbishop of Bologna, delivered a speech that unexpectedly reinforced the arguments of the minority, Pius angrily summoned him to the pontifical presence and furiously upbraided him for expressing unworthy and heretical ideas. But, replied Guidi, in surprise, he had merely argued that the bishops were witnesses of tradition. 'Witnesses of tradition?' cried Pius in scorn. 'There is only one. *La tradizione son' io. I* am tradition.'[2]

But by June the Council's proceedings were nearly over. It was clear that the powers would not intervene, and the only danger that still threatened the smooth transaction of business was the possibility of war, which slowly grew into an ugly probability and, in the second week of July, turned to a black certainty. It was a question whether fighting would begin before the new dogma was voted. In the event the dogma won—by a day. Fifty-five bishops of the minority signed a joint letter to the Pope in which they explained that 'out of filial love and reverence' they would absent themselves from the final session. On July 18th in the midst of a great storm that plunged St. Peter's in darkness, the constitution *Pater aeternus* was at last voted to an accompaniment of rolls of thunder and sheets of

[1] Quoted by E. and F. Veuillot, *Louis Veuillot*, IV, pp. 162–3.
[2] For the authority of this story, see Butler, II, p. 98; Mourret, p. 299; E. L. Woodward, *Three Studies in European Conservatism*, p. 338.

lightning. 'In the crowd', says Veuillot, 'some thought of Gallicanism and said: It is a funeral rite! Others thought of the future and said: We are on Sinai.' Still others interpreted the weather as a sign of heaven's disapproval. On July 19th, while bishops began to leave Rome in large numbers, France declared war on Prussia.

CHAPTER IV

Rome and Paris

T he war had an immediate result on the Vatican Council: it caused France to withdraw her army from Rome, and almost exactly two months after the voting of *Pater aeternus* Italian troops took possession of the city. The Pope, who throughout August had maintained an attempt to carry on the Council, found himself technically a prisoner in the Vatican—though, be it said, an unusually independent prisoner —and in October he issued an Apostolic Letter postponing the Council till more propitious times. As a result, the interpretation of papal infallibility, which would certainly have been clarified had the Council met again during the winter, is still a matter of argument and conjecture.

It is easy to assume that the definition of papal infallibility was the only work of the Vatican Council. Certainly the unrealistic hopes of reunion with the Protestant and Orthodox Churches were speedily dashed. But the Council was also active in other spheres—so active, indeed, that the chances of Christian reunion were probably killed for good; for a doctrine that received final authority without any opposition from the minority, was that of papal primacy. No dissentient Church could henceforth claim parity with the Roman Communion: it must either submit or remain apart. The crystallization of this doctrine consummated the divisions of Christendom, and Rome, by setting her house in order, permanently destroyed any prospect of reunion short of the capitulation of her rivals.

But however important the question of primacy may be in its ultimate implications, the dogma that rightly caught the imagination of the world was that of papal infallibility. At a time when the average man in the western hemisphere thought of science as the only corpus of knowledge possessing infallibility, it came as a shock to be told that an old man in the Vatican claimed the exclusive exercise of that power. Infallibility, of course, was a word that had often been used. Protestants sometimes applied it rather incautiously to the inspiration of the Bible: for centuries many Christians had conceived of it as appertaining to the general decisions of the Church. From 18th July 1870, however, every orthodox Roman Catholic has believed that the Pope, speaking *ex cathedra* in matters of faith and morals, is preserved from error and that his definitions are of themselves irreformable. It sounded plain enough at the time: only when one came to analyse the doctrine did it appear vague and unsatisfactory. For when did the Pope speak *ex cathedra*? How was one to recognize an irreformable definition? Fessler, in an authoritative work, declared that the Pope possessed infallibility only as 'the supreme teacher of truths necessary for salvation revealed by God'; Pius himself announced that the deposing power was not, and never had been, part of the doctrine; and Dublanchy, some years later, taught that there had only been twelve papal utterances in the whole of Church history that fulfilled the necessary conditions. But against these attempts to limit the exercise of the power there were corresponding attempts to extend it. Schulte and Ward both argued that whenever the Pope invoked his apostolic office and the plenitude of his power he was using his infallible prerogative: by these signs infallibility could be recognized. Manning, as one might expect, considered that the power covered dogmatic facts, censures less than heresy, canonizations of saints and approbations of religious orders. Even so liberal-minded a theologian as Von Hügel, writing in 1888, declared, 'I myself should say that authoritative Catholic theologians are agreed in ascertaining infallibility to canonizations, papal solemn approvals of religious orders, and to the clenching of doctrinal definition and condemnations through the settling of dogmatic facts.'[1] It is not even certain whether any relevant *ex cathedra*

---

[1] Michael de la Bedoyere, *The Life of Baron von Hügel*, p. 58. On the doctrine on infallibility see particularly, on the Catholic side, Butler's *Vatican Council* (a restrained interpretation), and on the Protestant side, George Salmon's *Infallibility of the Church*, which has recently been republished in a convenient abridgement.

pronouncement has been made since 1870. It seems that the dogma of the bodily Assumption of Our Lady falls in that category. Otherwise the situation is marked by a convenient but peculiar obscurity. As a Catholic lawyer observed, 'When you are infallible, you have to be very careful not to make a mistake.'

Now if this confusion resulted partly from the enforced interruption of the Council, it was also due to the representations of the minority. They could not disprove the dogma; they could not defer its promulgation; but at least, by learned arguments and continuous pressure, they could ensure that its terms fell short of the sweeping definition desired by Manning and Veuillot. Their defeat, though resounding, was not absolute.

No doubt it is necessary to be a Roman Catholic to feel that the dogmas promulgated and the devotions approved in the last thousand years have, under the guidance of the Holy Spirit, led to an increasingly exact formulation of the truth already implicit in the New Testament. The curious admixture of popular piety and scholastic learning which marks this period in the history of the Church appears to have fostered doctrines which would have puzzled and bewildered the apostles. Unless one believes in a divine inspiration that preserves the visible Roman Church from serious error, the corpus of doctrine now taught in all sees dependent on Rome has a paradoxical flavour of archaic novelty, combining the parochialism of the past with the embellishments of the present. But this is not a new process: it has a history of many centuries. Only because of the singularly inept and aggressive policy of Pius IX towards the modern world did it appear in 1870 that the Roman Church had unexpectedly succumbed to an attack of arteriosclerosis. Both the spokesmen and the enemies of Catholicism exaggerated the theological significance of papal infallibility: to the former it was a new suit of armour, to the latter an old talisman. But its real importance was political, for by converting the theory of the pope's doctrinal supremacy into a dogma, it enforced the closer adhesion of all Catholics to the Holy See. Whereas they had hitherto been driven by circumstances and linked by self-interest, they were henceforth bound. In other fields, as anyone who reads the documents can perceive, the Vatican Council did no more than reaffirm traditional teachings in a reasonable

VEUILLOT'S TRIUMPH

form. In some respects it even atoned for the rigours of the
Syllabus. One finds, for example, in Chapter IV of the Dogmatic Constitution of Catholic Faith, given on 24th April 1870:
'The Church neither ignores nor despises the benefits to
human life which result from the arts and sciences, but con-
fesses that, as they came from God, the Lord of all science, so,
if they be rightly used, they lead to God by the help of his grace.
Nor does the Church forbid that each of these sciences in its
sphere should make use of its own principles and its own
method.'[1]

This is the reason why the Vatican Council failed to provoke
the schism that was confidently predicted. Apart from the Old
Catholic Movement in Germany which took its impetus from
the historical scholarship of Döllinger, there were only isolated
defections. When it came to the point, submission was easier
than revolt. Men who had spent their lives within the Roman
Communion had to feel very sure of their history and very
certain of their theology before they dared to defy the might of
their Church. Of the bishops who had formed the minority,
not one failed, in time, to declare his adhesion to *Pater aeternus*.
And even Michon followed their example.

The Intransigents were jubilant and merciless. The Bishop of
Rodez curdled the blood of his clergy by referring to Dupanloup
as 'a second Erostratus' and to Gratry as 'a crack-brained
insulter of the Roman Church'; indeed thanks to such generous
abuse Gratry was reduced to the barest poverty, dying shortly
after his declaration of submission.

But the pleasures of doctrinal conquest were cut short by
war and the prospect of military defeat. The French and
German bishops who had attained such a remarkable degree of
unanimity in Rome, hastened home in immediate discord, calling with inharmonious voices for God's blessing on their respec-
tive armies. In a matter of weeks French resistance was broken,
the Emperor deposed and the future of the State cast into
uncertainty. So distressed and perplexed were Frenchmen at
their own problems that even Catholics could spare only a hasty
expression of sympathy when Rome was overrun and the Pope's

[1] Quoted from Butler, II, p. 267. The whole Constitution is given in
Latin and English, pp. 248–75.

VEUILLOT

temporal sovereignty reduced to an area rather smaller than Hyde Park.

Down at Sainte-Radegonde Michon himself proclaimed the Republic, and it needed all his firmness to avoid election as the village *maire*. In Paris Darboy decided to co-operate with the Government of National Defence and ordered *Domine, salvam fac rempublicam* to be sung once more in the churches of his diocese. Throughout the country priests and monks strove by prayer and supplication to revive the flagging fortunes of French arms. But in spite of the energetic intervention of Gambetta and the occasional successes of his scratch troops, there could be no question of military recovery, and when Paris surrendered at the end of January, it was clear that an armistice could not be long delayed. The preliminaries of peace were, in fact, voted on March 1st—by a new National Assembly which had been elected the previous month. It was a sardonic comment on the state of the country that in this Assembly, which was the first representative body of the new Republic, monarchists out-numbered republicans by two to one. It was the republicans' misfortune that by their adoption of the revolutionary tradition they stood for war, glory and sacrifice; for only the industrial workers who hankered after military glory of the Napoleonic order and had no vested interest in the stability of society voted for the new regime. In rural districts the electors, feeling that they had less to lose from an immediate peace than from a prolongation of hostilities, and fearing that the republicans, even if peace were concluded, would hasten to launch them on a war of revenge, voted conservative. But this was not the only cleavage in the National Assembly. There was a further division, following almost exactly the same lines, which, while testifying eloquently to the politics of the two previous decades, suggested a grim forecast of the years to come: almost without exception, the republican deputies were freethinkers and the conservatives supported the Church.

Not that the Republic showed itself hostile to religion. In the first excitement of Napoleon's fall there had been sporadic out-bursts of violence; but Gambetta's Government was too heavily involved in the prosecution of war to trifle with the luxury of anticlericalism, and once the National Assembly was elected, the Church considered its safety assured. But self-congratulation was premature. On March 18th the revolutionary movement which history knows as the Commune broke out in Paris and eight days later its triumph was consummated in the municipal elections. The club orators who for months had been expending their eloquence on the sloth and corruption of the Church found themselves carried to power on a wave of savage self-pity and bitter hatred. Into the long-term causes of the Commune there is no need for us to inquire: it is enough that the workers, humiliated by the signature of peace preliminaries, resentful at the complexion of the National Assembly, exacerbated by the privations they had undergone during the siege, were all too eager to defy the Government and to name a scapegoat for their present misfortunes. They were not, as the legend has it, devils thirsting for capitalist blood; they were rough, ordinary people, badly treated, ill advised, unwisely led, who allowed their passions to be exploited by conspirators and demagogues, and were glad to avenge themselves for the Days of June.

Thus the anticlericalism which had hitherto been confined to clubs, cabarets and lodges, suddenly erupted in a vicious jet. A fortnight after the beginning of the insurrection the Communards declared the separation of Church and State and the suppression of the Budget des Cultes. Three days later they issued the famous 'decree of hostages', by which all persons suspected of complicity with the Government at Versailles were to be arrested, forming a body of hostages from which suitable victims would be chosen if any of the Commune prisoners were shot. In pursuance of this decree, one hundred and twenty priests were apprehended in a few days, including 'citizen Darboy, calling himself Archbishop of Paris'.

The artificial frenzy that marked the deeds and decisions of the Communards resulted partly from their isolation from the rest of France; but as soon as it became evident that the Government troops were much stronger and better organized than their own unruly forces, this frenzy degenerated into a kind of madness, as though time were running out and every contemplated excess, however wild or bloody, must be perpetrated before the occasion vanished. The Masons, rumour said, were insisting on their pound of flesh. Had they not marched defiantly to the ramparts of Paris, led by venerables who publicly wore their aprons and other insignia? Had they not planted their banners in the face of the regular army? Whatever the complicity of the Masons as a corporate body, the week of bloody fighting, *la semaine sanglante*, which preceded the overthrow of the Commune, was marked by indiscriminate slaughter on either side. The Government troops, fighting their way into the city street by street, sometimes house by house, were excited to a degree of savagery which is seldom reached except in civil war. In the course of a few days they killed about twenty thousand men and women without trial. The Communards replied to this carnage with a butchery as appalling, if less widespread. On May 22nd, after the Commune had met for the last time, responsibility for decisions passed into the hands of individuals. On the same day Darboy and his companions were ordered out of the prison of Mazas to that of La Roquette, and on the 24th a member of the Commune, delivering judgement on his own authority, commanded six of them, including Darboy, to be shot. At half-past seven the same evening, under a sky blackened by the smoke from the burning city, the victims were led out to the end of the rampart and lined against a wall. As the volley rang out all but Darboy crumpled and fell; but he remained, a tall pale figure, tottering slightly, his hand raised in a final benediction. There was a shout of anger from the firing squad. 'The brute must be armour-plated!' one of them cried: 'here comes *our* blessing!' There was a second shot and Darboy sank down in his turn, twitching as the last traces of life were beaten out with the butt-end of a bayonet. In all, out of the seventy-four hostages who were executed in this week, there were twenty-four priests; and so high a proportion grimly indicates the deep anticlericalism of the Commune.

When the news of Darboy's death reached Rome, the Pope, who had been gratified by his belated but unqualified adhesion to the Vatican decrees, remarked contentedly that 'Mgr Darboy has washed out his errors with his blood'. Of Guibert, the new Archbishop of Paris, he was far more confident: at last a man had taken possession of the ancient headquarters of Gallicanism who could be relied on to pursue without deviation the policy of the Holy See. The Government, which would gladly have nominated Dupanloup, was forced to desist on the realization that Pius would never consent. To eyes that looked on the world from Rome, it still appeared that liberalism in any form was more dangerous than the violent creeds of social unrest and that Darboy armed with a mitre offered a greater menace than a Communard provided with a gun. Reinforced in his authority, Pius frowned still more fiercely on the few Catholics whose opinions diverged from his own, and let slip no opportunity to emphasize his distrust and disapproval of those whom he suspected of Erastian compromise. 'What I fear for you', he told a group of French priests and laymen in 1871, 'is not that miserable band of Communards—demons escaped from Hell—but Catholic Liberalism. I do not mean those Catholics once called Liberal (they have often deserved well of the Holy See) but that fatal system which dreams of reconciling two irreconcilables— Church and Revolution. I have already condemned it, but if need be, I would condemn it forty times more.'

The vigour of Pius's condemnation inevitably coloured the interpretation which was given throughout the world to the doctrine of papal infallibility. Tightening the strings which bound the members of the Church to the Holy See, he intensified the conflict which was already developing between Church and State in France, in Germany and in Italy. But the vigour of his condemnation was unmatched by any vigour of mind. He was an old man who had realized his dream. Now that the Vatican Council was over, he had no policy. His attitude to the world was of carping petulance. He insisted on regarding himself as a prisoner in the Vatican, an islet of sublime understanding in a sea of wickedness, till his plaintive protests became tiresome even to his supporters and they spoke softly of the need for another pope. By 1876 even Manning could write: 'At this moment the Holy See seems to me reduced very low in its counsellors and men of action. . . . Six years have passed over the Holy See since 1870, and its organization has been dying out year after year. . . . I find some looking for miracles, some for inaction, and some for action. The inactive unite with the first class in doing nothing, letting everything get worse, and speaking against them who would act as *conciliatori*.'[1]

The years that immediately followed the Vatican Council were years of relative calm in ecclesiastical affairs. After the first full meeting of the bishops since the Council of Trent and the promulgation of a dogma whose terms and purport were

[1] E. S. Purcell, *Life of Cardinal Manning*, II, p. 575.

eagerly agitated all over the Catholic world, it was strange to
return to placid teaching and humdrum administration. The
decade that preceded the Vatican Council had seen the ideas
and conflicts of centuries speedily brought to boiling-point, and
as the heat subsided, interest died away. There was a sense of
anticlimax. The old Pope and his white-headed advisers stuck
to their ingrained attitude, only heeding the changes of Europe
in order to denounce them. Habits of mind which had been
antiquated under Gregory XVI still prevailed at the Vatican,
and outside it even Veuillot and Dupanloup, though abating not
a jot from their habitual violence of expression, were unable to
command the passion which had been theirs under the spur of
a new dogma. There was a finality about the Vatican Council
which had a depressive effect. The Pope, being infallible,
seemed to commit his successors to a repetition of his own
policy, and though this impression was doubtless illogical, it
conjured up a picture which even Pius's most aggressive supporters could not find enlivening. All the decisions, all the
excitements, belonged to the past. Few troubled about the
future. A blanket seemed to have dropped over the entire
Catholic world; sounds were stilled; voices were muffled; and
only the heavy breathing of the older prelates ruffled the silence
and showed that life still went on.

CHAPTER V

The Royalist Republic

But this quiet was deceptive. Prolonged struggles were impending. In France, as in other countries, anticlerical organizations were building up their forces for a trial of strength with the Church, a trial which they hoped would be decisive. Meanwhile, as Pius surveyed Europe from the vantage point of Rome, his eye halted with some uneasiness on France; for in France, where Ultramontanes enjoyed all the satisfaction of theological rectitude and approval, the Liberal Catholics, by some tiresome quirk of fortune, had attained power. Though lacking support in the country, they were predominant in an Assembly that was elected by universal suffrage. The Republic had brought them political triumph.

This accident, if accident it was, possessed the highest significance. The country had elected an assembly which regarded the Third Republic as a mere preparation for another monarchy. But which monarchy? For there were two candidates—the Comte de Chambord, who represented the elder Bourbon line, and the Comte de Paris, who claimed Orleanist allegiance. Intransigents tended to support the former; Liberal Catholics the latter. But as long as the two parties could not agree, the monarchy remained in abeyance, and France presented the curious spectacle of a monarchical Assembly slowly strengthening and establishing a republic.

The clergy, almost without exception, believed in a monarchy, applauding the efforts of Veuillot, who spared no epithet in praising the Comte de Chambord. 'Henri de Bourbon's programme', he wrote of the manifesto of 8th May 1871, 'leaves a deep impression. One is astonished at this simplicity, this serenity, this grandeur. . . . No man has spoken thus.' Nor was Veuillot's astonishment lessened by the fact that he had himself composed the manifesto. He felt a natural affinity with this pretender who conceived of himself as a Most Christian King and cultivated ideas which Louis XIV would have found out of date. For Chambord's shining virtues as a private citizen were matched by his conspicuous vices as a public man. His deep faith in the Christian religion accompanied a profound belief in the mystic significance of royalty; his unfaltering love of France coexisted with an antique paternalism towards the people. Living most of his life far from the practicalities of politics, he insisted on his natural right to a restoration: all conditions, bargains and compromises were swept away by his rigid acceptance of heredity as an absolute title to power. As early as July 1871 he refused to accept the tricolour, announcing that the flag which had floated above his cradle would over-shadow his tomb. 'It is', said Falloux regretfully, 'the suicide of the Comte de Chambord.'

There were, of course, other ways of regarding the decision. Veuillot issued a panegyric. 'No circumstances', wrote the *Dublin Review* when Chambord's affirmation was repeated, 'could be better calculated to reveal the chivalrous sense of honour, the sublime disinterestedness, the blameless and candid soul of the Prince.'[1] But however blameless and candid, he was destroying his future as a king. The moderate legitimists and the Liberal Catholics in the Assembly combined to deplore the stubbornness with which he refused to face the fact of the Revolution. There was some hope of an agreement between the two Bourbon lines, but so long as Chambord persisted in his demands, that hope was frustrated: in time it would fade.

There were, in fact, two aims which were continually urged by *L'Univers*—the restoration of a monarchy in France and an amelioration of the Pope's situation in Rome. Despite the efforts of the Liberal Catholics the first aim was defeated by Chambord's refusal to listen to all counsels of prudence: the second, even if desirable, could not conceivably be executed by a country which had just been defeated in a major war. Veuillot, however, was expert in conceiving of the incon-

[1] 'The Situation in France'. *Dublin Review*, 1874 (New Series), XXII, p. 206.

ceivable. Organizing petitions, invoking Chambord's approval, advancing the familiar arguments of national duty, he did much to create a state of opinion in which France was brought to the brink of further hostilities. When Thiers, with Dupanloup's support, deprecated a discussion of the Italian question, Veuillot's fury even exceeded its habitual bounds. But for once he overreached himself. The Pope, in an allocution, rebuked the Intransigent party for 'entirely forgetting the laws of charity'; and in a personal brief to Veuillot reproved him for 'a bitter zeal which is foreign to the charity of a Catholic'.

The reproof, though explicit, was not severe: it was expressed in affectionate terms and included in a letter which praised Veuillot's high services to the Holy See. But Veuillot, who was proof against all the innuendoes and animadversions of his enemies, staggered in bewildered wretchedness now that his self-erected idol lifted a finger in admonishment. A word of blame from Pius struck him like a thunderbolt from Jove. Though he protested miserably and abjectly of his entire submission to the will and judgement of the Pope, the rebuke annihilated his self-confidence and courage, leaving him weak and disheartened. The brief he thought harsh and cruel, but he could not believe it altogether misguided. Were, then, his methods as a journalist altogether unsuited to the Catholic cause? If he was wrong in 1872, had he been wrong all his life? Could there be something in Liberal Catholicism after all? Should he resign? This battery of questions shook him as he had never been shaken before. For some months his personality shrank into a pale image of its normal robustness: the past seemed hollow, the present a misery, and the future a void. His friends were grieved and uneasy at the sight of this terrible warrior reduced to a self-doubting impotence. Only when Pius, who had intended merely to administer a mild reproach, learnt with dismay that he had shattered the energy of his foremost champion, did rumours at last arrive from Rome that the Pope still loved Veuillot and was seeking some occasion on which to repair the injury which he had involuntarily caused. Slowly Veuillot recovered: first came a feeling of reassurance, then of justification, then of urgent duty, and by the end of the year he was waging battle with all his old angry verve. But from this moment the obscure nervous symptoms, which for some time had been disturbing his mind and weakening his body, were to grow in frequency and severity until at last they forced him to abandon his pen and to watch events with the helpless irritation of an unnecessary spectator.

Meanwhile, if the Intransigents encountered difficulties in both foreign and domestic policy, they could derive some satisfaction from their position in the Church. In spite of the power of Liberal Catholics in the National Assembly, the new Minister of Religion, Jules Simon, displayed a subservience to the Vatican which would have been exceptional under the Second Empire and inconceivable under the Bourbons. Himself a deist, he consulted with the Papal Nuncio on all matters of episcopal nomination, inquiring with an ingratiating earnestness when each candidate's name was mooted, 'Is he sound in doctrine?' As Dupanloup maliciously remarked, 'M. Simon will be a cardinal before I am'.

The war, as is usual, had provoked a superficial revival of religious fervour, and although republicans pointed out that the army was predominantly Catholic in education and belief, its defeat was interpreted in ecclesiastical circles as a spur to further devotion. This devotion, if linked with the military past, was not unconnected with the political future; for the mystical movement which swept the country, and the great number of pilgrimages which were encouraged by the Church and facilitated by the introduction of cheap railway fares, were seized on by ecclesiastical spokesmen as an opportunity to inculcate the virtues of a monarchy. The climax of these demonstrations took place at Paray-le-Monial, a small township in the diocese of Autun, where in 1689 Marguerite Marie Alacoque had seen a vision of the Sacred Heart. At Paray, on 29th June 1873, fifty members of the National Assembly arrived with a banner given by one hundred and fifty of their colleagues; and their spokesman dedicated his country 'in the measure of their powers' to the Sacred Heart, muttering, when his speech was over, 'Pardon! pardon!' as though it had not expressed the real depth of his feeling or the true extent of his thought. One month later, as part of the same movement, the National Assembly approved the project to erect a great basilica of the Sacred Heart on the hill of Montmartre, in partial atonement for the sins of the nation.

But Catholics committed one great blunder. They talked, acted and thought as though the majority of Frenchmen still believed in the Catholic faith; and they deluded themselves, despite the evidence of by-elections, that the country wished for a monarchical restoration. Every day it became clearer that the conservative landslide of 1871 had been a vote for peace and for nothing else. Even the peasants, who were traditionally the most docile supporters of the monarchy, feared the return of a Bourbon king as a renewal of ancient malpractices. With however little justification, the republicans played on this theme: the *gabelle*, the *dîme*, the *droit de seigneur*, the privileges of nobles and priests—who wished to see these things brought back? Chambord, by insisting on his white flag, confirmed the suspicion that his real aim was to restore the *ancien régime* with all its outworn abuses: and such a restoration the country would never tolerate. The nobles of the Faubourg Saint-Germain who prepared their coaches for the return of the king, and the decrepit dowagers who even ordered sedan-chairs for the coronation procession, were no more foolish than the legitimists of the Assembly or the journalists of the popular Press who supposed that by flamboyant demonstrations and incessant propaganda they could eliminate a century of political development and force the country to conform to a picture which existed only in their overheated imaginations.

When Broglie came to power in 1873, Veuillot's pleasure in the advent of a Catholic Prime Minister soon gave way to indignation at his obedience to a parliamentary majority. For Veuillot, hoping persistently for a Bourbon triumph, looked to the Government for speedy action. And he advocated it in the plainest terms.

'His post', he said of President MacMahon, 'is not only that of a sentinel, as he modestly declares, but of a pilot, watching for hostile winds and dangerous reefs. Keeping his hand on the tiller, let him steer ahead without heeding the shouts raised wildly against him. He is in charge of the ship, not of the opinions of the crew. If danger presses, his duty is to suppose that the majority agrees with the indications of sounding-line, compass and wind.'

In other words, let MacMahon prepare for an immediate *coup d'état*, ignoring the wishes of the country and the majority of its elected representatives.

It is interesting to speculate on the course of events had Chambord been more accommodating and MacMahon less scrupulous. There is little doubt that a restoration could have been achieved; but there is also little doubt that the enthronement of a Most Christian King, the establishment of a regime favourable to the Church, and the return to a political credo which ascertained the opinion of the country only in order to defy it would soon have provoked a rising far more bloody than that which set Charles X on the road back to Edinburgh, exposing the Church to reprisals as violent as the Commune but far more widespread and prolonged.

Veuillot, however, was always ready to diagnose the diseases of his opponents and to prescribe drastic remedies. Smarting at the indifference with which his counsels were heard by the French Government, he visited Rome, where he was always welcome. Pius received him with joy; and Veuillot listened with awestruck admiration while the Pope spoke sadly of Darboy's death (one must pray that he had expiated his misdeeds) and even expressed a pious hope for a second Commune to bring Broglie and MacMahon to their senses. 'Caro Veuillot!' 'Très Saint-Père!'

Thus encouraged in his dark suspicions of Broglie and Dupanloup, Veuillot proceeded to blacken their reputations by disinterring an obscure and unimportant episode that had taken place in 1862 when the leading Liberal Catholics had met for a few days at Montalembert's château. As always, his motives were of the best and his methods of the worst. What did it matter if his facts were uncertain, his allegations offensive and his deductions mischievous, provided only that he convinced his readers of the potential heresy of the most skilful Catholic statesman and the most eminent Catholic bishop in the country? In the event it profited him little. His vigorous polemic on behalf of the German bishops had already aroused Bismarck's resentment, and Broglie, scurrilously abused, was all the more willing to yield to diplomatic pressure and to inflict on L'Univers two months of chastening silence.

The Liberal Catholics were, in fact, politicians: they moved within the circumscribed limits of the possible, leaving the ideal to the prolix attention of their journalist opponents. The early years of the Third Republic witnessed the passing of two measures which, had they survived, would have been of cardinal importance in the educational development of the country. In 1873 the Church regained control of the Conseil supérieur de l'Instruction publique—a control which Napoleon III, in the heyday of clerical influence, had seen fit to take into his own hands; and in 1875 a law was passed which permitted the establishment of Catholic universities.

But these were sandcastles set up against a flowing tide. So long as the Church is a party issue, it is bound to remain a political organization. The concessions which the Liberal Catholics won with such skill and patience were regarded by their opponents as temporary alterations in the structure of society, which would be rectified as soon as there was a shift in power. What the Church achieved today would be destroyed tomorrow. Perhaps, left to themselves, the Liberal Catholics might have reached a political philosophy which allowed some continuity to the process of legislation: perhaps they might even have instilled such a philosophy into their opponents. But alongside the Liberal Catholics there were always the Intransigents, making vast claims, fomenting bitter quarrels; and even the Liberals were not prepared, in 1875, to accept the Republic as anything more than a provisional form of government.

The Church, therefore, was regarded less as a permanent institution in French life than as a conservative pressure group. While Catholics based their policy on the outworn theory that all Frenchmen were Christians, the republicans behaved as though the country were converted to Masonry. It seems that the number of Masons in France has never exceeded sixty thousand, but numbers are less important than position and influence. Between 1871 and 1914 Masonry, gaining hold of the professional classes, played a part in French politics out of all proportion to its numerical strength. The doctors and lawyers, the shopkeepers, industrialists and tradesmen who formed its basis were penetrated with a belief in the perfectibility of man. None responded more readily to Gambetta's cry, 'Le cléricalisme, voilà l'ennemi'. No doubt the freedom of speech which the country had welcomed in 1870 meant that the lodges, which had hitherto represented the only safe forum for the expression of republican opinions, forfeited their pre-eminent position; but they remained the headquarters of radicalism.

THE ROYALIST REPUBLIC

That they were also the headquarters of anticlerical theory was indicated in 1877 when the Grand Orient, by a momentous decision, ceased to demand from its members any belief in God or in the immortality of the soul.

By this time indeed the republicans had the smell of victory in their nostrils. They had swept the country in the elections of 1876, and MacMahon's dissolution of the Chamber in the following year had cost them few seats and merely proved that the President must submit to his deputies. It is true that the conservative majority in the Senate still denied them the full exercise of power. But in due course new senators would be elected: then the country would enjoy a government which actually believed in the constitution. France, which at the beginning of 1871 had been prepared to consider a restoration, already displayed doubts in the summer. Each new year of successful republican government combined with the successive failures of monarchist ambition to promote confidence in the regime, till in the end the Republic was consolidated not so much by its own efforts as by the bankruptcy of its opponents. *Il n'y a que le provisoire qui dure.* The Church, from the oldest bishop to the youngest priest, from the timidest nobleman to the fiercest journalist, regarded with foreboding this ascent from transience to durability.

CHAPTER VI

End of an Epoch

Michon must have been one of the few priests who believed in the Republic and yet contrived to evade the temptation of schism and the danger of expulsion. It is true that his sudden bursts of discretion, if they kept him in the Church, did not betoken any change of heart. He seems indeed to have grown more bitter and disillusioned after 1870, for his name occurs sooner or later in the account of nearly every heterodox movement. From time to time one catches a glimpse of his earnest, tortured face before he vanishes again into his dissident obscurity. In 1878 he calls on Hyacinthe Loyson who notes bleakly: 'He will die a Roman Catholic, saying his Mass every day, but without faith! The Immaculate Conception and papal infallibility are absurdities, the Roman Church has destroyed itself, and so on. But it is not only faith in Rome he lacks; his faith in Catholicism is vague in the extreme. His moral judgements are most accommodating; he readily excuses Jules Favre's "marriage", Victor Hugo's bigamy [sic], and so on. I prefer the Ultramontanes. His visit left me profoundly sad.'[1]

Probably Hyacinthe was slightly unfair. Why, after all, if Michon had lost his faith, should he continue to say Mass daily? There is in fact no evidence that he was any nearer to solving the dilemma which had deranged his life. He remained far from port, tossing on the high seas, refusing to seek shelter, refusing to scuttle. But if his career ends on the same discordant note that marked its commencement, Michon continues to display in his declining years that freshness of outlook which always distin-

[1] Albert Houtin, *Le Père Hyacinthe*, II, p. 216.

guished his thought—that flash of talent which redeems his life from the banality of failure. Indeed, his last decade was concentrated on the work that was to preserve his name from utter oblivion. Secluded from disturbance in the small village of Baignes-Sainte-Radegonde, thirty kilometres south-west of Angoulême and only a short distance from his first parish, he devoted his energies to the study of handwriting and its relation to character. If graphology (he even coined the word) is taken far more seriously in France than in England, the blame and the credit alike go to Michon. He founded several papers and wrote a number of books. Waging a bitter war on the advocates of palmistry, he defended graphology in the name of science, and with such success that before he died the interest of doctors and alienists was assured. With as little compunction as he had shown in attacking Veuillot and Pius IX, he analysed the writing of his more celebrated contemporaries, attributing to them characteristics that were seldom flattering and often repellent. Flaubert, who remembered Michon from their meeting at Constantinople, was indignant at the news that his signature bore a suggestive likeness to those of Fouquier-Tinville and Collet d'Herbois. But whatever his vagaries, Michon established graphology as a force to be reckoned with. In July 1880, the summer before he died, the first congress of graphologists acclaimed as their master the man who, after forty years of private observation, had at last succeeded in establishing a new department of knowledge. Today, even if his followers deny his theories, his achievement stands; in practice he hardly ever went wrong; he was, as a modern exponent declares, 'a born empiricist'.[1]

Nor was graphology his only occupation. With the few sous which survived his generous but indiscreet practice of charity, he erected extensions to his manor at Montausier—a building which became more curious as it grew. The four relatives with whom he shared its narrow rooms may have consoled themselves with the reflection that if it lacked space, it did not lack character. From afar the traveller could see something like a sheet of zinc, glinting white in the sun, while as he drew nearer, he slowly made out the threat of two crenellated towers and the splendid incongruity of two Moorish galleries running along-

[1] Robert Saudek, *The Psychology of Handwriting*, p. 14.

side. Michon was his own architect, his own bricklayer, his own carpenter and mason, and the visitor who persevered in his approach found that the building which looked so ludicrous at a distance assumed a more friendly aspect at close quarters, till even the convolutions on the pediments and cornices, which the celebrated Abbé had carved with his own hand, were united in a tolerable and unique ensemble.

That is the end of Michon, an end not unworthy of his past. He lived out his last years in this preposterous manor which for all its eccentricity was something more than a freak. Graphology and botany, religious polemic and novel-writing, occupied his leisure. While Veuillot and the Ultramontanes still mentioned his name with that slight snigger which befits the indecent, he was known to his fellow graphologists as an affable old man with an unpredictable temperament and no sense whatever of practical difficulties. None ever impugned his good-nature. To the peasants he was a more familiar figure—an ageing priest with an uproarious laugh who shambled into Baignes to say Mass, and trudged back to Montausier with a handful of newly bought mussels caught in the flap of his tattered soutane. And thus in May 1881 he died, fortified by the rites of the Church, doubtless still clinging to his idiosyncratic conception of the Catholic faith. He left a few sous, a few debts, a number of manuscripts and a memory which has not died at Baignes after the passage of seventy years.

It was characteristic of Michon to be aware of the social problem whose existence the Liberal Catholics virtually denied. In 1868 he delivered a series of *conférences* at Saint-Eloi in Paris, urging the need for mutual comprehension between priests and workmen. His words, if they did not go unheeded, merely enhanced his eccentric reputation. Those who perceived the frightening gulf between Catholics and the new industrial classes were in fact not Liberals but Intransigents. By 1868 the two sociologists Le Play and Keller had already attacked individualism as the cause of poverty, but not till after the war, with its sudden increase in charitable works, did the social movement begin to make headway. Under the leadership of Albert de Mun and with the keen encouragement of Veuillot, who was ever ready to boast of his own plebeian origins, the Cercles catholiques d'ouvriers sprang into vigorous life, first in Paris and then all over the country. But this vigour belied their future. Meetings at which bourgeois and nobles consented rather self-consciously to talk of religion with their social inferiors were not the true way of introducing Catholicism to the working class. Catholicism, if it were to come at all, must come from equals and not from social superiors whose intrinsic superiority was already being questioned. Albert de Mun, despite his deep sincerity and splendid eloquence, was too rigid a nobleman to understand the necessary approach, and his placid insistence on the doctrine of the Syllabus alienated men who might have tolerated, if they could not accept, his implicit faith in the permanence of current social distinctions. Desiring to return to medieval guild corporations, he was suspected of favouring the *ancien régime*, and to workers the *ancien régime* evoked an idea of gross poverty and exploitation. In spite, therefore, of their brilliant inception, the Cercles catholiques counted only sixty thousand members in 1900 and speedily declined as the twentieth century progressed.

By about 1878 indeed the Church seemed to have reached a full stop. Either it proposed no remedies for the diseases of the modern world, or its cures were painfully reminiscent of medieval quackery. In politics it was allied, both on the Intransigent and on the Liberal Catholic wing, with monarchist forces which, though still powerful, were clearly marching to ultimate defeat. In the realm of thought its pronouncements commanded no respect outside the ranks of the faithful. Even in the limited domain of social reform it failed to arouse general support from either workers or employers. Apart from the Protestant minority, who were to exercise a disproportionate political influence throughout the Third Republic, there was no Christian whose religion enhanced his standing with the unbelieving masses: the average worker, like the average intellectual, regarded the Christian as a credulous idealist and the Catholic as an obscurantist idiot. Only in the traditionally devout regions of the countryside did the priest maintain his hold on the minds and consciences of the people, and even there his influence was not always powerful enough to prevent his wilful penitents from voting republican.

In 1879, in fact, the inevitable evolution was complete: the

R   257

monarchists lost control of the Senate, and the republicans, with majorities in both houses, were free to work their will on the country. But by 1879 much had happened. The spectator who for forty years had contemplated the passionate drama of Catholicism being played out before his eyes seemed to have reached the fifth act of a tragedy in which all the principal characters were successively borne away to the accompaniment of solemn music. On 3rd September 1877 it was the shrewd and evasive Thiers, a politician whose role in religious affairs was largely conducted in the wings. 'We may well imagine him', wrote Veuillot with lugubrious satisfaction, 'in the ranks of those who wish they had never lived.' In January 1878 it was the leading villain, Victor Emmanuel, whose sudden disappearance evoked from Catholics a number of fitting but sombre reflections on the theme, *memento mori*. A month later came the greatest exit of all, an event which the Chancelleries of Europe had confidently predicted a decade and a half before: the big bell of the Capitol at last tolled for Pius IX, dead in his eighty-sixth year after one of the longest and most obstreperous pontificates of modern times. Scarcely had the Catholic world grown reconciled to the unusual silence of the Vatican than Dupanloup, who had been one of Pius's most strenuous defenders and one of his most stubborn enemies, himself left the stage, choosing a time when the cardinal's hat, which he had so signally deserved, was at last within reach. And the final great departure was that of the quick-tempered, courageous Pie, who, laying down a pen which had never shirked the expression of outrageous opinions and never disclaimed a close familiarity with the political purposes of the Almighty, died in the splendour of a serene but outmoded legitimism.

For each life that ended, Veuillot composed an obituary, surveying its pattern with the authority, if not the impartiality, of the recording angel. Dupanloup recalled to him a quarter-century of battle between *L'Univers* and Liberal Catholicism. Pie evoked memories of Intransigence at its boldest and greatest; Pius represented the supreme inspiration of almost every word that had adorned the editorial columns of *L'Univers* since 1846. But as he wrote these articles resuming and justifying his past, Veuillot felt that he too was the proper subject for an obituary. His health, impaired by the gruelling labours of early journalism and undermined by a life of unremitting effort, had never recovered from the stresses of the Franco-Prussian War. The Pope's reproof in 1872, and the realization that despite his every exertion the destiny of France was drifting beyond his control, may have induced his final illness. At all events, during those years after the Vatican Council when he might have savoured his greatest triumph, his sense of political impotence was reinforced by a sense of physical impotence—a condition which his doctors vaguely ascribed to neurasthenia. His periods of silence and recuperation grew steadily longer. He was assailed by the most distressing affliction which could overtake a writer —a sudden mood in which the world lost all its colour and relief and he forgot that it had ever appeared otherwise, a mood in which thoughts dried up like grapes in the sun and words were removed behind a high wall against which he ran and battered in vain. If he walked, he stumbled. If he spoke, his tongue knotted itself in his mouth. From time to time he emerged from this condition to write perhaps an article in praise of the egregious Antonelli or in abuse of the ineffable Voltaire. But, the article once written, his disease took hold of him again, and on each occasion he found it harder to break out, harder to climb over the wall in search of words, harder to protect his thoughts from a relentless desiccation. In 1878 he collected his poems in the last volume of his works that was to be published during his lifetime; in 1879 he achieved only fifteen articles; in 1880 he mustered energy for an agonized forty lines to commemorate the death of Pie. Then the great silence fell. Left only with his shrewish sister and his bustling brother, he lingered for three years, a pale mute old man sitting beside the fire, following the conversation around him with an occasional thin smile and rarely interrupting with an abrupt and painful monosyllable. It was a pathetic end for the greatest journalist of the century, but an end whose pathos Veuillot accepted without resentment. Truly the sword had outworn the sheath.

But while the actors vanished one by one, a new play was in preparation. Rome had seen the enthronement of Cardinal Pecci as Leo XIII—a prelate who had never been a favourite with Pius IX. In France, where the republicans prepared to execute their policy of secularization, royalists, churchmen and conservatives all sought nervously to divine the portents of the future. Veuillot's theological triumph had been followed by his political defeat. But fortune's wheel was still turning. Would his victims of yesterday prove the conquerors of tomorrow? Would the accidents of the past determine the chances of the future? Would the old for ever exclude the new? To some of those questions there would be a clear and startling answer.

Epilogue

B ut if we cannot stay to see the new play, at least we can look over the acts of the old. Between 1831, when the rioters burst through the doors of Saint-Germain-l'Auxerrois, and 1883, when the long-prepared obituaries of Veuillot were at last sent down to the printer, the Church of France had known changing fortunes of extraordinary complexity and scope. There had been mob violence; there had been mass enthusiasm. Crowds such as the cathedral had not seen since the Middle Ages jostled across the Parvis of Notre-Dame to hear a preacher as eloquent as Bossuet or Bourdaloue; yet twenty years later, when the Church was reaping rich rewards by its alliance with a clerical regime, the same preacher was reduced to virtual retirement and disgrace. A prophet had arisen, had hurtled brilliantly like a meteor across a darkened sky, then dived to earth, burnt out. Old arguments for the faith had given way to new methods; but at the same time new techniques of intellectual exploration had chilled the ardour of many a heart and bred paralysing doubt. Societies whose one aim was to strangle the Church and to choke all belief in Christianity had spread their tentacles across the country and gained a tight hold on the schools and the central administration. Gallicanism, whose tenets once ruled the Church of France, had gone down to a desperate end at the Vatican Council, and in its place Ultramontanism held undisputed sway. For half a century the Church had been *the* domestic problem, the central point of interrogation around which all other problems revolved, and in that half-century, though its position was still precarious, its outlook and composition had entirely changed. Blood had flowed across the altars; three out of four successive Archbishops of Paris had died a violent death. Passions had smouldered and flared, strange resentments had taken root. And while old conceptions—royalism, legitimism— still lived on, slowly turning sour in the unfriendly air of the Third Republic, fresh problems sprang up to test the resilience and capacity of the leaders of the Church.

But by 1880 had any of the old problems been settled? As the familiar figures glide into the wings and the footlights fade, can we strike a pencil through a list of questions and draw up new posers for the following generation? These men who have occupied the stage for so long—Lacordaire, Lamennais, Dupan-loup, Michon, Pius, Darboy, Veuillot—has any of them dealt with a point so conclusively that it can be tied up and pushed into a pigeon-hole of history?

No doubt some of them have. Pius, for instance, has erased Gallicanism from the agenda of all succeeding pontiffs. But on the whole the play ends rather than concludes. If, taking Lacordaire, Michon and Veuillot, we refine each man's life down to a particular problem, we shall see that each problem, though carried further, persists with an uncomfortable clarity.

Lacordaire's first and essential task was to adapt Christianity to the nineteenth century, to make religion emotionally accep-table, to sell it (as it were) to his contemporaries. He had to strip dogma of the irrelevant trappings of the *ancien régime*; he had to show that faith could be not only a formula such as the eighteenth-century *philosophes* had understood, but an inspira-tion such as the nineteenth-century Romantics were longing for. All this he achieved; and he did more than launch a revival— he created a new spirit. But that spirit, which had already faltered before he died, seemed nothing but a memory twenty years later, when the republicans were preparing to take over the regime and to wreak vengeance on a Church that was linked to their bitterest adversaries. One might be forgiven for thinking that Lacordaire had failed; and fail he certainly did within the limits of his lifetime. But the eclipse of his ideas was temporary. If we look forward to the 1920's, we see Pius XI, in the plenitude of his disciplinary power, imposing on the Church a doctrine of political modernity which, in spite of the autocratic method employed, would have delighted Lacordaire.

EPILOGUE

If Christianity was to survive in France, it could not afford to be hampered by antique shibboleths. Sooner or later Rome had to allow men to die, as Lacordaire died, a 'penitent Catholic and an impenitent liberal'.

Lacordaire's aim was, then, ultimately achieved. But with Michon it is a different story. Brushing aside his temperamental quirks and eccentricities, we can see him as a man ceaselessly racked by the discrepancy between faith and reason, clinging to both, refusing to believe that a real contradiction between the two can exist yet unable either to abandon his faith or to quell his inquiring mind. Michon held so fast to his Christianity that he was prepared to risk his Catholicism; he cared so deeply for reasonable belief that as a last resort he was ready to forsake the Pope. But in fact he was never driven to any such public act of rebellion. At the price of all kinds of evasions, subtleties and prevarications, he managed somehow to stay within the Church—to incur blame without condemnation. In this he was fortunate. For the problem remained starkly posed, and the scholars and philosophers who were later to tread the same path were either, like Loisy, forced out of the Church or, like Laberthonnière and Blondel, pressed into recantation and submission. Twenty years after Michon was dead, the world learned from the full-scale attack which Pius X launched on modernism that for an orthodox Catholic intellectual specula-tion was unwise and biblical criticism wellnigh fatal. Better men than Michon—more profound, more obedient, more scholarly and more orthodox—felt their hopes wilt and their courage snap under the relentless persecution of their saintly Pope.

Nor does Veuillot's life end with a conclusive full stop and the final demonstration of an established fact. His career sets the problem of toleration. Veuillot—the believer, the absolutist, the rigid logician—faced a world in which his belief was shared by a minority and his logic was shirked. As to the absolutisms that were to spread across Europe after his death, they had nothing in common with his own political doctrine, for they relied on mass opinion, on majority support, on popular acclaim, on anything rather than a permanent and divine authority. He would have found nothing essentially to admire in any modern system of government—liberal democracy, Commun-

EPILOGUE

ism, National Socialism, even Fascism. If the latter tempted him the most, it would still have been a makeshift, an authoritarian structure with the wrong man perched on top. Veuillot represents the good antihumanist; and perhaps for this reason he has never had a true successor. Maurras, who possessed a comparable talent, had none of his faith and preached a political doctrine which, in spite of an apparent similarity, rested on quite different foundations. While Maurras's theory provided the mould in which the Vichy Government was cast, Veuillot's theory provided no mould and produced no government. He was, as Michon used to say in a favourite gibe, a theocrat; but whether, in order to bring about a theocracy, one could bully and coerce those members of society who held opposite—and fallacious—views, Veuillot never really decided.

The question-marks therefore stand. The problems of Michon and Veuillot are not—and never will be—solved. Even Lacordaire's problem, the emotional adaptation of religion to society and of society to religion, has to be grappled with afresh in each new generation; while the problems of intellectual integrity and toleration are part of the eternal paradox of belief. These three men fought out their part in a continuous and age-long war. The Church and its acceptance; fact and faith; the toleration of heresy—such are the points of tension which, continually re-created, vex the original minds of every epoch. Lacordaire, Michon, Veuillot stand at the nodes of conflict; their lives are episodes in the ceaseless dialectic of religion; the doubts that beset them, their frustrations and failures, their difficulties and temptations, the nagging fear of spiritual impotence, are all part of that pattern which forms the crux of survival.

So when the curtain rises again, there will be new dramatis personae and another cast; the scene-shifters have been busy and the backcloth has changed; the actors cut unfamiliar postures and use a strange language. To us in the auditorium it all seems very different. But if we attend carefully, we shall see that the plot is much the same.

APPENDIX

The Gallican Articles

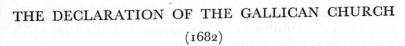

THE DECLARATION OF THE GALLICAN CHURCH

(1682)

(French text in Emil Reich, *Select Documents illustrating Mediaeval and Modern History* (London, 1905), pp. 379–80.)

MANY people are seeking to overthrow the decrees of the Gallican Church and its liberties, so zealously upheld by our forefathers, and to destroy their foundations, which are based on the sacred canons and on the tradition of the Fathers; others, under the pretext of defending them, have the audacity to attack the primacy of Saint Peter and the Roman pontiffs, his successors, instituted by Jesus Christ, to prevent them from receiving the obedience which they are owed by the whole world, and to lessen the majesty of the Holy Apostolic See, which is respected by all nations where the true doctrine of the Church is taught and its unity observed. The heretics, for their part, are doing their utmost to make this power, which maintains the peace of the Church, intolerable to kings and peoples, and they have recourse to this device in order to separate simple souls from the Communion of the Church. Wishing therefore to remedy these ills, we, archbishops and bishops assembled in Paris by order of the King, with the other deputed priests, representing the Gallican Church, have seen fit, after mature deliberation, to make the following rules and declaration:

ARTICLE I. That Saint Peter and the Vicars of Christ, his successors, and the whole Church have received power from God in spiritual matters and matters touching salvation only,

265

and not in temporal and civil matters. . . . We therefore declare that kings and sovereigns are not, by God's command, subordinate to any ecclesiastical power in temporal matters, that they cannot be deposed either directly or indirectly by the authority of the heads of the Church, that their subjects cannot be dispensed from due submission and obedience or absolved from the oath of allegiance. . . .

ARTICLE II. That the plenitude of power exercised in matters spiritual by the Holy Apostolic See and by the Vicars of Christ, the successors of Saint Peter, is such that the decrees of the Holy Oecumenical Council of Constance . . . retain their force and strength. . . .

ARTICLE III. That the use of the apostolic power must thus be regulated according to the canons made by the Holy Spirit and consecrated by universal respect. That the rules, customs and constitutions received in the realm and the Church of France must retain their force and strength, and the usages of our fathers must remain intact; that it is even required by the greatness of the Holy Apostolic See that the laws and customs established with the consent of this venerable see and of the churches should remain invariable.

ARTICLE IV. That although the Pope has the chief voice in questions of faith, and his decrees concern all churches and each particular church, his judgement is not irreformable unless the consent of the Church is given.

ARTICLE V. We have decided to send to all the French bishops and churches these maxims received by us from our fathers, that we may all say the same thing, hold the same opinions, and follow the same doctrine.

Bibliography

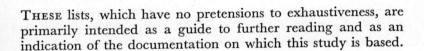

THESE lists, which have no pretensions to exhaustiveness, are primarily intended as a guide to further reading and as an indication of the documentation on which this study is based.

1. GENERAL

ACTON, LORD: *The History of Freedom and Other Essays*. Edited with an introduction by J. N. Figgis and R. N. Lawrence (London, 1907).

BAUNARD, MGR L.: *Un Siècle de l'Eglise de France*. 18ᵉ mille (Paris, 1922).

BAZIN, ABBÉ G.: *Vie de Mgr Maret, évêque de Sura, etc.* 3 vols. (Paris, 1891).

BEDOYERE, MICHAEL DE LA: *The Life of Baron Von Hügel* (London, 1951).

BETTENSON, HENRY (ed.): *Documents of the Christian Church* (London, 1943).

CAHILL, REV. E.: *Freemasonry and the Anti-Christian Movement* (2nd edition, Dublin, 1930).

DANSETTE, ADRIEN: *Histoire religieuse de la France contemporaine*. 2 vols. (Paris, 1948–51) (with bibliography).

DU CAMP, MAXIME: *Les Convulsions de Paris*. 4 vols. (Paris, 1878–80).

DUROSELLE, J. B.: *Les Débuts du catholicisme social en France (1822–1870)* (Paris, 1951) (with bibliography).

FAGUET, EMILE: *L'Anticléricalisme* (Paris, 1905).

FOULON, MGR J. A.: *Histoire de la vie et des œuvres de Mgr Darboy* (Paris, 1889).

BIBLIOGRAPHY

GALTON, ARTHUR: *Church and State in France, 1300–1907* (London, 1907).

GUETTÉE, R. F. W.: *Mémoires pour servir à l'histoire de l'Eglise de France pendant le XIXe siècle*. Only one volume published (Paris and Brussels, 1881).

— *Souvenirs d'un prêtre romain devenu prêtre orthodoxe* (Paris and Brussels, 1889).

GUILLEMANT, CHARLES: *Pierre-Louis Parisis*. 3 vols. (Paris, 1916–24).

GUILLEMIN, HENRI: *Histoire des catholiques français au XIXe siècle* (1815–1905) (Geneva, 1947).

HAYWOOD, H. L. and CRAIG, JAMES E.: *A History of Freemasonry* (New York, 1927).

KLEIN, ABBÉ FÉLIX: *L'Evêque de Metz. Vie de Mgr Dupont des Loges*. (New edition, Paris, 1925.)

LE BRAS, GABRIEL: *Introduction à l'Histoire de la pratique religieuse en France*. 2 vols. (Paris, 1942–5).

LECANUET, LE R. P.: *Montalembert*. 3 vols. (Paris, 1895–1912).

— *L'Eglise de France sous la Troisième République*. 4 vols. (Paris, 1930).

LOTH, A.: *Le Miracle en France au dix-neuvième siècle* (Paris, 1894).

MENCZER, B. (ed.): *Catholic Political Thought, 1789–1848* (London, 1952).

MOINE BÉNÉDICTIN, UN: *Dom Guéranger, Abbé de Solesmes*. 2 vols. (8th edition, Paris, 1909–10).

MONTALEMBERT, M. LE COMTE DE: *Œuvres*. 9 vols. (Paris, 1860–8).

NÉDONCELLE, M.: *Les Leçons spirituelles du XIXe siècle* (Paris, 1937).

NIELSEN, FREDRIK: *The History of the Papacy in the Nineteenth Century*. Translated under the direction of Arthur James Marsh. 2 vols. (London, 1906).

PAGUELLE DE FOLLENAY, J.: *Vie du Cardinal Guibert*. 2 vols. (Paris, 1896).

PHILLIPS, C. S.: *The Church in France, 1789–1907*. 2 vols. (London, 1929–36) (with bibliography).

PONTMARTIN, A. DE: *Souvenirs d'un vieux critique*. 6e série (Paris, 1885).

PURCELL, E. S.: *Life of Cardinal Manning*. 2 vols. (London, 1896).

BIBLIOGRAPHY

RENARD, EDMOND: *Le Cardinal Mathieu, 1839–1908* (Paris, 1925).

RICARD, MGR: *L'Abbé Combalot, missionnaire apostolique. L'action catholique de 1820 à 1870* (new edition, Paris, 1892).

SAINTE-BEUVE, C. A.: *Nouveaux lundis.* Vol. I (Paris, 1870).

SCHWEITZER, ALBERT: *Von Reimarus zu Wrede, eine Geschichte der Leben-Jesu-Forschung* (Tübingen, 1906). English translation as: *The Quest of the Historical Jesus* (London, 1910).

SÉCHÉ, LÉON: *Les Derniers Jansénistes (1710–1870).* 3 vols. (Paris, n.d.).

SIMPSON, W. J. S.: *Religious Thought in France in the Nineteenth Century* (London, 1935).

SOLTAU, ROGER: *French Political Thought in the Nineteenth Century* (London, 1931).

TAINE, H.: *Les Origines de la France contemporaine. Le Régime moderne.* 2 vols. (Paris, 1891–4).

WARD, WILFRID: *William George Ward and the Catholic Revival* (London, 1893).

WEILL, GEORGES: *Histoire du Catholicisme libéral en France, 1828–1908* (Paris, 1909).

— *Histoire de l'idée laïque en France au XIXe siècle* (new edition, Paris, 1929).

— 'Le Protestantisme français au XIXe siècle.' *Revue de Synthèse historique,* Vol. 23 (1911), pp. 210–39.

WOODWARD, E. L.: *Three Studies in European Conservatism* (London, 1929).

— *French Revolutions* (Oxford, 1934).

See also the files of the religious periodicals, in particular, *L'Ami de la Religion, Le Semeur,* and *L'Univers.*

2. LACORDAIRE'S HOUR

(a) Lacordaire's works

All references are to the Poussielgue edition in six volumes, 1857–61. There is a later edition by the same publisher in nine volumes, 1872, and a critical edition by Lethielleux in four volumes, 1912. See also: *Lettres du R.P. Lacordaire à des jeunes gens recueillies et publiées par M. l'Abbé Henri Perreyve* (5th edition, Paris, 1865).

BIBLIOGRAPHY

DEVAS, RAYMUND: *Ex Umbris.* Letters and Papers hitherto un-published of the Fathers Lacordaire, Jandel, Danzas . . . (Hawkesyard, Rugely, Staffs, 1920).

DUINE, F.: *Documents Ménaisiens* (Paris, 1919).

MONTALEMBERT, LE COMTE DE: *Le Testament du P. Lacordaire* (Paris, 1870).

(b) Period 1830–48

ALLIES, THOMAS WILLIAM: *Journal in France in 1845 and 1848, with Letters from Italy in 1847* (London, 1849).

ALLIGNOL, C. and A.: *De l'Etat actuel du clergé en France* (Paris, 1839).

BÉRANGER: *Chansons.* 2 vols. (Paris, 1869).

BERNIS, PAUL: *Lacordaire et sa prédication* (Strasburg, 1869).

BERTHIER DE SAUVIGNY, G. DE: 'Mgr Quélen et les incidents de Saint-Germain-l'Auxerrois en février 1831.' *Revue d'histoire de l'Eglise de France,* Vol. 32, pp. 110–20.

BLANC, LOUIS: *Histoire de dix ans, 1830–1840.* 5 vols. (4th edition, Paris, 1844).

BOUTARD, CHARLES: *Lamennais. Sa vie et ses doctrines.* 3 vols. (Paris, 1905–13).

CARNÉ, LE COMTE LOUIS DE: *Souvenirs de ma jeunesse au temps de la Restauration* (Paris, 1872).

CASTAN, E.: *Histoire de la vie et de la mort de Monseigneur Denis-Auguste Affre* (Paris, 1855).

CHASLES, PHILARÈTE: 'Les Prédicateurs du carême.' *Revue de Paris,* Vol. 17 (1835), pp. 5–25.

CHOCARNE, P. B.: *Le R.P. H. D. Lacordaire.* 2 vols. (7th edition, Paris, 1886).

DEVAS, RAYMUND: *The Dominican Revival in the Nineteenth Century* (London, 1913).

DUMAS, ALEXANDRE, *père*: *Mémoires.* 2 series. 26 vols. (Brussels, 1852–6).

DUPANLOUP, M. L'ABBÉ: *De la pacification religieuse* (2nd edition, Paris, 1845).

FAVRE, JULIEN: *Lacordaire orateur* (Paris, 1906).

FOISSET, M.: *Vie du R.P. Lacordaire.* 2 vols. (Paris, 1870).

GIBSON, W.: *The Abbé de Lamennais and the Liberal Catholic Movement in France* (London, 1896).

BIBLIOGRAPHY

GIRARD, HENRI: 'La Pensée religieuse des Romantiques.' *Revue d'Histoire littéraire de la France* (1925), pp. 79–97.

GUÉRIN, MAURICE DE: *Journal, lettres et poèmes* (2nd edition, Paris, 1862).

GUTTINGUER, ULRIC: *Arthur* (Paris, 1837 and 1925).

HAUSSONVILLE, LE COMTE D': *Lacordaire* (Paris, 1895).

LA GORCE, PIERRE DE: *Louis-Philippe (1830–1848)* (Paris, 1931).

LAMENNAIS, F. DE: *Œuvres.* 10 vols. (Paris, 1844).

LEAR, H. L. S.: *Henri Dominique Lacordaire* (new edition, London, 1887).

LUCAS-DUBRETON, J.: *Le Comte d'Artois. Charles X* (Paris, 1927).

MONTALEMBERT, LE COMTE DE: *Le Père Lacordaire* (2nd edition, Paris, 1862).

— *Lettres à La Mennais* (Publiées par G. Goyau et P. de Lallemand, Paris, 1932).

O'MEARA, KATHLEEN: *Frederic Ozanam* (2nd edition, London, 1878).

OZANAM, FRÉDÉRIC: *Lettres, 1831–1853.* 2 vols. (Paris, 1865).

POISSON, JACQUES: *Le Romantisme social de Lamennais* (Paris, 1931).

POUTHAS, C. H.: 'Le Clergé sous la Monarchie constitutionnelle.' *Revue d'histoire de l'Eglise de France*, Vol. 28, pp. 19–53.

RENAN, ERNEST: *Souvenirs d'enfance et de jeunesse* (Paris, 1883).

RICARD, A.: *L'Ecole menaisienne. Lacordaire* (Paris, 1882).

ROUSSEL, ALFRED: *Lamennais intime d'après une correspondance inédite* (Paris, 1897).

SACY, SILVESTRE DE: *Variétés littéraires, morales et historiques.* 2 vols. (Paris, 1858).

SAINTE-BEUVE, C. A.: *Causeries du lundi.* Vol. 15 (Paris, 1862).

— *Nouveaux lundis.* Vol. 5 (Paris, 1865).

SOURIAU, MAURICE: *Histoire du Romantisme en France.* Vol. 2 (Paris, 1927).

THACKERAY, W. M.: *The Paris Sketch Book* (London, 1840).

THUREAU-DANGIN, P.: *L'Eglise et l'Etat sous la monarchie de juillet* (Paris, 1880).

— *Histoire de la monarchie de juillet.* 4 vols. (Paris, 1884–7).

TOCQUEVILLE, A. DE: *Œuvres et correspondances inédites.* 2 vols. (Paris, 1861).

VIATTE, A.: *Le Catholicisme chez les romantiques* (Paris, 1922).

WOODGATE, M. V.: *Père Lacordaire, Leader of Youth* (London, 1939).

BIBLIOGRAPHY

WORDSWORTH, CHRISTOPHER: *Diary in France* (London, 1845).

See also the following anonymous articles:

Dublin Review: 'The Religious and Social Condition of France.' Vol. 16 (March 1844), pp. 1–36.

— 'Lacordaire and the Conferences of Notre-Dame.' New series, Vol. 15 (October 1870), pp. 356–93.

London and Westminster Review: 'The Political and Social Condition of France.' By Δ (i.e. A. de Tocqueville). Vol. 3 (April 1836), pp. 137–68.

Revue de Paris: 'Avec le clergé catholique. Revue politique.' Vol. 23 (1831), pp. 187–95.

3. MICHON'S DILEMMA

(*a*) *Michon's works*

Michon's novels are as follows: *Le Maudit.* 3 vols. (1864). *La Religieuse* (1864). *Le Jésuite.* 2 vols. (1865). *Le Moine* (1865). *Le Confesseur.* 2 vols. (1866). *Le Curé de campagne.* 2 vols. (1867). *Les Mystiques* (1869). *Le Fils de Prêtre. Roman posthume* (1885).

Of his large and ephemeral production, only the following have even historical interest:

Statistique monumentale de la Charente (Paris, 1844).

Le Femme et la Famille dans le catholicisme (Paris, 1845).

De la Scission du parti catholique (Paris, 1856).

Lettre à l'Evêque de Montauban sur les dangers de la polémique religieuse (Paris, 1856).

Les Archevêques de Paris (Paris, 1857).

La Révolution et le clergé (Paris, 1858).

Du Progrès et de l'importance des idées gallicanes (Paris, 1858).

Vie de Jésus suivie des Evangiles parallèles (Paris, 1866).

La Grande Crise du catholicisme (Paris, 1870).

Various documents bearing on Michon are in private hands at Baignes-Sainte-Radegonde (Charente).

(*b*) *Period 1848–64*

ALBRIGHT, W. F.: *The Archaeology of Palestine* (London, 1949).

ALMÉRAS, H. d': *La Vie Parisienne sous la République de 1848* (Paris, n.d.).

BIBLIOGRAPHY

ARDOUIN-DUMAZET: *Voyage en France*. 16th series (Paris, 1898).

BALFOUR, R. E.: 'Notes on the History of the Breviary in France.' *Journal of Theological Studies*, Vol. 33, pp. 365–71.

BÉLET, P.: *La Religieuse selon l'auteur du Maudit* (Paris, 1864).

BOUIS, C.: *Calottes et Soutanes* (Paris, 1870).

CABANE, H.: *Histoire du Clergé en France pendant la Révolution de 1848* (Paris, 1908).

COBBAN, ALFRED: 'The Influence of the Clergy, etc., April 1848.' *English Historical Review*, Vol. 57, pp. 334–44.

CUVILLIER-FLEURY: *Etudes et Portraits* (Paris, 1865).

DEBIDOUR, A.: *Histoire des rapports de l'Eglise et de l'Etat de 1789 à 1870* (Paris, 1898).

DELORD, TAXILE: *Histoire du Second Empire*. 6 vols. (Paris, 1869–75).

DUROSELLE, J. B.: 'L'Attitude politique et sociale des catholiques français en 1848.' *Revue d'histoire de l'Eglise de France*, Vol. 34, pp. 44–62.

FALLOUX, LE COMTE DE: *Mémoires d'un royaliste*. 2 vols. (Paris, 1888).

GASTINEAU, B.: *Les Crimes des prêtres et de l'Eglise* (Paris, 1880).

GUERARD, A. L.: *French Prophets of Yesterday* (London, 1913).

HAVET, ERNEST: *Le Christianisme et ses origines*. 4 vols. (Paris, 1871–84).

HOUTIN, ALBERT: *La Question biblique chez les catholiques de France au XIXe siècle* (2nd edition, Paris, 1902).

— *La Controverse de l'apostolicité des églises en France au XIXe siècle* (3rd edition, Paris, 1903).

— *Un dernier gallican. Henri Bernier, chanoine d'Angers* (2nd edition, Paris, 1904).

— *Un prêtre marié. Charles Perraud* (Paris, 1908).

— *Autour d'un prêtre marié. Histoire d'une polémique* (Paris, 1910).

LAMARTINE, A. DE: *Le Conseiller du Peuple* (Paris, 1849).

LEPROUX, MARC: *Quelques Figures charentaises en Orient* (Paris, 1939).

MADAME ***: *Le Vrai Maudit*. 2 vols. (Paris, 1866).

MAURAIN, JEAN: *Le Saint-Siège et la France* (Paris, 1930).

— *La Politique ecclésiastique du Second Empire* (Paris, 1930).

MEIGNAN, ABBÉ: 'D'un mouvement antireligieux en France.' *Le Correspondant*, New series, Vol. 10, pp. 225–50.

MICHELET, J.: *Du Prêtre, de la Femme, de la Famille* (4th edition, Paris, 1845).

NORMANBY, MARQUIS OF: *A Year of Revolution.* 2 vols. (London, 1857).

POUJADE, E.: *Essai . . . à propos du Maudit* (Paris, 1864).

SALBERG, MME DE: *Quelques mots sur Michon* (Paris, 1906).

SAULCY, F. DE: 'Les Ruines de Masada.' *Revue des Deux Mondes*, Vol. 1 (1852), pp. 401–20.

SENIOR, NASSAU WILLIAM: *Conversations with M. Thiers, etc.* 2 vols. (London, 1878).

— *Conversations with Distinguished Persons during the Second Empire.* 2 vols. (London, 1880).

TALMADGE, W.: *Letters from Florence* (London, 1866).

TRANNOY, ANDRÉ: 'Les Responsabilités de Montalembert en 1848.' *Revue d'histoire de l'Eglise de France*, Vol. 35, pp. 177–206.

VARINARD, ADRIEN: *J.-H. Michon, fondateur de la graphologie* (Paris, n.d.) (1881?).

VIEL CASTEL, LE COMTE HORACE DE: *Mémoires sur le règne de Napoléon III.* 6 vols. (Paris, 1883–4).

See also the following anonymous articles:

Dublin Review: 'France since the Revolution of February.' Vol. 24 (September 1849), pp. 91–122.

— 'De Saulcy's Dead Sea and Bible Lands.' Vol. 35 (September 1853), pp. 139–72.

— 'Renan's "Vie de Jésus".' New series, Vol. 2 (April 1864), pp. 386–419.

Quarterly Review: 'The Gallican Church.' Vol. 118 (July and October 1865), pp. 498–529.

4. VEUILLOT'S TRIUMPH

(a) Veuillot's works

All references to Veuillot's correspondence are to the Retaux edition in nine volumes, 1883–1913. There is a 51-volume edition of his complete works, published by Lethielleux, 1924–39.

(b) *Period 1864–80*

ANON.: *Ce qui se passe au Concile* (Paris, 1870).

BAUNARD, MGR L.: *Histoire du Cardinal Pie.* 2 vols. (2nd edition, Poitiers and Paris, 1886).

BUTLER, CUTHBERT: *The Vatican Council. The Story told from inside from Bishop Ullathorne's letters.* 2 vols. (London, 1930).

DELPIT, JULES: *Réponse d'un campagnard à un parisien* (Paris, 1857).

DEVOUCOUX, MGR: 'Lettres d'un évêque français pendant le Concile du Vatican.' *Revue d'histoire de l'Eglise de France,* Vol. 13, pp. 199–213.

FERNESSOLE, P.: *Les Origines littéraires de Louis Veuillot (1813–1843)* (Paris, 1923).

— *Bio-bibliographie de la jeunesse de Louis Veuillot* (Tarbes, 1923).

GIRAUD, VICTOR: 'Louis Veuillot d'après sa correspondance.' *Revue des Deux Mondes,* Vol. 1 (1935), pp. 458–70.

HOUTIN, ALBERT: *Le Père Hyacinthe.* 3 vols. (Paris, 1920–4).

LAGRANGE, F.: *Vie de Mgr Dupanloup.* 3 vols. (3rd edition, Paris, 1883–4).

MAYNARD, U.: *Monseigneur Dupanloup et M. Lagrange son historien* (2nd edition, Paris, 1884).

MOURRET, F.: *Le Concile du Vatican d'après des documents inédits* (Paris, 1919).

OLLIVIER, EMILE: *L'Eglise et l'Etat au Concile du Vatican.* 2 vols. (2nd edition, Paris, n.d.).

PRICE, LEWIS C.: *Archbishop Darboy and some French tragedies (1813–1871)* (London, 1915).

SIMPSON, W. J. S.: *Roman Catholic Opposition to Papal Infallibility* (London, 1909).

VEUILLOT, E. and F.: *Louis Veuillot.* 4 vols. (Paris, 1899–1914).

See also the following anonymous articles:

Dublin Review: 'The Situation in France.' New series, Vol. 22 (January 1874), pp. 204–10.

— 'Marshal MacMahon's Appeal to France.' New series, Vol. 29 (July 1877), pp. 222–30.

Almost every French newspaper printed a long obituary of Veuillot in 1883.

Index

INDEX

Boyer, Abbé, 38
Brienne, Loménie de, 31
Brizeux, 165
Broglie, Léonce Victor, Duc de, 109
Broglie, Albert, Duc de, 151, 178, 250, 251
Brutus, 67
Buckle, 183
Bulls, Papal: *Qui Christi Domini* (1801), 82, 84; *Ineffabilis Deus* (1855), 146–7
Butler, Cuthbert, 223, 226, 231

Calas, 72, 218
Calderon, 67
Calvin, 189
Carmelite Order, 228
Carmes, Ecole des, 179
Carné, L. de, 26–7, 51–2, 151
Carrière, Abbé, 92
Catherine II (of Russia), 55
Cavaignac, General, 129
Cavour, 146, 168–9, 193, 226
Cayla, Mme du, 25, 29, 59
Chambord, Comte de, 167, 246–248, 250, 251
Champollion, 161
Charlemagne, 140, 169
Charles X (Comte d'Artois), 17, 18, 26–9, 30, 31, 33, 53, 85, 98, 107, 140
Charroux, Abbey of, 206
Chateaubriand, 36, 56, 63, 67, 95, 98, 165
Chesnaie, La, 39, 40, 41, 48, 49, 71, 78
Church in France: strength of, 25, 50 ff., 72, 110, 127, 164 ff. 171–2, 173 ff., 208–9; revival, 71–2, 74–7; political affiliations of, 21–4, 26, 29–34, 40–2, 43–6, 50, 53, 66, 74–7, 79–81, 82–8, 94, 96, 110, 113–15,
119 ff., 127–30, 133–4, 135–6, 139–42, 145, 167–72, 175 ff., 192–7, 203, 222, 241–4, 246–253, 256–7, 262–4
Circourt, 219–20
Civiltà Cattolica, 224, 227
Clovis, 83
Cobden, 106
Cochin, 151
Cognat, Abbé, 152
Collet d'Herbois, 256
Combalot, Abbé, 148, 149
Commune, 242–4, 251
Comte, A., 77, 162, 164, 175
Concordat (1801), 22, 84, 88
Congregation of the Blessed Virgin, the, 26–7
Constance, Council of, 223
Constitution of the Clergy, Civil, 22
Constitutionnel, Le, 30, 45, 61
Coquerel, A., 181
Cornelius Nepos, 69
Correspondant, Le, 151, 196, 213
Courier, P. L., 27
Cousin, Victor, 50–1, 109, 110, 164
Cousseau, Mgr (Angoulême), 142, 159
Coux, Comte de, 44 *n.*, 124
Craven, Mme Augustus, 231
Creuzer, 51
Cuvier, 55, 161
Cuvillier-Fleury, 185

Dalcy, G., 98
Darboy, Mgr (Paris), 220–2, 227, 228, 229, 230, 232, 233, 241, 242–4, 251, 262
Delessert, E., 155
Denis, 180
Descartes, 164
Desgenettes, Abbé, 72, 74
Devoucoux, Mgr (Evreux), 230

278

INDEX

INDEX

Lamartine, A. de, 36, 52, 56, 63, 98, 120–1
La Mennais, Abbé Jean de, 86
Lamennais: appearance, 39; character, 39, 44, 46, 79; doctrines, 39–41, 44–5, 49, 78–9, 85; and Lacordaire, 41–2, 48–9, 54, 78–9; launches *L'Avenir*, 43 ff.; visits Rome, 46–7; leaves Church, 48–9; 50, 58, 64, 68, 71, 74, 76, 77, 84, 86, 88, 91, 98, 99, 103, 107, 114, 119, 122, 124, 125, 145, 154, 157, 162, 204, 261, 262
Laprade, 151
La Salette, 176–7
Lawrence, D. H., 216
Leconte de Lisle, 165
Ledru-Rollin, 121–2
Leo XII, 39
Leo XIII, 193, 219, 225, 259
Le Play, 256
Leroux, 51, 119
Le Sage, 216
Le Verrier, 161–2, 163
Lévi, E., 165–6
Liautard, Abbé, 26, 29, 59
Liberal Catholics, 134, 136, 147 ff., 159, 163–4, 169, 170–2, 177–8, 192 ff., 205, 208, 212, 219 ff., 239, 244, 246–8, 251–252, 256, 257, 258
Libre Parole, La, 217
Littré, 164, 175
Loisy, 263
Longchamp, 63
Loreto, 218
Louis, Saint, 26, 30, 83, 169
Louis XIV, 64, 247
Louis XVI, 22
Louis XVIII, 22, 25–6, 104
Louis Napoleon, *see* Napoleon III
Louis Philippe, 17, 18, 28, 30,

33, 43, 53, 86, 104, 110, 114, 119, 121, 128, 139, 169, 202, 203, 208
Lourdes, 176–7, 218
Luther, 189, 218

Macé, J., 206
MacMahon, Marshal, 250–1, 253
Magnan, Marshal, 221
Maistre, J. de, 55, 85
Malines, Congress of, 192–3, 194, 195
Mallet, 173–4
Manning, Cardinal, 220, 224, 230, 231–2, 238, 239, 244
Marengo, 82
Maret, Mgr (Sura), 124, 163, 180 n., 220, 229, 234
Marie Antoinette, 18
Martin du Nord, 98
Masonry, 207, 221, 229, 242–3, 252–3
Massillon, 64
Massol, 207
Mathilde, Princess, 221
Maurras, 217, 264
Meignan, Cardinal (Tours), 177, 179, 181
Ménard, L., 180
Mentana, 210
Merivale, 183
Metternich, 46, 98
Michelet, 52, 69, 95, 111, 114, 165, 183, 190
Michon: stands for Assembly, 122–3; journeys to Near East, 134–5; character and interests, 153–60; and need for scholarship, 179; as novelist, 182–91; and Vatican Council, 229–30, 240; last years, 254–256; 125, 170, 178, 192, 204, 220, 241, 262, 263, 264

281

INDEX